# INTRODUCTION TO SOFTWARE ENGINEERING

CS-70

For

Bachelor of Computer Applications [B.C.A.]

**Dinesh Verma**

(MCA, BCA, 'A', 'O' Level, SCJP(USA), JP, DAST)

**Dr. A.K. Saini**

Ph.d., M.PHIL., MCA, M.Sc., MBA

IGNOU Course Writer

CLOSER TO NATURE

WE USE RECYCLED PAPER



***Useful For***

IGNOU, Nalanda University, Lalit Narayan Mithila University, Andhra University, Pt. Sunderlal Sharma (Open) University (Bilaspur), Annamalai University, Bangalore University, Bharathiar University, Bharathidasan University, HP University, Jamia Millia Islamia, Kakatiya University (Andhra Pradesh), KSOU (Karnataka), KOU (Rajasthan), MPBOU (MP), MDU (Haryana), Punjab University, Tamilnadu Open University, Sri Padmavati Mahila Visvavidyalayam (Andhra Pradesh), Sri Venkateswara University (Andhra Pradesh), UCSDE (Kerala), University of Jammu, YCMOU, Rajasthan University, UPRTOU (UP) and all other Indian Universities.

**GULLYBABA PUBLISHING HOUSE (P). LTD**

AN ISO 9001:2008 CERTIFIED CO.

Developed and Produced by:
**GullyBaba Publishing House Pvt. Ltd**
2525/193, 1st Floor, Onkar Nagar-A, Tri Nagar, Delhi-110035
Landmark: Kanhaiya Nagar Metro Station
E-mail: info@gullybaba.com
Website: www.GullyBaba.com

**Edition:** 2012


**ISBN:** 978-81-89086-62-6



---

# Preface

This book (CS-70) is mainly targeted for the exam of 'Introduction To software Engineering' for all Universities. This topic has been in demand and is the need of current scenario. Providing well researched material to the learners, with focus on examination and learning has been a constant pursuit for us. We at GPH, believe in the power of educato and respect the growth and positive contribution that education can contribute to a society.

The unavailability of material in the market is a demotivating factor for the students and searching and collecting it, becomes a tough task for the student community. We, at GPH wish to strive for excellence as we perceive it not only as earning a degree but a step towards the growth and enrichment.

GPH Books are the pioneers in the field and an effort to provide a Strategy and a unique methodology so as to give you excellent performance in the examination. Your goal of attaining a higher grade and securing your future can be made accessible by the use of our published material Your goal can thus be achievable and realistic! Hoping for your better, brighter, and a promising and successful future!

*Our website is www.gullybaba.com. It is a vital resource for your exams and can have manifold effect on our meticulous preparation Now you can access us on the net through* ***www.doeacconline.com, www.ignouonline.com,*** *and* ***www.astrologyeverywhere.com.***

We gratefully acknowledge the significant contributions of our experts in bringing out this publication.

Dear Reader,

Welcome in the world of GullyBaba Publishing House (P) Ltd. Profound, In-depth study and research can guarantee you the most reliable, latest & accurate information on the subject. However, as the saying goes, nothing is perfect, but we still believe that there is always a scope for improvement. And we wish to be nothing less but aim for the best.

You, the reader can be our best guide in making this book more interesting and user friendly.

Your valuable suggestions are welcome!

***Feedback about the book can be sent at*** **feedback@gullybaba.com.**

Publisher.

# Contents



## Question Papers

# CHAPTER-1

# INTRODUCTION

## SOFTWARE ENGINEERING AND COMPUTER SCIENCE

**Q1. Define the term "Software Engineering" and distinguish it from Computer Science.**

The application of a systematic, disciplined, quantifiable approach to the development, operation, and maintenance of software; that is, the application of engineering to software. A branch of knowledge concerned with information processes, the structures and procedures representing these processes, and their implementation in information-processing systems.

Computer science sometimes defined as the study of information encompasses a wide range of deep and fascinating topics. Computer science is a core scientific discipline with unique intellectual challenges and, at the same time, an enabling discipline for all of science and engineering. Computer science serves as a foundation for thinking about and understanding all forms of computation; it builds insight into analyzing and solving problems of every imaginable variety; and it develops sophisticated knowledge and skills that will be in increasing demand in academic, business, and government for the foreseeable future.

Here software engineering is a subset of computer science, while computer science incorporates science and engineering both.

## SOFTWARE

**Q2. Explain the term Software & its role ?**

Computer software has become a driving force. It is the engine that drives business decision making. It serves as the basis for modern scientific investigation and engineering problem solving.

The software community continually attempts to develop technologies that will make it easier, faster, and less expensive to build high-quality computer programs. Some of these technologies are targeted at a specific application domain (e.g., Web-site design and implementation); other focus on a technology domain (e.g., object-oriented system); and still other are broad-based (e.g., operating system such as LINUX).

Today, software takes on a dual role. It is a product and, at the same time, the vehicle for delivering a product. As a product, it delivers the computing potential embodied by computer hardware or, more broadly, a network of computers that are accessible by local hardware. Whether it resides within a cellular phone or operates inside a mainframe computer, software is an information transformer producing, managing, acquiring, modifying, displaying, or transmitting information that can be as simple as a single bit or as complex as a multimedia presentation.

## 🗁ISSUES

**Q3. Give some Issues related to software development.**

Why does it take so long to get software finished?
Why are development costs so high?
Why can't we find all the error before we give the software to customers?
Why do we continue to have difficulty in measuring progress as software is being developed?

## 🗁SOFTWARE vs HARDWARE

**Q4. How is a software product different from a hardware product? Give five features. [JUNE01, Q2(a)]**

Software product is different from a hardware product in following manner :

**i)** Software is developed or engineered, it is not manufactured in the classical sense. Although some similarities exists between software development and hardware manufacturing, the two activities are fundamentally different. In both activities, high quality is achieved through good design, but the manufacturing phase for hardware can introduce quality problems that are nonexistent (or easily corrected) for software.

**ii) Software does not "wear out."**

Following Figure depicts failure rate as a function of time for hardware. The relationship, often called the "bathtub curve," indicates that hardware exhibits relatively high failure rates early in its life (these failures are often attributable to design or manufacturing defects); defects are corrected and the failure rate drops to a steady state level (ideally, quite low) for some period of time. As time passes, however, the failure rate rises again as hardware components suffer from the cumulative affects of dust, vibration, abuse, temperature extremes and many other environmental maladies. Stated simply, the hardware beings to wear out.

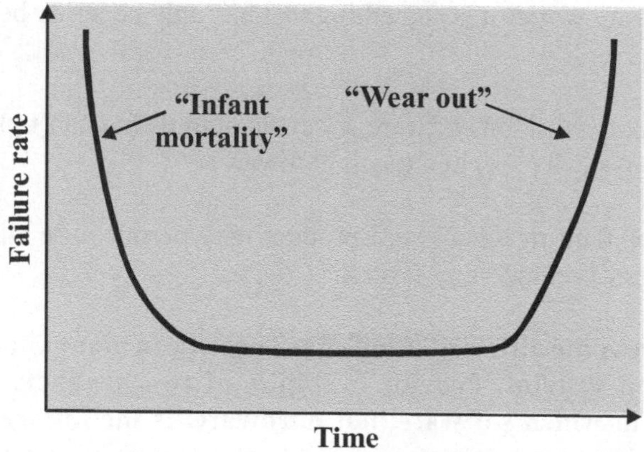


Software is not susceptible to the environmental maladies that cause hardware to wear out. In theory, therefore, the failure rate curve for software should take the form of the "idealized curve" shown in the following Figure. Undiscovered defects will cause high failure rates early in the life of a program. However, these are corrected (ideally, without introducing other errors) and the curve flattens as shown.

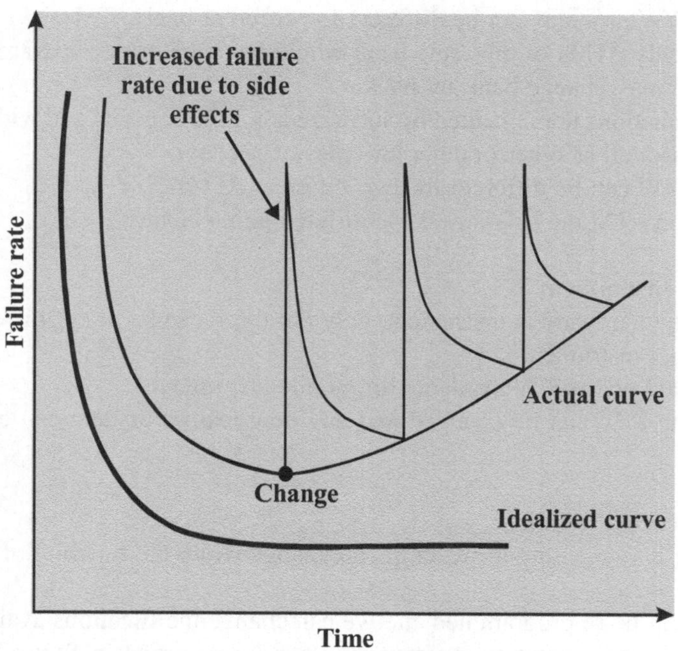


**Fig : Idealized and actual failure curves for software**

**iii)** In hardware world, component reuse is a natural part of engineering process. In software world, it is something that has only begun to be achieved on a broad scale.

**iv)** You can only work on software & see its outputs but can't physically feel it. You can physically feel and touch hardware.

**v)** Any minor fault in a hardware product may permit it be still usable but software doesn't enduce any errors.

**Q5. Software is the differentiating characteristic in many computer based products and systems. Provide examples of two products and at least one system in which software, not hardware, is the differentiating element. Explain your answers.**

**[DEC01, Q1(a)][DEC04, Q1(a)][DEC03, Q1(b)]**

**System in which software is differentiating element :**

**ATM Machine :**

ATM Machine is a system from which a user can withdraw money.

**1.** The other functions of ATM are to view balance, deposits etc.

**2.** In this case the hardware is same.

**3.** The function of the S/W is integrated with S/W program installed on it.

**4.** The S/W program can be different for different bank ATMs.

**5.** Naturally ATMs of the same bank would have the same software, but the software may change bank by bank.

**6.** The functions implemented by software is for the deposits and withdraw of money as well as other options for types of account.

**7.** The S/W can be different for two different ATMs.

**8.** Thus in ATM the software is the differentiating element.

**Mobile Instrument :**

In this the hardware is instrument, only but these can be no. of different s/w to run that instrument

- There are no. of S/W available for mobile instrument.
- And the S/W can be changed and any new feature or item can be downloaded.

**Microprocessor chip :**

This the S/W residing in the chip can change while the function of the chip remains same.

- Chip can be re-programmed and we can change the functions available.
- Once the chip has been written they can be modified in future for more enhancement.

## 🗁SOFTWARE MYTHS

**Q6. Describe some of the myths associated with software development community.**

There are number of myths associated with software development community. Some of them really affect the way, in which software development should takes place. In this section, we list few myths, and discuss their applicability to standard software development

**1.Software is easy to change :**

It is true that source code files are easy to edit, but that is quite different than saying that software is easy to change. This is deceptive precisely because source code is so easy to alter. But making changes without introducing error is extremely difficult, particularly in organizations with poor process maturity. Every change requires that the complete system be re-verified. If we do not take proper care this will be an extremely tedious and expensive process.

**2. Computers provide greater reliability than the devices they replace :**

It is true that software does not fail in the traditional sense. These are no limits to how many times a given piece of code can be executed before it "wears out". In any event, the simple expression of this myth is that our general ledgers are still not perfectly accurate, even though they have been computerized.

**3. Testing software or "proving" software correct can remove all the errors :**Testing can only show the presence of error. It cannot show the absence of errors. Our aim is to design effective test cases in order to find maximum possible error. The more we test more we are confident about our design.

**4. Reusing software increases safety :** This myth is particularly troubling because of the false sense of security that code re-use can create. Code re-use is a very powerful tool that can yield dramatic improvement in development efficiency, but it still requires analysis to determine its suitability and testing to determine if it works.

**5. Software can work right the first time :** If we go to an aeronautical engineer, and ask him to build a jet fighter craft, he will quote us a price. If we demand that it is to be put in production without building a prototype, he will laugh and may refuse the job. Yet, software engineers are often asked to de precisely this sort of work, and they often accept the job.

**6. Software can be designed thoroughly enough to avoid most integration problems :** There is an old saying among software designers: "too bad, there is no compiler for specifications": This point out the fundamental difficulty with detailed specifications. They always have inconsistencies, and there is no computer tool to perform consistency checks on them. Therefore, special care is required to understand the specifications, and if there is an ambiguity, that should be resolved before proceeding for design.

**7. Software with more features is better software :** This is, of course, almost the opposite of the truth. The best, most enduring programs are those which do one thing well.

**8. Addition of more software engineers will make up the delay :** This is not true in most of the cases. By the process of adding more software engineers during the project, we may further delay the project. This does not serve any purpose here, although this may be true for any civil engineering work.

**9. Aim is to develop working programs :** The aim has been shifted from developing working programs to good quality, maintainable programs. Maintaining software has become a very critical and crucial area for software engineering community.
This list is endless. These myths, poor quality of software, increasing cost and delay in the delivery of the software have been the driving forces behind the emergence of software engineering as a discipline. In addition, following are the contributing factors:
**a.** Change in ratio of hardware to software costs
**b.** Increasing importance of maintenance
**c.** Advances in software techniques
**d.** Increased demand for software
**e.** Demand for larger and more complex software system

## 🗁LAYERED MODEL

**Q7. Software engineering is a layered approach, Comment.**

**[JAN01, Q1(c)]**

The bedrock that supports software engineering is a quality focus. The foundation for software engineering is the process layer. Software engineering process is the glue that holds the technology layers together and enables rational and timely development of computer software. Software engineering methods provide the technical how-to's for building software. Methods encom-

pass a broad array of tasks that include requirements analysis, design, program construction, testing
and support. Software engineering tools provide automated or semi-automated support for the process and the methods. When tools are integrated so that another, a system for the support of software, can use information created by one tool are development, called *Computer-Aided Software Engineering(CASE), is established.*

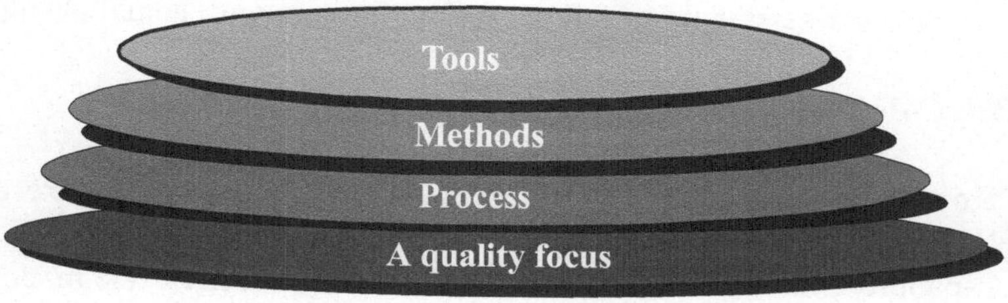


## THE PROCESS

**Q8. Explain the term process.** **[JAN01, Q1(b)]**

A common process framework is established by defining a small number of framework activities that are applicable to all software projects, regardless of their size or complexity. A number of task sets-each a collection of software engineering work tasks, project milestones, work products, and quality assurance points-enable the framework activities to be adapted to the characteristics of the software project and the requirements of the project team. Finally, umbrella activities-such as software quality assurance, software configuration management, and measurement-overlay the process model. Umbrella activities are independent of any one framework activity and occur throughout the process.

Few reasons why it is difficult to improve software process :

**1. Not enough time :** Unrealistic schedules leave insufficient time to do the essential project work. No software groups are sitting around with plenty of spare time to devote. Customers and senior managers are demanding more software, of higher quality in minimum possible time. Therefore, there is always a shortage of time. One consequence is that have to ship release 1.0 on time, but then they have to ship release 1.01 almost immediately thereafter to fix the recently discovered bugs.

**2. Lack of knowledge :** A second obstacle to widespread process improvement is that many software developers do not seem to be familiar with industry best practices.

**3. Wrong motivations :** Some organizations launch process improvement initiatives for the wrong reasons. May be an external entity, such as a contractor, demanded that the development organization to climb on the CMM bandwagon.

**4. Insufficient commitment :** Many times, the software process improvement fails, despite best of intentions, due to lack of true commitment. It starts with a process assessment but fails to follow through with actual changes.

## THE CMM

**Q9. How many process maturity levels are defined by software engineering institute ? Define them.**

The Capability Maturity Model(CMM) is not a software life cycle model. Instead, it is a strategy for improving the software process, irrespective of the actual life cycle model used.

CMM is used to judge the maturity of the software processes of an organization and to identify the key practices that are required to increase organization and to identify the key practices that are required to increase the maturity of these process. The CMM is organized into five maturity levels.

### MATURITY LEVELS

**1. Initial (maturity level 1) :** At this, the lowest level, there are essentially no sound software engineering management practices in place in the organization instead, everything is done on an adhoc basis.

**2. Repeatable (Maturity Level 2) :** At this level, policies for managing a software project and procedures to implement those policies are established. Planning and managing new projects is bases on experience with similar projects.
Instead of functioning in crisis mode as in level 1, managers identify problems as they arise and take immediate corrective action to prevent them from becoming crisis.

**3. Defined (Maturity level 3) :** At this level, the standard process for developing and maintaining software across the organization is documented, including both software engineering and management process. This standard process is referred to throughout the CMM as the organization's standard software process.

**4. Managed (Maturity level 4) :** At this level, the organization sets quantitative quality goals for both software products and processes. Productivity and quality are measured for important software process activities across all projects as part of an organizational measurement program. The software process capability at level 4 organizations can be summarized as "predicable " because the process is measured and operates within measurable limits.

**5. Optimizing (Maturity level 5) :** At this level, the entire organization is focused on continuous process improvement. The organizations have means to identify weaknesses and strengthen the process proactively, with the goal of preventing the occurrence of defects. Data of the effectiveness of the software process is used to perform cost benefit analysis of new technologies and proposes changes to the organization's software process.

## PROCESS MODELS

**Q10. List at least seven factors that influence the software development methodologies. [DEC04, Q6(b)] [JUNE04, Q5(a)]**

Six developments that influence the way software development methodologies are being look at are :

**1)** Evolving role of computers in day to day life.
**2)** Drastic changes in hardware performance, computing architectures etc.
**3)** Replacement of a lone programmer with team of specialists.
**4)** Customization of products.
**5)** Component based construction.
**6)** Introduction of fourth generation (4GT) techniques.

### WATERFALL MODEL OR SEQUENTIAL MODEL

**Q11. Write short note on waterfall model.**

Most familiar model is the waterfall model, which is given in figure. This model has five phases; Requirements analysis and specification, design, implementation and unit testing, integration & system testing, and operation & maintenance.

**1. Requirement analysis and specification phase :** The goal of this phase is to understand the exact requirements of the customer and to document them properly. This activity is usually executed together with the customer, as the goal is to document all functions, performance and interfacing requirements for the software.

The resultant document is known as Software Requirement Specification (SRS) document.

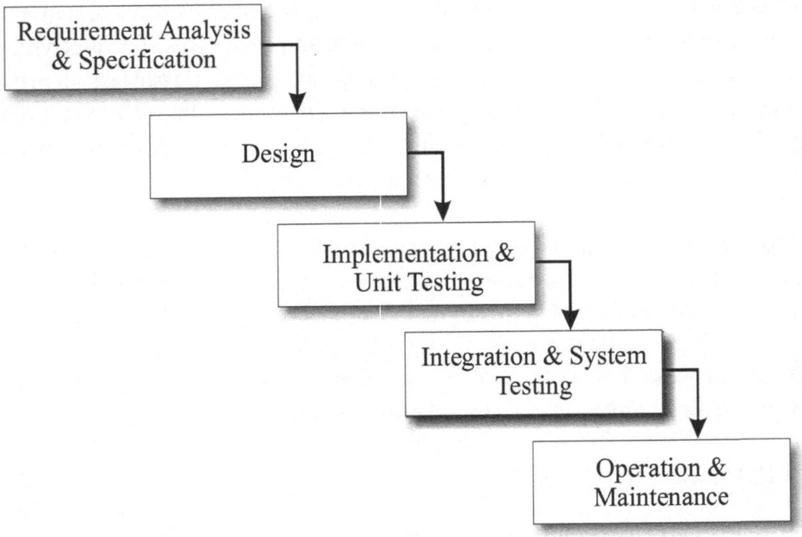


Fig : Waterfall model

**2. Design phase :** The SRS document is produced in the previous phase, which contains the exact requirements of the customer. The goal of this phase is to transform the requirement specification into a structure that is suitable for implementation in some programming language.

**3. Implementation and unit testing phase :** During this phase, design is implemented. If the SDD is complete, the implementation or coding phase proceeds smoothly, because all the information needed by the software engineers is contained in the SDD.

**4. Integration and system testing phase :** This is a very important phase. Effective testing will contribute to the delivery of higher quality software products, more satisfied users, lower maintenance costs, and more accurate and reliable results.

**5. Operation & maintenance phase :** Software maintenance is a task that every development group has to face, when the software is delivered to the customer's site, installed and is operational.

**Q12. What are the shortcomings of the Waterfall Model ? Propose a Software Development Life Cycle (SDLC) model which is a modified version of the Waterfall model but overcomes all the disadvantages of the Waterfall Model. [JUNE04, Q1(a)]**

Waterfall model is the oldest and widely used model for software engineering but it has some drawbacks as well, specially if we look at practical aspects of it.

**1)** It is often difficult for the customer to state all requirements explicitly. Thus natural uncertainty is not covered that exists at inception of projects.

**2)** Customer must have patience as working session of program is only available later in the project. That means if a major defect is detected after delivery, it becomes nearly impossible to correct.

**3)** Importantly, rear projects rarely follow the sequential flow that this model proposes. There is iteration, but it is indirect. Thus changes can cause confusion as project proceeds. A software development life cycle(SDLC) model that is better one and overcomes disadvantages mentioned above is incremental model.

The incremental model combines elements of the linear sequential model (applied repetitively) with the iterative philosophy of prototyping. Referring to Figure, the incremental model applies linear sequences in a staggered fashion as calendar time progresses. Each linear sequence produces a deliverable "increment" of the software.

When an incremental model is used, the first increment is often a core product. The core product is used by the customer (or undergoes detailed review). As a result of use and/or evaluation, a plan is developed for the next increment. The plan addresses the modification of the core product to better meet the needs of the customer and the delivery of additional features and functionality. This process is repeated following the delivery of each increment, until the complete product is produced.

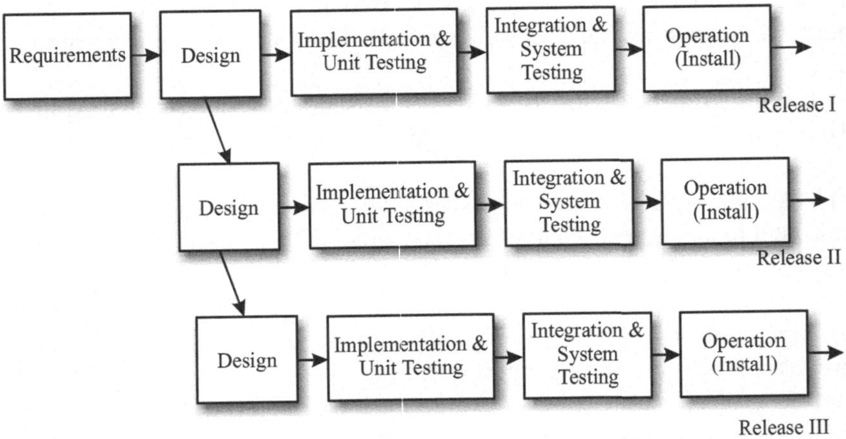


Fig : Iterative enhancement model.

## SEQUENTIAL MODEL

**Q13. Write in detail about "Sequential Model".**

**System/information engineering and modeling :** Because software is always part of a larger system (or business), work begins by establishing requirement to software.

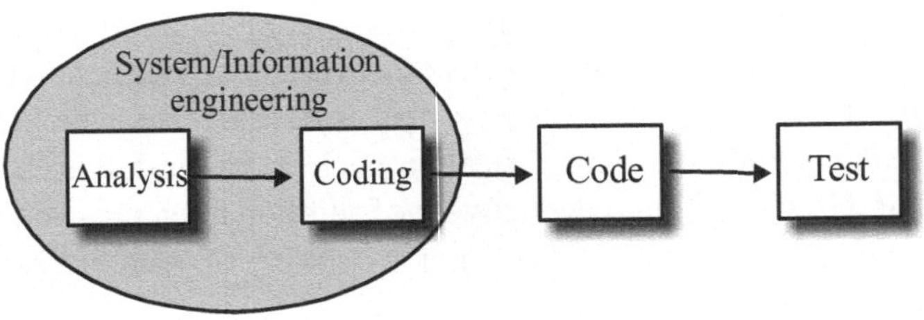


**Software requirements analysis :** The requirements gathering process is intensified and focused specifically on software. To understand the nature of the program(s) to be built, the software engineer(analyst) must understand the information domain for the software, as well as required function, behavior, performance, and interface.

**Design :** Software design is actually a multistep process that focuses on four distinct attributes of a program: data structure, software architecture, interface representations, and procedural (algorithmic) detail.

**Code Generation :** The design must be translated into a machine-readable form. The code generation step performs this task.

**Testing :** Once code has been generated, program testing begins.

**Support :** Software will undoubtedly undergo change after it is delivered to the customer (a possible exception is embedded software). Change will occur because error have been encountered, because the software must be adapted to accommodate changes.

Among the problems that are sometimes encountered when the linear sequential model is applied are:

**1.** Real projects rarely follow the sequential flow that the model proposes.

**2.** It is often difficult for the customer to state all requirements explicitly.

**3.** The customer must have patience. A working version of the program(s) will not be available until late in the project time –span.

## Prototyping Model

**Q14. Explain prototyping model. Give areas of problem related to it.**

A disadvantage of waterfall model is that the working software is not available until late in the process, thus delaying the discovery of serious error. An alternative to this is to first develop a working prototype of the software instead of developing the actual software. The working prototype is developed as per current available requirements.

The developers use this prototype to refine the requirements and prepare the final specification document.

The developers should develop prototype as early as possible to speed up the software development process.

After the finalization of software requirement and specification (SRS) document, the prototype is discarded and actual system is then development using the waterfall approach. Thus, it is used as an input to waterfall model and produces maintainable and good quality software.

Prototyping can be problematic for the following reasons:

**1.** The customer sees what appears to be working version of the software, unaware that the prototyping is held together "with chewing gum and baling wire." Unaware that in the rush to get it working no one has considered over all software quality or long-term maintainability.

**2.** The developer often makes implementation compromises in order to get a prototype working quickly. An inappropriate operating system or programming language may be used simply because it is available and known; an inefficient algorithm may be implemented simply to demonstrate capability.

## Evolutionary Model

### Q15. Write short note on evolutionary model.

There is growing recognition that software, like all complex system, evolves over a period of time. Business and product requirements often change as development proceeds, making a straight path to an end product unrealistic; tight market deadlines make completion or a comprehensive software product impossible, but a limited version must be introduced to meet competitive or business pressure.

## The Incremental Model

### Q16. Write short note on incremental model.

The incremental model combines elements of the linear sequential model (applied repetitively) with the iterative philosophy of prototyping. Referring to figure, the incremental model applies linear sequences in a staggered fashion as calendar time progresses. Each linear sequence produces a deliverable "increment" of the software.

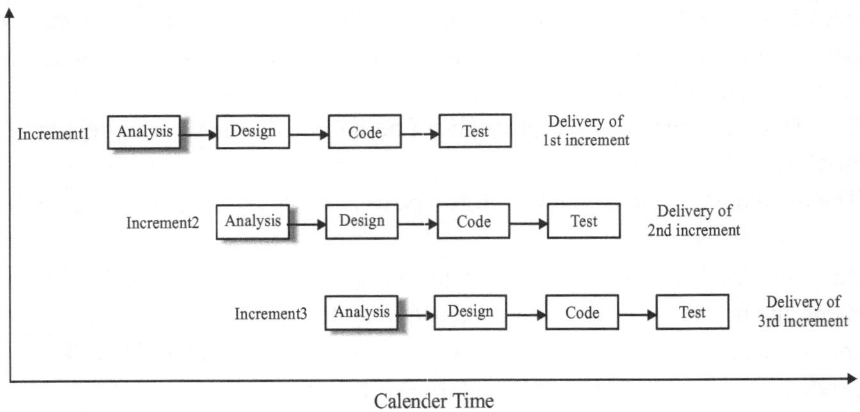


## Spiral Model

### Q17. Write short note on spiral model. [DEC03, Q6(ii)]

The spiral model, originally proposed by Boehm, is an evolutionary software process model that couples the iterative nature of prototyping with the controlled and systematic aspects of the linear sequential model. It provides the potential for rapid development of incremental versions of the software.

A spiral model is divided into a number of framework activities, also called task regions. Typically, there are between three and six task regions. Figure depicts a spiral model that contains six task regions:

- **Customer communication** – tasks required to establish effective communication between developer and customer.
- **Planning** – tasks required to define resources, timelines and other project related information.
- **Risk analysis** – tasks required to assess both technical and management risks.
- **Engineering** – tasks required to build one or more representations of the application.
- **Construction and release** – tasks required to construct, test, install and provide user support (e.g., documentation and training).

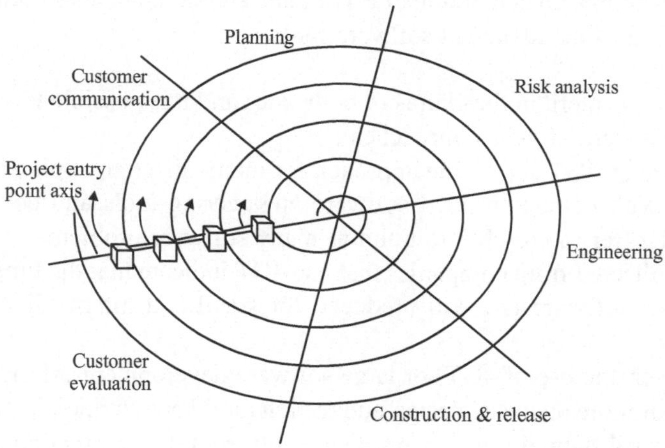


**Figure : A typical spiral model**

**Customer evaluation** – tasks required to obtain customer feedback based on evaluation of the software representations created during the engineering stage and implemented during the installation stage.

Each of the regions is populated by a set of work tasks, called a task set, that are adapted to the characteristics of the project to be undertaken. For small projects, the number of work tasks and their formality is low. For larger, more critical projects, each task region contains more work tasks that are defined to achieve a higher level of formality.

As this evolutionary process begins, the software engineering team moves around the spiral in a clockwise direction, beginning at the center. The first circuit around the spiral might result in the development of a product specification; subsequent passes around the spiral might be used to develop a prototype and then progressively more sophisticated versions of the software.

### 4TH GENERATION TECHNIQUES

**Q18. What are 4th Generation Techniques ? Give its merits.**

The term fourth generation techniques (4GT) encompasses a broad array of software tools that have one thing in common: each enables the software engineer to specify some characteristic of software at a high level.

Currently, a software development environment that supports the 4GT paradigm includes some or all the following tools: nonprocedural languages for database query, report generation, data manipulation, screen interaction and definition, code generation; high-level graphics capability; spreadsheet capability and automated generation of HTML and similar languages used for Website creation using advanced software tools.

There is some merit in the claims of both sides and it is possible to summarize the current state of 4GT approaches :

**1.** The use of 4GT is a viable approach for many different application areas. Coupled with computer-aided software engineering tools and code generators, 4GT offers a credible solution to many software problems.

**2.** Data collected from companies that use 4GT indicate that the time required to produce software is greatly reduced for small and intermediate applications.

**3.** However, the use of 4GT for large software development efforts demands as much or more analysis, design and testing (software engineering activities) to achieve substantial time savings that result from the elimination of coding.

**Q19. Which is more important the product or the process?**

If the process is weak, the end product will undoubtedly suffer. All of human activity may be a process, but each of us derives a sense of self-worth from those activities that result in a representation or instance that can be used or appreciated either by more than one person, used over and over, or used in some other context not considered. That is, we derive feelings of satisfaction from reuse of our products by ourselves or others. About every ten years, give or take five, the software community redefines "the problem" by shifting its focus from product issues to process issues. There is precedence in the scientific community to advance notions of duality when contradiction in observations cannot be fully explained by one competing theory or another. Thus, while the rapid assimilation or reuse goals into software development potentially increases the satisfaction software practitioners derive from their work, it also increases the urgency for acceptance of the duality of product and process. "A creative software professional should also derive as much satisfaction from the process the end-product".

The work of software people will change in the years ahead. The duality of product and process is one important element in keeping creative people engaged as the transition from programming to software engineering is finalized.

**Q20. Describe the type of situations where iterative enhancement model might lead to difficulties.**

An iterative enhancement model would start by developing a very simplistic, but usable database. On the completion of each cycle, the system would become more sophisticated. It would, however, provide all the critical functionality by the end of the first cycle. Evolutionary development and iterative enhancement are somewhat interchangeable. Evolutionary development should be used when it is not necessary to provide a minimal version of the system quickly.

This model has the same phases as the waterfall model, but with fewer restrictions. Generally the phases occur in the same order as in the waterfall model, but they may be conducted in several cycles. A usable product is released at the end of the each cycle, with each release providing additional functionality. This model is useful for projects using new technology that is not well understood. This is also used for complex projects where all functionality must be delivered at one time, but the requirements are unstable or not well understood at the beginning.

It may be difficult to convince customers ( particularly) in contract situations that the evolutionary approach is controllable. It demands considerable risk assessment expertise, and relies on this expertise for success. If a major risk is not uncovered and managed, problems will undoubtedly occur. Finally, the model itself is relatively new and has not been used as widely as the linear sequential or prototyping paradigms. It will take a number of years before the efficacy of this important new paradigm can be determined with absolute certainly.

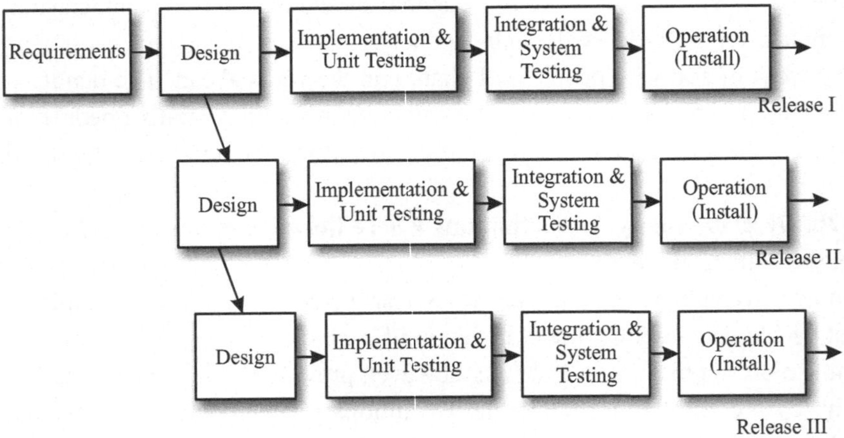


Fig : Iterative enhancement model.

**Q21. Give five examples of Software Development Projects that would be amenable to prototyping. Explain your answer. [JUNE02, Q2(a)]**

Mathematical Algorithms
Subset of Command Driven Systems
Vector 3 D Graph Generator
Speed Calculators
Route Monitoring System

Software applications that are relatively easy to prototype almost always involve human-machine interaction and/or heavy computer graphics. Other applications that are sometimes amenable to prototyping are certain classes of mathematical algorithms, subset of command driven systems and other applications where results can be easily examined without real-time interaction.

**Q22. Name three software applications that would be difficult for prototyping. Explain your answer. [JUNE02, Q2(b)]**

Applications that are difficult to prototype include control and process control systems. Also all mission critical applications are difficult to apply prototyping :

**1.** Satellite launching
**2.** Weather forecasting
**3.** Space Shuttle Monitoring

Because under prototype model - The first version that comes one - having minimum core functionality and later subsequent versions get updated and finally the full-functional model comes into existence. As mission critical system can't work on partly functional models. These are highly sensitive to the inputs and may prove highly destructive if experimented with partly functional models.

CHAPTER-2

# PROJECT PLANNING AND SOFTWARE METRICS

## ISSUES

**Q1. What are the main factors to consider in project planning?** **[JAN01, Q3(a)]**

Main factors to be considered in project planning are :

**a.** Estimation techniques used; accuracy required

**b.** Lifecycle model, control functions, and reviews

**c.** Organizational structure

**d.** Level of formality in specifications, test plans

**e.** Level of verification and validation

**f.** Level of configuration management and quality assurance

**Q2. Why early planning is not possible?**

Early planning is not possible because precise information regarding project goals, customer needs, and product constraints, whose clarification is a major purpose of planning, are not available at the beginning of a software project.

**Q3. What are the major activities during planning?**

Major activities during planning:

**a.** Defining the problem,

**b.** Perform feasibility study,

**c.** Develop a recommended solution strategy,

**d.** Planning the development process.

**Q4. What is the format of a project planning?**

**a.** LCM Terminology/ Milestones/ Work products,

**b.** Organization Structure

**c.** Preliminary Staffing and resource requirements; Staffing and resource schedule,

**d.** Preliminary development schedule,

**e.** Preliminary cost estimate,
**f.** Project Monitoring and control mechanisms,
**g.** Tools and techniques to be used,
**h.** Programming Languages,
**i.** Testing Requirements,
**j.** Supporting Documents required,
**k.** Manner of documentation and delivery,
**l.** Training Schedule and materials,
**m.** Installation Plan,
**n.** Maintenance consideration,
**o.** Method and time of delivery,
**p.** Sources of information.

## 🗁SOFTWARE TEAM STRUCTURES

**Q5. Explain various team structures in brief. [JUNE01, Q1(a)]**

The "best" team structure depends on the management style of your organization, the number of people who will populate the team and their skill levels, and the overall problem difficulty. Mantei suggests three generic team organizations :

**Democratic Decentralized (DD)** – This software engineering team has no permanent leader. Rather, "task coordinators are appointed for short durations and then replaced by others who may coordinate different tasks." Decisions on problems and approach are made by group consensus. Communication among team members is horizontal.

**Controlled Decentralized (CD)** – This software engineering team has a defined leader who coordinates specific tasks and secondary leaders that have responsibility for subtasks. Problem solving remains a group activity, but implementation of solutions is partitioned among subgroups by the team leader. Communication among subgroups and individual is horizontal. Vertical communication along the control hierarchy also occurs.

**Controlled Centralized (CC)** – Top-level problem solving and internal team coordination are managed by a team leader. Communication between the leader and team members is vertical.

Because a centralized structure completes tasks faster, it is the most adaptable in handling simple problems. Decentralized teams generate more and better solutions than individuals. Therefore such teams have a greater probability of success when working on difficult problems. Since the CD team is centralized for problem solving, either a CD or CC team structure can be successfully applied to simple problems. A DD structure is best for difficult problems.

## 🗁COMMUNICATION & COORDINATION TECHNIQUES

**Q6. Explain the basic coordination techniques related to software project.**
Project coordination techniques are categorized in the following manner :

**Formal, impersonal approaches** include software engineering documents and deliverables (including source code), technical memos, project milestones, schedules and project control tools, change requests and related documentation, error tracking reports and repository data.

**Formal, interpersonal procedures** focus on quality assurance activities applied to software engineering work products. These includes status review meetings, design and code inspections.

**Informal, interpersonal procedures** include group meetings for information dissemination, problem solving and "colocation of requirements and development staff."

**Electronic communication** encompasses electronic mail, electronic bulletin boards and by extension, video-based conferencing systems.

**Interpersonal networking** includes informal discussions with team members and those outside the project who may have experience or insight that can assist team members.

**Q7. What are the various software team organizations ? Also, give one example each, with justification, of a software project that fits for each type of team organization. [JUNE04, Q5(b)]**
The "best" team structure depends on the management style of your organization, the number of people who will populate the team and their skill levels, and the overall problem difficulty. Mantei suggests three generic team organizations :

**Democratic Decentralized (DD)** – This software engineering team has no permanent leader. Rather, "task coordinators are appointed for short durations and then replaced by others who may coordinate different tasks." Decisions on problems and approach are made by group consensus. Communication among team members is horizontal.

**Controlled Decentralized (CD)** – This software engineering team has a defined leader who coordinates specific tasks and secondary leaders that have responsibility for subtasks. Problem solving remains a group activity, but implementation of solutions is partitioned among subgroups by the team leader. Communication among subgroups and individual is horizontal. Vertical communication along the control hierarchy also occurs.

**Controlled Centralized (CC)** – Top-level problem solving and internal team coordination are managed by a team leader. Communication between the leader and team members is vertical.

Because a centralized structure completes tasks faster, it is the most adaptable in handling simple problems. Decentralized teams generate more and better solutions than individuals. Therefore such teams have a greater probability of success when working on difficult problems. Since the CD team is centralized for problem solving, either a CD or CC team structure can be successfully applied to simple problems. A DD structure is best for difficult problems.

e.g. DD

You have been appointed as a Project Manager within an information systems organisation. Your job is to build an application that is quite similar to the other that your team has built, although this one is larger and more complex. Requirement have been thoroughly documented by the customer.

Regarding the said project

- Since project is large more number of personnel will participate
- since project is complex, project will require the experts level professional.
- Expert professional need to have freedom to work, they are just needed the deadlines to meet, should be having free hand to deal with, since they know their job on hand and have maturity and experience.

All of the above scenario points advocate for the DD (Democratic Decentralized) team structure if the professionals involved with the project are from the organization itself.

e.g. CD

You have been appointed as a Project Manager within an information systems organisation. Your job is to build an application that is quite similar to the other that your team has built, although this one is larger and more complex. Requirement have been thoroughly documented by the customer.

Regarding the said project :

- Since project is large, more number of personnel will participate
- Since project is complex project will require the experts level professional

- All the requirements are thoroughly documented
- Already similar system had been built in past, basic guidelines are ready

All of the above points advocate for the **CD (Controlled Decentralized)** team structure if the professionals involved with the project are from the organization itself.

e.g. CC

You have been appointed as a Project Manager for a major software products company. Your job is to manage the development of the next generation version of its widely used word-processing software. Because competition is intense, tight deadlines have been established and announced.

Regarding the said project

- Since a project is a new version for the product already in the market, the requirements are properly documented. Need to just follow up with accommodating the certain new requirement which also had been properly defined.
- Because of tight deadlines, the work activity need to be focused and certain work discipline need to be introduced so that the tight control is enforced.
- Above point suggests that the personnel working on the project are from the organization only, so the understanding with each other and understanding of the software is also very good since right now new version is going to be developed, and tight deadlines enforced to have good leader who can motivate and control the project, which clearly suggest the Controlled Centralized team structure, where the top level problem solving and internal team coordination are managed by a team leader.

Communication between the leader and team members is vertical since requirements are already defined properly, no discussion and brain storming session are required with experts.

## 🗁SOFTWARE METRICS

### Q8. What is a metric ?

The term software metrics designates here "a unit of measurement of a software product or software related process". The continuous application of measurement based techniques to the software development process and its products to supply meaningful and timely management information, together with the use of those techniques to improve that process and its products".

Within the context of software project management, we are concerned primarily with productivity and quality metrics – measures of software development "output" as a function of effort and time applied and measures of the "fitness for use" of the work products that are produced.

**MEASURE**

Within the software engineering context, a measure provides a quantitative indication of the extent, amount dimension, capacity or size of some attribute of a product or process.

### Measurement

Measurement occurs as the result of the collection of one or more data points (e.g., a number of module reviews are investigated to collect measures of the number of errors for each).

### Indicators

An indicator is a metric or combination of metrics that provide insight into the software process, a software project, or the product itself. An indicator provides insight that enables the project manager or software engineers to adjust the process, the project, or the process to make things better.

**Q9. What are the set of attributes that should be encompassed by effective software metrics? Explain them.**

The set of attributes that should be encompassed by effective software metrics are as follows :

**1) Simple and computable :** It should be relatively easy to learn how to derive the metric, and its computation should not demand inordinate efforts or time. Empirically and intuitively persuasive. The metric should satisfy the engineer's intuitive notions about the product attribute under consideration (e.g., a metric that measures module cohesion should increase in value as the level of cohesion increases).

**2) Consistent and objective :** The metric should always yield results that are unambiguous. An independent third party should be able to derive the same metric using the same information about the software. Consistent in its use of units and dimensions. The mathematical computation of the metric should use measure that do not lead to bizarre combinations of units. For example, multiplying people terms by programming language variables in the program results in a suspicious mix of units that are not inclusive persuasive.

**3) Programming language independent :** Metrics should be based on the analysis model, The design model, or the structure of the program itself. They should not be dependent on vagaries of programming language syntax or semantics.

**4) An effective mechanism for high-quality feedback :** That is, the metric should provide a software engineer with information that can lead to a higher quality end product.

**Q10. Describe the difference between Process and Project metrics, with appropriate examples.**

**a) Process Metrics**

The only rational way to improve any process is to measure specific attributes of the process, develop a set of meaningful metrics based on these attributes and then use the metrics to provide indicators that will lead to a strategy for improvement.

We measure the efficacy of a software process indirectly. That is, we drive a set of metrics based on the outcomes that can be derived from the process. Outcomes include measures of errors uncovered before release of the software, defects delivered to and reported by end-users, work products delivered (productivity), human efforts expended, calendar time extended, schedule conformance and other measures. We also derive process metrics by measuring the characteristics of specific software engineering tasks. For example, we might measure the effort and time spent performing the umbrella activities.

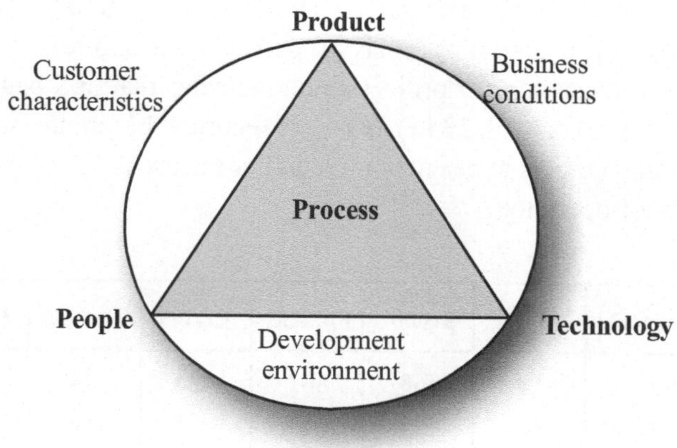


**b) Project Metrics**

Software process metrics are used for strategic purposes. Software project measures are tactical. That is, project metrics and the indicators derived from them are used by a project manager and a software team to adopt project work flow and technical activities.

The first application of project metrics on most software projects occurs during estimation. Metrics collected from past projects are used as a basis from which effort and time estimates are made for current software work. The intent of project metrics is two fold. First, these metrics are used to minimize the development schedule by making the adjustments necessary to avoid delays and mitigate potential problems and risks. Second, project metrics are used to assess product quality on an outgoing basis and, when necessary, modify the technical approach to improve quality. Every project should measure :

- Inputs – measures of the resources (e.g., people, environment) required to do the work.
- Outputs – measures of the deliverables or work products created during the software engineering process.
- Results – measures that indicate the effectiveness of the deliverables.

**Q11. Write short note on size oriented metrics ?**

Size-oriented software metrics are derived by normalizing quality and/or productivity measures by considering the size of the software that has been produced. A table of size-oriented measures, such as the one shown can be created. The table lists each software development project that has been completed over the past few years and corresponding measures for that project. It should be noted that the effort and cost recorded in the table represent all software engineering activities (analysis, design, code and test), not just coding. Further information for project alpha indicates that 365 pages of documentation were developed, 134 errors were recorded before the software was released, and 29 defects were encountered after release to the customer within the first year of operation.

| Project | LOC | Effort | $ (000) | Pp. doc. | Errors | Defects | People |
|---|---|---|---|---|---|---|---|
| alpha | 12,100 | 24 | 168 | 365 | 134 | 29 | 3 |
| beta | 27,200 | 62 | 440 | 1224 | 321 | 86 | 5 |
| gamma | 20,200 | 43 | 314 | 1050 | 256 | 64 | 8 |
| • | • | • | • | • | • | | |
| • | • | • | • | • | • | | |
| • | • | • | • | • | • | | |

In order to develop metrics that can be assimilated with similar metrics from other projects, we choose lines of code as our normalization value. From the rudimentary data contained in the table, a set of simple size-oriented metrics can be developed for each project:

- Errors per KLOC (thousand lines of code).
- Defects per KLOC.
- $ per LOC.
- Page of documentation per KLOC.

In addition, other interesting metrics can be computed:

- Errors per person-month.
- LOC per person-month.
- $ per page of documentation.

Size-oriented metrics are not universally accepted as the best way to measure the process of software development. Most of the controversy swirls around the use of lines of code as a key measure. Proponents of the LOC measure claim that LOC is an "artifact" of all software development projects that can be easily counted, that many existing software estimation models use LOC or KLOC as a key input, and that a large body of literature and data predicated on LOC already exists. On the other hand, opponents argue that LOC measures are programming language dependent, that they penalize well-designed but shorter programs, that they cannot easily accommodate nonprocedural languages, and that their use in estimation requires a level of detail that may be difficult to achieve.

**Q12. Write short note on function oriented metrics. [DEC03, Q6(i)]**

Function-oriented software metrics use a measure of the functionally delivered by the application as a normalization value. Since 'functionality' cannot be measured directly, it must be derived indirectly using other direct measures.

Function points are derived using an empirical relationship based on countable (direct) measures of software's information domain and assessments of software complexity.

| | | | Weighting factor | | | | |
|---|---|---|---|---|---|---|---|
| **Measurement parameter** | **Count** | | **Simple** | **Average** | **Complex** | | |
| Number of user inputs | | × | 3 | 4 | 6 | = | |
| Number of user outputs | | × | 4 | 5 | 7 | = | |
| Number of user inquiries | | × | 3 | 4 | 6 | = | |
| Number of files | | × | 7 | 10 | 15 | = | |
| Number of external interfaces | | × | 5 | 7 | 10 | = | |
| Count total ------------------------→ | | | | | | | |

**Number of user inputs** – Each user input that provides distinct application-oriented data to the software is counted.

**Number of user outputs** – Each user output that provides application-oriented information to the user is counted.

**Number of user inquiries** – An inquiry is defined as an on-line input that results in the generation of some immediate software response in the form of an on-line output.

**Number of files** – Each logical master file (i.e., a logical grouping of data that may be one part of a large database or a separate file) is counted.

**Number of external interfaces** – All machine readable interfaces (e.g., data files on storage media) that are used to transmit information to another system are counted.

To compute function points (FP), the following relationship is used:

$$FP = \text{count total} \times [0.65 + 0.01 \times (F_i)]$$

The $F_i$ (i = 1 to 14) are "complexity adjustment values"

## THE SCOPE

### Q13. What is meant by scope ?

Software scope describes the data and control to be processed, function, performance, constraints, interfaces and reliability.

The most commonly used technique to bridge the communication gap between the customer and developer and to get the communication process started is to conduct a preliminary meeting or interview. The analyst might ask:

- Who is behind the request for this work?
- Who will use the solution?
- What will be the economic benefit of a successful solution?
- Is there another source for the solution?

The next set of questions enables the analyst to gain a better understanding of the problem and the customer to voice any perceptions about a solution:

- How would you (the customer) characterize "good" output that would be generated by a successful solution?
- What problem(s) will this solution address?
- Can you show me (or describe) the environment in which the solution will be used?

The final set of questions focuses on the effectiveness of the meeting

- Are you the right person to answer these questions? Are answers "official"?
- Am I asking too many questions?

## THE COCOMO MODEL

**Q14. Write short note on cocomo Model.**

COCOMO is a hierarchy of software cost estimation models, which include basic, intermediate and detailed sub models.

### Basic Model

The basic model aims at estimating, in a quick and rough fashion, most of the small to medium sized software projects. There modes of software development are considered in this model: organic, semi-detached and embedded.

In the organic mode, a small team of experienced programmers develops software in a very familiar environment. The size of the software development in this mode ranges from small (a few KLOC) to medium (a few tens of KLOC), while in other two modes the size ranges from small to very large (a few hundreds of KLOC).

In the embedded mode of software development, the project has tight constraints, which might be related to the target processor and its interface with the associated hardware.

The semi detached mode is an intermediate mode between the organic mode and embedded mode. Depending on the problem at hand, the team might include a mixture of experienced and less experienced people with only a recent history together. The basic COCOMO equations take the form

$$E = a_b \text{ (KLOC) } b_b$$
$$D = c_b \text{ (E) } d_b$$

Where E is effort applied in Person-Months and D is the development time in months. The coefficient $a_b$, $b_b$, $c_b$ and $d_b$ are given in the following table.

| **Project** | A1 | B1 | C1 | D1 |
|---|---|---|---|---|
| Organic | 2.4 | 1.05 | 2.5 | 0.38 |
| Semidetached | 3.0 | 1.12 | 2.5 | 0.35 |
| Embedded | 3.6 | 1.20 | 2.5 | 0.32 |

### INTERMEDIATE MODEL

The basic model allowed for a quick and rough estimate, but it resulted in a lack of accuracy. Boehm introduced an additional set of 15 predictors called cost drivers in the intermediate model to take account of the software development environment. Cost drivers are used to adjust the nominal cost of a project to the actual project environment, hence increasing the accuracy of the estimate.

The cost drivers are grouped into four categories:

**1. Product attributes**

**(a)** Required software reliability (RELY)
**(b)** Database size (DATA)
**(c)** Product complexity (CPLX)

**2. Computer attributes**

**(a)** Execution time constraint (TIME)
**(b)** Main storage constraint (STOR)
**(c)** Virtual machine volatility (VIRT)
**(d)** Computer turnaround time (TURN)

**3. Personal attributes**

**(a)** Analyst capability (ACAP)
**(b)** Application experience (AEXP)
**(c)** Programmer capability (PCAP)
**(d)** Virtual machine experience (VEXP)
**(e)** Programming language experience (LEXP)

**4. Project attributes**

**(a)** Modern programming practices (MODP)
**(b)** Use of software tools (TOOL)
**(c)** Required development schedule (SCED)

Each cost driver is rated for a given project environment.

The intermediate COCOMO equations take the form:

$$E = a_i (KLOC)^{b_i} \times EAF$$

$$D = c_i (E)^{d_i}$$

The coefficients $a_i$, $b_i$, $c_i$ and $d_i$ are given in the following Table:

| Project | A1 | B1 | C1 | D1 |
|---|---|---|---|---|
| Organic | 3.2 | 1.05 | 2.5 | 0.38 |
| Semidetached | 3.0 | 1.12 | 2.5 | 0.35 |
| Embedded | 2.8 | 1.20 | 2.5 | 0.32 |

**Table: Coefficients for intermediate COCOMO**

### DETAILED COCOMO MODEL

The detailed model introduces two more capabilities :

**1. Phase-sensitive effort multipliers :** Some phases (design, programming, integration/test) are affected by factors defined by the cost drivers.

**2. Three-level product hierarchy :** These are modules, subsystem and system levels. The ratings of the cost drivers are done at appropriate level; that is, the level at which it is most susceptible to variation.

## MAKE/BUY DECISION

In many software application areas, it is often more cost effective to acquire than developing computer software. Software engineering managers are faced with a make/buy decision that can be further complicated by a number of acquisition options: **(1)** software may be purchased (or licensed) off-the-shelf, **(2)** "full-experience" or "partial-experience" software components may be acquired and then modified and integrated to meet specific needs, or **(3)** software may be custom built by an outside contractor to meet the purchaser's specifications.

### Creating a decision tree

**Q15. Write short note on decision tree.**

Once the data elements are defined in the data dictionary, we begin to focus on the process. For example, we need to know what goes into particular transaction. For example, particular transaction. For example, particular book store gets various discount on the purchase of the book from the publishers, let us assume the following discount policy:

Book stores get a trade discount of 40% for orders from libraries and individuals, 50% allowed on orders of 6-19 copies for a book title: 10% on order for 20-49 copies per book title: 15% on orders for 50 copies or more per book title.

A policy statement like this can be time-consuming to describe and confusing to implement. The analyst needs to use tools to implement the logic of the policy. The first such tool is DECISION TREE. Decision Tree has many branches as there are logical alternatives. It is excellent tool, below is an example of Decision Tree:

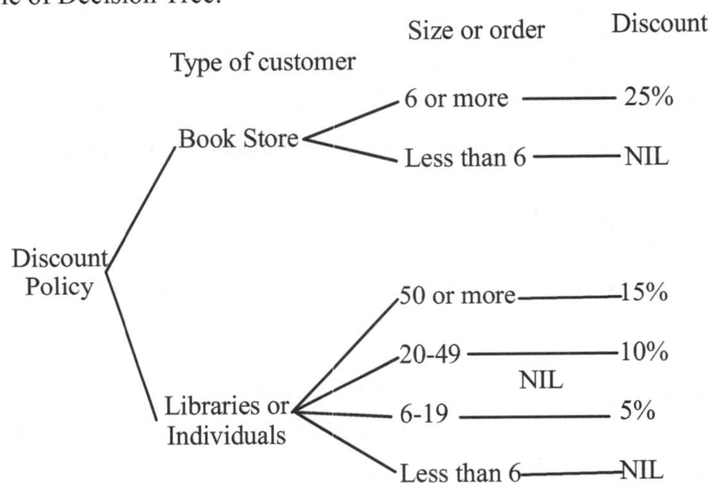


## OUTSOURCING

**Q16. Write short note on outsourcing. [DEC02, Q6(iii)]**

In concept, outsourcing is extremely simple. Software engineering activities are contracted to a third party who does the work at lower cost and, hopefully, higher quality. Software work conducted within a company is reduced to a contract management activity.

The decision to outsource can be either strategic or tactical. At the strategic level, business managers consider whether a significant portion of all software work can be contracted to others. At the tactical level, a project manager determines whether part or all of a project can be best accomplished by subcontracting the software work.

A brief review of the pros and cons of the decision is worthwhile.

On the positive side, cost savings can usually be achieved by reducing the number of software people and the facilities (e.g., computers, infrastructure) that support them. On the negative side, a company loses some control over the software that it needs. Since software is a technology that differentiates its systems, services, and products, a company runs the risk of putting the fate of its competitiveness into the hands of a third party.

## RISK MANAGEMENT

**Q17. Describe risk management concepts and strategies to manage risks. [JAN01, Q1(f)]**

Risk analysis and management are a series of steps that help a software team to understand and manage uncertainty. Many problems can plague a software project. A risk is a potential problem – it might happen, it might not.

### REACTIVE RISK STRATEGY

At best, a reactive strategy monitors the project for likely risks. Resources are set aside to deal with them, should they become actual problems. More commonly, the software team does nothing about risks until something goes wrong. Then, the team flies into action in an attempt to correct the problem rapidly.

### PROACTIVE RISK STRATEGY

A more intelligent strategy for risk management is to be proactive. A proactive strategy begins long before technical work is initiated. Potential risks are identified, their probability and impact are assessed, and they are ranked by importance. Then, the software team establishes a plan for managing risk. The primary objective is to avoid risk, but because not all risks can be avoided.

## FACTORS CAUSING RISKS

**Q18. Give at least 4 factors that can cause risk in a project.**

**Dependencies**

Many risks arise due to dependencies of project on outside agencies or factors. Some typical dependency-related risk factors are:

- Availability of trained, experienced people.
- Inter-component or inter-group dependencies.
- Customer-furnished items or information.

**Requirement Issues**

Many projects face uncertainty and turmoil around the product's requirements. While some of this uncertainty is tolerable in early stages, but the threat to success increases if such issues are not resolved as the project progresses. Some typical factors are :

- Lack of clear product vision.
- Lack of agreement on product requirements.
- Un-prioritized requirements.

**Management issues**

Project Managers usually write the risk management plan and most people do not wish to air their weaknesses (assuming they even recognize them) in public. Some of these risk factors are :

- Inadequate planning and task identification
- nadequate visibility into actual project status
- Unclear project ownership and decision making
- Unrealistic commitments made, sometimes for the wrong reasons
- Managers or customers with unrealistic expectations.

**Lack of Knowledge**

The rapid rate of change of technologies and the increasing change of skilled staff, mean that our project teams may not have the skills we need to be successful

Some of the factors are :

- Inadequate training
- Poor understanding of methods, tools and techniques
- Inadequate application domain experience.

## SOFTWARE SAFETY AND HAZARD ANALYSIS

**Q19. Describe five Software application areas in which software safety and hazard analysis would be a major concern. [JUNE04, Q2(a)]**

Following are the five application areas in which S/W safety and hazard analysis would be a major concern :

**1. Computer based control for automobile :** if significant hazards that can effect software for automobile are not identified & accessed then it may cause malfunctioning of automobile.

**2. Computer based system for nuclear reactions :** potential hazards related to reaction formation should be assessed in advance so as to ensure proper reactions taking place inside the reactor, otherwise loss of life may occur.

**3. Aircraft flight control :** safety analysis required to ensure that the software is capable of controlling the flight in all cases so as to be reliable & safe for humans.

**4. Weapons systems :** safety & hazard analysis is of utmost concern when weapon formation & automation is based on a software. We must make sure that all the latest modules & techniques are incorporated in software.

**5. Large scale industrial processes :** Industrial processes as iron and steel carrying, chemical works etc. need safety analysis for proper & efficient working of machines & tools that can prove to be of significant aid in human.

## 🗁RMMM PLAN

A risk management strategy can be included in the software project plan or the risk management steps can be organized into a separate Risk Mitigation, Monitoring and Management Plan. The RMMM plan documents all work performed as part of risk analysis and is used by the project manager as part of the overall project plan.

Risk mitigation is a problem avoidance activity. Risk monitoring is a project tracking activity with three primary objectives: (1) to assess whether predicted risks do, in fact, occur; (2) to ensure that risk handling steps defined for the risk are being properly applied; and (3) to collect information that can be used for future risk analysis.

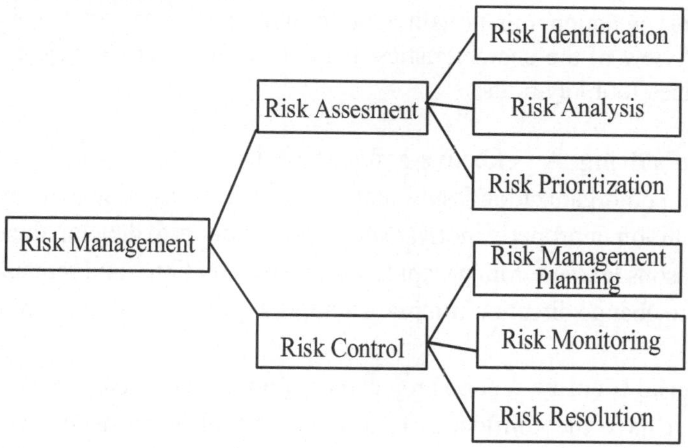


Fig:Risk Management Activities

**Q20. What kind of leaders we select someone to lead a Software Project?**
**# Explain why the intangibility of software systems poses special problems for the software project management.**
**# What are the important issues of Project Management ?**

**[JUNE01, Q5(b)]**

Project management is a people-intensive activity, and for this reason, competent practitioners often make poor team leaders. They simply don't have the right mix of people skills. And yet, as Edgemon states: Unfortunately all individuals just fall into a project manager role and become accidental project managers.

In an excellent book of technical leadership, Jerry Weinberg suggests a MOI model of leadership:

**Motivation**. The ability to encourage (by "push or pull") technical people to produce to their best ability.

**Organization**. The ability to mold existing processes (or invent new ones) that will enable the initial concepts to be translated into a final product.

**Ideas or innovation**. The ability to encourage people to create and feel creative even when they must work within bounds established for a particular software product or application.

Weinberg suggests that successful project leaders apply a problem solving management style. That is, a software project manager should concentrate on understanding the problem to be solved, managing the flow of ideas, and at the same time, letting everyone on the team know (by words and, far more important, by actions) that quality counts and will not be compromised.

Another view of the characteristics that define an effective project manager emphasizes four key traits:

**Problem solving.** An effective software project manager can diagnose the technical and organization issues that are most relevant, systematically structured solution or properly motivate other practitioners to develop the solution, apply lessons learned from past projects to new situations, and remain flexible enough to change direction if initial attempts at problem solution are fruitless.

**Managerial Identity**. A good project manager must take charge of the project. She must have the confidence to assume control when necessary and the assurance to allow good technical people to follow their instincts.

**Achievement.** To optimize the productivity of a project team, a manager must reward initiative and accomplishment and demonstrate through his own actions that controlled risk taking will not be punished.

**Influence and team building.** An effective project manager must be able to "read" people; she must be able to understand verbal and nonverbal signals and react to the needs of the people sending these signals. The manager must remain under control in high-stress situations.

**Q21. What questions need to be answered in order to develop a Project Plan?**

**# What are the main factors to consider in project planning?**

In an excellent paper on software process and projects, Barry Boehm states: "you need an organizing principle that scales down to provide simple plans for simple projects." Boehm suggests an approach that addresses project objectives, milestones and schedules, responsibilities, management and technical approaches, and required resources. He calls it the WWWWWHH principle, after a series of questions that lead to a definition of key project characteristics and the resultant project plan:

**Why is the system being developed?** The answer to this question enables all parties to assess the validity of business reasons for the software work. Stated in another way, does the business purpose justify the expenditure of people, time and money?

**What will be done, by when?** The answers to these questions help the team to establish a project schedule by identifying key project tasks and the milestones that are required by the customer.

**Who is responsible for a function?** The role and responsibility of each member of the software team must be defined. The answer to this question helps accomplish this.

**Where are they organizationally located?** Not all roles and responsibilities reside within the software team itself. The customer, users, and other stakeholders also have responsibilities.

**How will be job be done technically and managerially?** Once product scope is established, a management and technical strategy for the project must be defined.

How much of each resource is needed? The answer to this question is derived by developing estimates based on answers to earlier questions.

**Q22. Describe Software metrics its areas of application & problem during implementation?**

**Definition**

Software metrics are applicable to the whole development life cycle from initiation, when costs must be estimated, to monitoring the reliability of the end product in the field, and the way that product changes over time with enhancement. It covers the techniques for monitoring & controlling the progress of the software development, such that the fact that it is going to be six months late is recognized as early as possible rather than the day before delivery is due. It even covers organizations determining which of its software products are the cash cows and which are the dogs.

**Areas of Applications**

Controlling software development projects through measurement is an area that is generating a great deal of interest. This has become much more relevant with the increase in fixed price contracts and the use of penalty clauses by customers who deal with software developers.

The prediction of quality levels for software, often in terms of reliability, is another area where software metrics have an important role to play. Again, there are proprietary models in the market that can assist this, but debate continues about their accuracy. The requirement is there both from the customer's point of view and that from the developer's, who needs to control testing and proving costs. Various techniques can be used now, and this area will become more and more important in future.

Software metrics are also used to provide management information. This includes information about productivity, quality and process effectiveness. It is important to realize that this should be seen as an ongoing activity. Snapshots of the current situation have their place, but the most valuable information comes when we can see trends in data.

**Problems during implementation**

There is a rule in software development that we do not try something new on a large or critical system and this translates, in the software metrics area, to 'do not try to do too much'. On the other hand, there is evidence that concentrating on too small area and can result in such a limited pay back so as to invalidate software metrics in an organization. It is always said, 'do not bet your career on a single metric'.

Another problem during implementation arises if we start measuring the performance of individual productivity, in terms of functionality divided by effort, as a major determinant of salary increase. While this may appear attractive to some managers, the organization later stated that this was one of the worst mistakes it ever made. Using measurement in this way is counter productive, divisive and simply ensures that developers will rig the data they supply. We may say that management has one chance and one chance only. The first time that a manager uses data supplied by an individual against that individual is the last time that the manager will get accurate or true data from that person. The reasoning behind such a statement is simple, ***"employees do not like upsetting the boss!"***

Software metrics cannot solve all our problems, but they can enable managers to improve their processes, to improve productivity and quality, to improve the probability of survival. But it is not an easy option. Many metrics programs fail. One reason for this is that organizations and individuals who would never dream of introducing a new system without a structured approach ignore the problems of introducing change inherent in software metrics implementation succeed. Hence the use of software metrics does not ensure survival, but it improves the probability of survival.

**Q23. Unreasonable deadlines are a fact of life in software business. How would you proceed if you are faced with one? Example with two examples. [DEC04, Q3(b)]**

The deadlines for the project has to be readied before project commences. To decide about a deadline is a part of Project Estimation activity. The Gantt Chart is used for scheduling the project work, and PERT chart is used to project the Maximum duration the project will take to finish. Since estimations are based on past experience, historical data, nature of the project work on hand, resources available, expertise required, complexity of the work. It is a fact for the software project that most of the project gets delayed, crosses the deadlines. The reasons for the delay could be as follows:

**1.** Complexity of the project

**2.** Man power shortage

**3.** Hardware failure

**4.** Electricity failure for long time

**5.** Unrealistic deadlines committed just to bag the order

**6.** End users are interrupting the project by adding new requirement every now and then.

**7.** Virus affection.

**8.** New technology has outdone the current work, now to develop project with the new technology.

If faced with the Unreasonable deadlines :

**1.** If the technology has outdated the current project, and new technology are just needed then it could be easy to convince the end user to approach the project with new technology. But this option requires the availability of knowledgeable expert.

**2.** If any resources shortage has been noticed, additional resources has to be added to the current project. (Resources could be manpower, hardware), this addition to new resources will cut the profit margin.

**3.** If resources are perfect still the deadlines is the problem. Project Manager need to reschedule the project Plan, project activity, the responsibilities of the personnel need to be reassigned. Team structure could be re-designed. This option may be having adverse effect, if the new team members are not experienced and not aware of the project nature, then deadline will be broken for sure.

# CHAPTER-3

# QUALITY ASSURANCE & CHANGE CONTROL (CONFIGURATION)

## INTRODUCTION

It's not enough to talk that software quality is important, you have to **(1)** explicitly define what is meant when you say 'software quality," **(2)** create a set of activities that will help ensure that every software engineering work product exhibits high quality, **(3)** perform quality assurance activities on every software project **(4)** use metrics to develop strategies for improving your software process and as a consequence, the quality of the end product.

**Q1. Is it possible to assess the quality of software if the customer keeps changing his/her mind about what it is supposed to do? Explain your answer with at least two examples. [DEC04, Q2(b)]**

It is not possible to assess quality of software if the customer keeps on changing his / her mind as all it leads to uncertainty that gives rise to risk in the project. It is very much required that in the analysis phase and system engineering phase, requirements are properly arrived at by discussion with customer else software hazards come up.

e.g.

**1)** Consider following project

It is demanded that a bank is computerized and a software product is needed for transaction. If the user initially states that for transaction he needs to have facility to process data of at most 3 customers at a time but later changes his mind to 5 customers, the application changes a lot and new modifications are to be made to design and code.

**2)** Consider a demand for a database management product where the initially stated demand was implicit locking of database, if not accessed frequently. Later it is demanded that such locking is not a need. Such changes can make the programmer's life stressful and dissatisfactory.

Both above examples show that quality is the outcome of good requirements **statement.**

**Q2. Under what circumstances is product quality likely to be determined by the quality of the development team? Give at least two examples of the types of software products that are particularly dependent on individual talent and ability. [JUNE04, Q1(b)]**

Product quality is determined by quality of development team when the demand is at a higher level. Some criterias are :

**1)** Problem is difficult so a better team is needed.
**2)** Required reliability of system to be build.
**3)** Rigidity of delivery date.
**4)** Size of resultant programs in lines of code.
**5)** Degree of sociability (communication) required for the project.
**6)** Time span of project because it effect time for which team will stay together.

Although, each and every software product is dependent on individual talent but some tend to have more stress on individual capability. Some examples are:

**i)** Software products where we have difficult customers.
**ii)** Software that uses a break through technology.

## 🗁QUALITY ASSURANCE

**Q3. Define quality assurance and its goal ?**

Quality assurance consists of the auditing and reporting functions of management. The goal of quality assurance is to provide management with the data necessary to be informed about product quality, thereby gaining insight and confidence that product quality is meeting its goals.

## 🗁CONFIGURATION MANAGEMENT

**Q4. How does software configuration management facilitate the changes that may occur during various stages of a system development life cycle ? Illustrate your explanation with an example at each stage.**

Software configuration management is a set of activities that have been developed to manage change throughout the life cycle of computer software. SCM can be viewed as a software quality assurance activity that is applied throughout the software process.

Configuration management allows a user to specify alternative configuration of the software system through the selection of appropriate versions. This is supported by associating attributes with each software version.

**Below is the description according to stages with examples :**

**1. Definition phase :** Budgetary or scheduling constraints can cause a redefinition of system or product. S/w configuration management here manage the change by identifying individual software configuration items (SCIs), then auditing of software configuration and finally reporting all changes applied.

**2. Development phase :** New business or market conditions can dictate changes in product requirements or business rules.
S/w configuration management should again identify configuration items according to market conditions & new version should be accessed, auditing should take place followed by reporting.

**3. Support phase :** New customer needs may demand modification of data produced by information systems, functionality delivered by products, or services delivered by a computer based system.
Here s/w configuration management requires formal steps.

## 🗁SQA ACTIVITIES

**Q5. Give activities performed by an SQA group.**

Software quality assurance is composed of a variety of tasks associated with two different constituencies – the software engineers who do technical work and an SQA group that has responsibility for quality assurance planning, oversight, record keeping, analysis and reporting.
The charger of the SQA group is to assist the software team in achieving a high quality end product. Activities performed (or facilitated) by an independent SQA group are :

**Prepares an SQA plan for a project** – The plan is developed during project planning and is reviewed by all interested parties. Quality assurance activities performed by the software engineering team and the SQA group are governed by the plan.

**Participates in the development of the project's software process description** – The software team selects a process for the work to be performed.

**Reviews software engineering activities to verify compliance with the defined software process** – The SQA group identifies documents and tracks deviations from the process and verifies that corrections have been made.

## MCCALL'S QUALITY FACTORS

**Q6. Write a note on McCall's Quality Factors. [JAN01, Q3(b)]**

Conformance to explicitly stated functional and performance requirements, explicitly documented development standards, and implicit characteristics that are expected from all professionally developed software.

McCall proposes a useful categorization of factors that affect software quality.

One of the major factors driving any production discipline is quality. In the current times, quality is the main "mantra" and business strategies are designed around quality. Clearly, developing methods that can produce high-quality software is another fundamental goal of software engineering. However, while cost is generally well understood, the concept of quality in the context of software needs further discussion. We can view quality of software product as having three dimensions:

* Product Operation
* Product Transition
* Product Revision

The first factor, product operation, deals with quality factors such a correctness, reliability, and efficiency. Product transition deals with quality factors like portability and inter operability. Product revision is concerned with those aspects related to modification of programs, including factors such a maintainability, and testability. These three dimensions and the different factors for each are shown in Figure below:

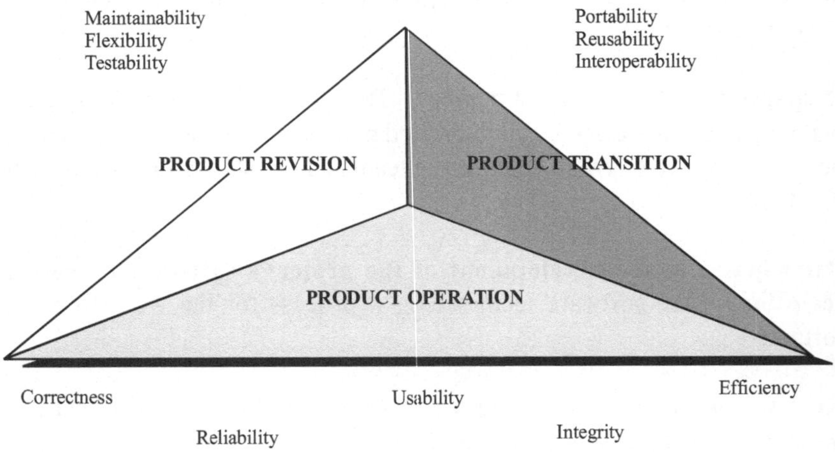


**McCAll's software quality factors**

Correctness is the extent to which a program satisfies its specifications. Reliability is the property that defines how well the software meets its requirements. Efficiency is a factor in all issues relating to the execution of software; it includes such consideration as response time, memory requirement, and throughput. Usability, or the effort required to learn and operate the software properly, is an important property that emphasized the human aspect of the system. Maintainability is the effort required to locate and fix errors in operating programs. Testability is the effort required to tests to ensure that the system or module perform its intended function. Flexibility is the effort required to modify an operational program (perhaps to enhance its functionality). Portability is the effort required to transfer the software from one hardware configuration to another. Reusability is the extent to which parts of the software can be reused in other related application. Inter operability is the effort required to couple the system with other systems.

There are two important consequences of having multiple dimensions to quality. First, software quality cannot be reduced to a single number (or a single parameter). And second, the concept of quality is project-specific. For some ultra-sensitive project, reliability amy be of utmost importance but not usability, while in some commercial package for playing games on a PC, usability may be of utmost importance and not reliability. Hence, for each software development project, a project-specific quality objective must be specified before the development starts, and the goal of the development process should be to satisfy that quality objective.

## 🗀FURPS QUALITY FACTORS.

### Q7. Write a short note on FURPS quality factors.

The quality factors described by McCall and his colleagues represent one of a number of suggested "checklists" for software quality. Hewlett-Packard developed a set of software quality factors that has been given the acronym FURPS- functionality, usability, reliability, performance and supportability. The FURPS quality factors draw liberally from earlier work, defining the following attributes for each of the five major factors:

**(i) Functionality** is assessed by evaluating the feature set and capabilities of the program, the generality of the functions that are delivered, and the security of the overall system.

**(ii) Usability** is assessed by considering human factors, overall aesthetics, consistency, and documentation.

**(iii) Reliability** is evaluated by measuring the frequency and severity of failure, the accuracy of output results, the Mean Time To Failure(MTTF), the ability to recover from failure, and the predictability of the program.

**(iv) Performance** is measured by processing speed, response time, resource consumption, throughput, and efficiency.

**(v) Supportability** combines the ability to extend the program (extensibility), adaptability, serviceability- these three attributes represent a more common term, maintainability in addition, testability, compatibility, configurability (the ability to organize and control elements of the software configuration, the ease with which a system can be installed, and the ease with which problems can be localized.

The FURPS quality factors and attributes just described can be use to establish quality metrics for each step in the software engineering process.

**🗁FTR**

**Q8. What is meant by "Formal Technical Review"? Should it assess both programming style as well as correctness of the software? Give reasons.**

A Formal Technical Review(FTR) is a software quality assurance activity performed by software engineers. The objectives of Formal Technical Review are :

**(i)** To uncover errors in function, logic, or implementation for any representation of the software;

**(ii)** To verify that the software under review meets its requirements;

**(iii)** To ensure that software has been represented according to predefined standards;

**(iv)** To achieve software that is develop in a uniform manner, and

**(v)** To make project more manageable.

Formal Technical Reviews (FTR) are one of the most important software quality Assurance activity.

The FTR is actually a class of reviews that includes walkthroughs inspections round-robin reviews and other small group technical assessments of software. It is not a good idea to argue that Formal Technical Review should assess programming style as well as correctness because the focus to FTR is on the technical correctness of the software design. The aim is to find errors. The assessment of programming style can be done by other means or by various CASE( Computer Aided Software Engineering) tools available for this purpose. A computer program is a mathematical object. A rigorous syntax and semantics is already defined for a programming language. The Formal Technical Review need not go into code/design style. Its two fold objective should be to identify problem areas within the product and uncover errors. Formal Technical Review does not even try to solve every technical problem it notes down. The focus is on work product and not its style but its contents. That is the main purpose for which FTR is used.

## CHANGE CONTROL

**Q9.Write short note on change control.**

Change control process comes into effect when the software and associated documentation are delivered to configuration management change request form, which should record the recommendations regarding the change. The recommendations may include assessment of the proposed change, the estimated costs and how the change should be implemented. This is submitted to a Change Control Authority (CCA), which decides whether or not the change is to be accepted. If change is approved by the CCA, it is applied to the software. The Software Quality Assurance (SQA) team to ensure that the change has not adversely affected other parts of the software. The changed software is handed over to the software configuration team and is incorporated in a new version of the system.

# CHAPTER-4

# SOFTWARE REQUIREMENT ANALYSIS AND SPECIFICATION

## PROBLEM ANALYSIS

**Q1. Describe the differences between functional and non-functional requirements? [DEC02, Q4(b);JAN01,Q1(d);JUNE01,Q3(c)]**

In general, requirements are partitioned into **functional requirements** and **non-functional requirements**. Functional requirements are associated with specific functions, tasks or behaviours the system must support, while non-functional requirements are constraints on various attributes of these functions or tasks. In terms of the ISO quality characteristics for evaluation, the functional requirements address the quality characteristic of functionality while the other quality characteristics are concerned with various kinds of non-functional requirements. Because non-functional requirements tend to be stated in terms of **constraints** on the results of tasks which are given as functional requirements (e.g., constraints on the speed or efficiency of a given task), a task-based functional requirements statement is a useful skeleton upon which to construct a complete requirements statement. That is the approach taken in this work. It can be helpful to think of non-functional requirements as adverbially related to tasks or functional requirements: how fast, how efficiently, how safely, etc., is a particular task carried out by a particular system?

**Q2. It seems odd that cost and schedule estimates are developed during software planning-before a detailed software requirement analysis or design has been conducted. Why do you think that this is done? Give at least four reasons. Are there circumstances when this should not be done? Give at least two such situations. [DEC04, Q2(a)]**

Cost and schedule estimates are developed during software project planning because

**1)** Cost and schedule estimates measure the uncertainty in the project.

**2)** They can measure the risk associated as an outcome of uncertainty then.

**3)** Cost and schedule are often formed out of historical information that strongly affects the project.

**4)** It leads to clear definitions of function, performance and interfaces.
Two situations where it should not be done are :
**i)** Where there is structural uncertainty i.e. requirements have not been clearly defined.
**ii)** Where project size is large i.e. larger the project more is the interdependency among various elements of software.

**Q3. What is problem analysis ? How is it related to SRS ?**
It is the activity that encompasses learning about the problem to be solved, understanding the needs of customers and users, trying to find out who the user really is, and understand all the constraints on the solution. As discussed earlier, requirement stage ends with creating a document called the Software Requirement Specification (SRS), which contains a complete description of the external behaviour of the software system.

Many analysis analyze the problem randomly by asking key questions, writing down the answers, asking other questions etc..
During problem analysis, different people may have different views of the problem. It is important to be able to track these different perspectives and relate them to each other. To be a really effective analyst, we must keep rich bag of tricks and know when and how to apply the right one at the right time. Most of the techniques for problem analysis use a combination of notations, including data flow diagrams, data dictionaries, Entity-Relation (E-R) diagrams.

## □SYSTEM ANALYST

**Q4. What is the job of a Systems Analyst ? What are two attributes of an effective System Analyst ? Explain them. [JUNE04, Q4(a)]**
System development generally consists of two major components : system analysis and system design. System analysis refers to the process of examining a business situation with the intent of improving it through better procedures and methods. System design is the process of planning a new business system of one to replace or complement an existing system.
System Analyst is a person, who analyzes the way the system works to identifies its problems. System analysts responsibilities vary among organizations. Below mentioned are the attributes of an analyst :

**1. Knowledge of business functions :** A systems analyst must know the environment in which he or she works. He must be aware of the peculiarities of management and the users at his installation and realize how they react to systems analyst. A working knowledge of accounting and marketing principles is a must since so many systems are built around these. Different sections in an organisation have conflicting needs and most systems are the result of compromise. The analyst's goal is to produce the system that will be the best for his organisation. This requires an open mind and flexibility in his ideas two areas. He must be familiar with his company's product and services and management's policies in areas concerning him.

**2. An analytical mind :** It takes an unusual person to see through problems facing an organisation and develop solutions that will work. Systems analysts often find themselves with more data than they can cope with. It requires an analytical mind to select pertinent data and concentrate on them in defining problems and forming solutions.

**Q5. Explain at least two technical and two interpersonal skills required for a System Analyst. When is one skill favoured over the other? Why? [DEC04, Q4(b)]**

Two interpersonal skills of system analysis

**1) Communication :** ability to speak language of user. Communication not just means reports, interviews but fulfilling, listening and reacting to one another.

Closed communication is not ideal open communication is needed.

**2) Understanding :** i.e. identifying problems and having grasp of company goals and objectives and showing sensitivity to impact of system on people.

Two technical skills of System Analyst

**1) Creativity :** helping users model ideas into concrete plans and developing candidate system.

**2) Problem Solving :** Reducing problems to their elemental levels and developing alternate solutions.

Necessity of both skills depends upon stages of system development.

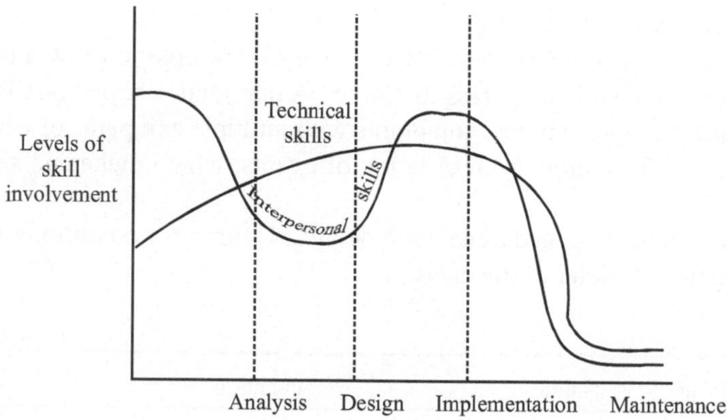


**During Analysis :** there is greater need of interpersonal skills - i.e. working with user to determine needs.

**During Design :** We need high technical skills even though interpersonal skills are required for user / analyst participation as a step to implementation.

**During Implementation :** Technical aspects focus on "proving" the software" Interpersonal aspects deal with "user training".

**During Maintenance :** Role of analyst drops off, except when an unanticipated problems appears.

## □DATA FLOW DIAGRAMS

**Q6. Define Data Flow Diagram. Differentiate between DFD & ERD.**
**# Define DFD. [JAN01, Q4(a)]**

Data flow diagrams (DFDs) have been used for many years prior to the advent of computers. DFDs show the flow of data through a system. The system may be a company, an organization, a set of procedures, a computer hardware system, a software system or any combination of the proceeding. The DFD is also known as a data flow graph or a bubble chart.

The following observations about DFDs are important :

**1.** All names should be unique. This makes it easier to refer to items of the DFD.
**2.** Remember that a DFD is now a flow chart. Arrows in a flow chart repre-

sent the order of events; arrows in DFD represent flowing data. A DFD does not imply any order of events.

**3.** Suppress logical decisions. If we ever have the urge to draw a diamond-shaped box in a DFD, suppress that urge! A diamond –shaped box is used in flow charts to represent decision points with multiple exit paths of which only one is taken. This implies an ordering of events, which makes no sense in a DFD.

**4.** Do not become bogged down with details. Defer error conditions and error handling until the end of the analysis.

| Symbol | Name | Function |
|---|---|---|
|  | Data Flow | Used to connect processes to each other, to sources or sinks; the arrowhead indicates direction of data flow. |
|  | Process | Perform some transformation of input data to yield output data. |
| 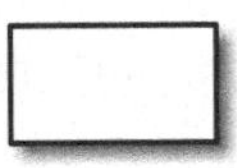 | Source or Sink (External Entity) | A source of system inputs or sink of system outputs. |
| 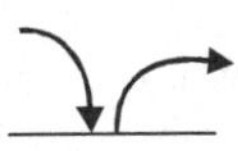 | Data Store | A repository of data; the arrowheads indicate net inputs and net outputs to store. |

Fig : Symbols for data flow diagrams

## LEVELLING

A level 0 DFD, also called a fundamental system model or context model represents the entire software element as a single bubble with input and output data indicated by incoming and outing arrows, respectively. Then the system is decomposed and represented as a DFD with multiple bubbles. Part of the system represented by each of these bubbles are then decomposed and documented as more and more detailed DFDs. It is important to preserve the number of inputs and outputs between levels; this concept is called leveling by DeMacro.

As the bubbles are decomposed into less and less abstract bubbles, the corresponding data flows may also need to be decomposed. For example, it may be sufficient to label the data flow between the employee data. However, when payroll is further decomposed into Obtain Salary and Dependents, Compute Deductions, and Print Check. We find that we must also decompose the data flow called Employee_Data into its constituent components namely, Number_of_dependents, each flowing into a unique (or possible multiplicity of) sub-bubbles. This parallel refinement of data is shown in figure :

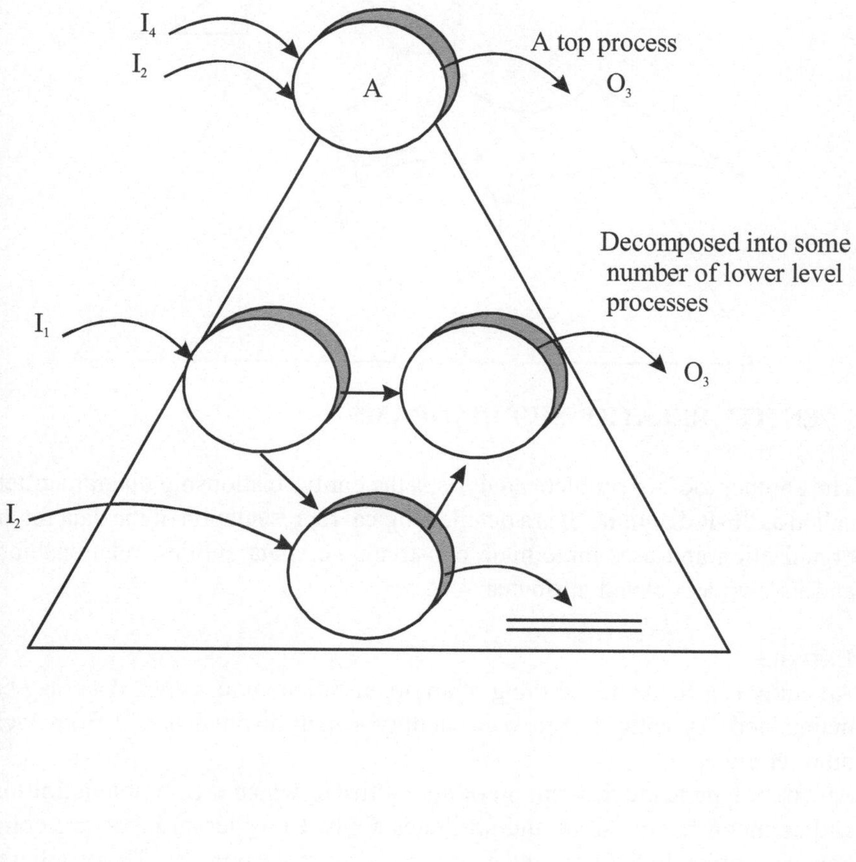

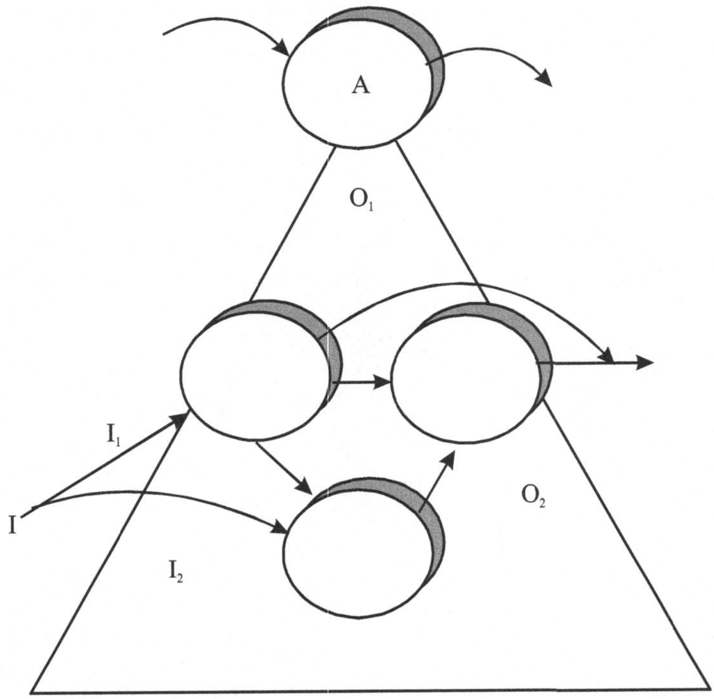


## ENTITY-RELATIONSHIP DIAGRAMS

The another tool for problem analysis is the entity-relationship diagram, often called as "E-R diagram". It is a detailed logical representation of the data for an organization and uses three main constructs i.e., data entities, relationships, and its own associated attributes.

### ENTITIES

An entity is a fundamental thing of an organization about which data may be maintained. An entity has its own identity, which distinguishes it from each other entity.

An entity type is the description of all entities to which a common definition and common relationships and attributes apply. Consider an insurance company that offers both home and automobile insurance policies. These policies are offered to individuals and businesses. POLICY and CUSTOMER are both entity types in this example, while home and automobile are entities of POLICY, and individual and business are entities of CUSTOMER.

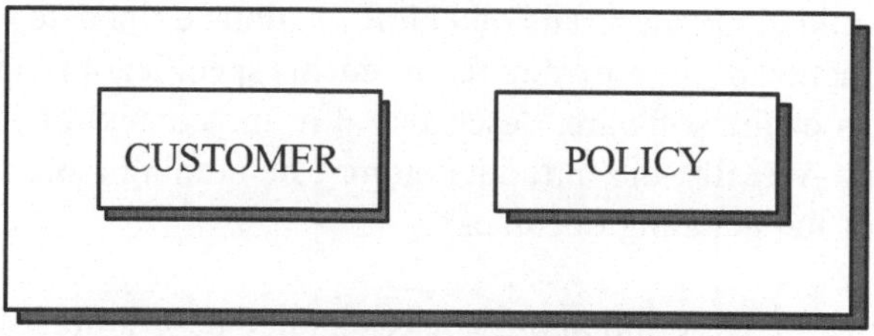


FIG: Two entity types in an E-R diagram

**RELATIONSHIPS**

A relationship is a reason for associating two entity types. These relationships are sometimes called binary relationships because they involve two entity types. Some forms of data model allow more than two entity types to be associated. A CUSTOMER is insured by a POLICY. A POLICY CLAIM is made against a POLICY

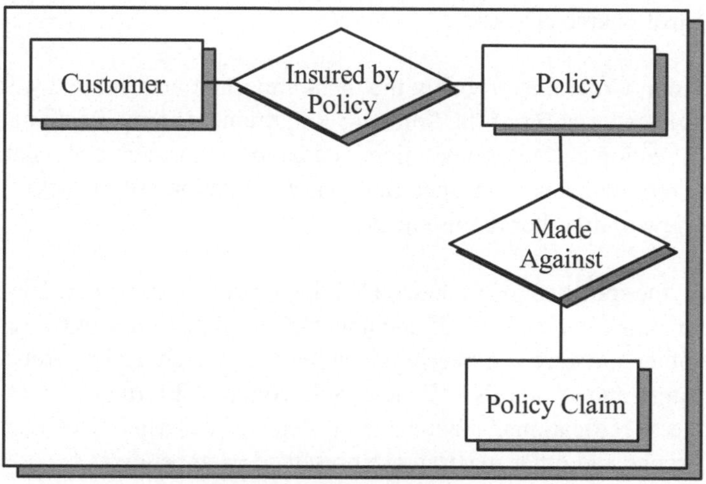


Fig: Relationship added to ERD

## SOFTWARE REQUIREMENT SPECIFICATION

### THE DOCUMENT

**Q7. What does the SRS document contain ?**

The Software Requirement Specification is produced at the culmination of the analysis task. The function and performance allocated to software as part of system engineering are refined by establishing a complete information description, a detailed functional description, a representation of system behaviour, an indication of performance requirements and design constraints,

appropriate validation criteria and other information pertinent to requirements.
**1.** The Introduction of the software requirements specification states the goals and objectives of the software, describing it in the context of the computer-based system. Actually, the Introduction may be nothing more than the software scope of the planning document.

**2.** The Information Description provides a detailed description of the problem that the software must solve. Information content, flow and structure are documented.

**3.** A description of each function required to solve the problem is presented in the Functional Description.

**4.** The Behavioral Description section of the specification examines the operation of the software as a consequence of external events and internally generated control characteristics.

**5.** Validation Criteria is probably the most important and ironically, the most often neglected section of the Software Requirements Specification. We neglect this section because completing it demands a thorough understanding of software requirements. Yet, specification of validation criteria acts as an implicit review of all other requirements.

**6.** Finally, the specification includes a Bibliography and Appendix. The bibliography contains references to all documents that relate to the software. These include other software engineering documentation, technical references, vendor literature and standards. The appendix contains information that supplements the specifications. Tabular data, detailed description of algorithms, charts, graphs and other material are presented as appendixes.

**PRINCIPLES**

**Q8. Five principles of specification.**

Following are the five principles of specification :

**1.** Separate functionality from implementation.

**2.** Develop a model of the desired behaviour of a system that encompasses data and the functional responses of a system to various stimuli from the environment.

**3.** Establish the context in which software operates by specifying the manner in which other system components interact with software.

**4.** Define the environment in which the system operates and indicate how "a highly inter-wined collection of agents react to stimuli in the environment (changes to objects) produced by those agents".

**5.** Create a cognitive model rather than a design or implementation model. The cognitive model describes a system as perceived by its user community.

## METRICS FOR ANALYSIS MODEL

### BANG METRIC

**Q9. Write short note on Bang Metric.**

The bang metric can be used to develop an indication of the size of the software to be implemented as a consequence of the analysis model. The bang metric is "an implementation independent indication of system size." To compute the bang metric, the software engineer must first evaluate a set of primitives – elements of the analysis model that are not further subdivided at the analysis level. Primitives are determined by evaluating the analysis model and developing counts for the following forms:

**Functional primitives (FuP)** – The number of transformations (bubbles) that appear at the lowest level of a data flow diagram.

**Data elements (DE)** – The number of attributes of a data object, data elements are not composite data and appear within the data dictionary.

**Objects (OB)** – The number of data objects.

**Relationship (RE)** – The number of connections between data objects.

**States (ST)** – The number of user observable states in the state transition diagram.

**Transitions (TR)** – The number of state transitions in the state transition diagram.

In addition to these six primitives, additional counts are determined for

**Modified manual function primitives (FuPM)** – Functions that lie outside the system boundary but must be modified to accommodate the new system.

**Input data elements (DEI)** – Those data elements that are input to the system.

**Output data elements (DEO)** – Those data elements that are output from the system.

**Retained data elements (DER)** – Those data elements that are retained (stores) by the system.

**Data token (TCi )** – The data tokens (data items that are not subdivided within a functional primitive) that exist at the boundary of the *i*th functional primitive (evaluated for each primitive).

**Relationship connections (REi)** -- The relationships that connect the *i*th object in the data model to other objects.

Most software can be allocated to one of two domains: function strong or data strong, depending upon the ratio RE/FuP. Function-strong application (often encountered in engineering and scientific applications) emphasize the transformation of data and do not generally have complex data structures. Data-strong applications (often encountered in information system applications) tend to have complex data models.

RE/FuP < 0.7 implies a function-strong application.
0.8 < RE/FuP < 1.4 implies a hybrid application.
RE/FuP > 1.5 implies a data-strong application.

**Q10. Consider the process of automation of a book distribution company. The details are given below:**

**"The library of Computer Sciences (LOCS) Corporation specializes in selling computer related books at low prices to computer specialists. It does this by mailing every month to every one of the current subscribers the following:**

- **A brief synopsis of the latest selection of the month book.**
- **A catalog of other available books.**
- **A postcard on which subscribers indicate whether or not they want the latest Selection of the month and/or other selections from the catalog.**

**When the company started its business three years ago, it did so with a small office and three employees, and all work was performed manually. The company now sells thirty thousand books per month and employs a full time staff of twenty. Unfortunately all work is still performed manually. The company recently purchased a computer system, thinking it would solve the problems. The company has contacted Software Company to evaluate its operations and develop an automated system. It is not at all clear at this point whether or not the solution will include automating any or all of the following: Payroll and human resources, inventory, conveyor belts, and robots to move books, accounts, payable and receivable, and so forth".**

This problem can be analyzed by both the ways, i.e., Structured Requirement Definition (SRD) and Structured Analysis & Design Techniques (SADT).

**Structured Requirements Definition**

To employ the SRD approach, we interview personnel from each of the major division of the company and ask them to tell us that what their job involves. As each person describes his or her role, we record on a DFD all the interfaces between that individual and others. Let us assume that we have been given the organization chart shown in fig.

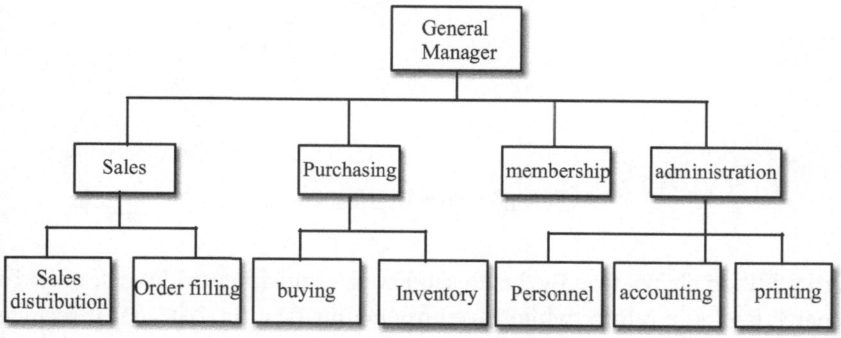


Fig 1 : LOCS Corporation Organization Chart

We decide to speak to representatives from the eight organizational units that show no subordinates, i.e., sales distribution, order filling, buying, inventory, membership, personnel, accounting, and printing.

Records the results of initial interviews. The next step in SRD is to merge the DFDs into one large DFD. When that is attempted, there arise three obvious inconsistencies in perspectives:

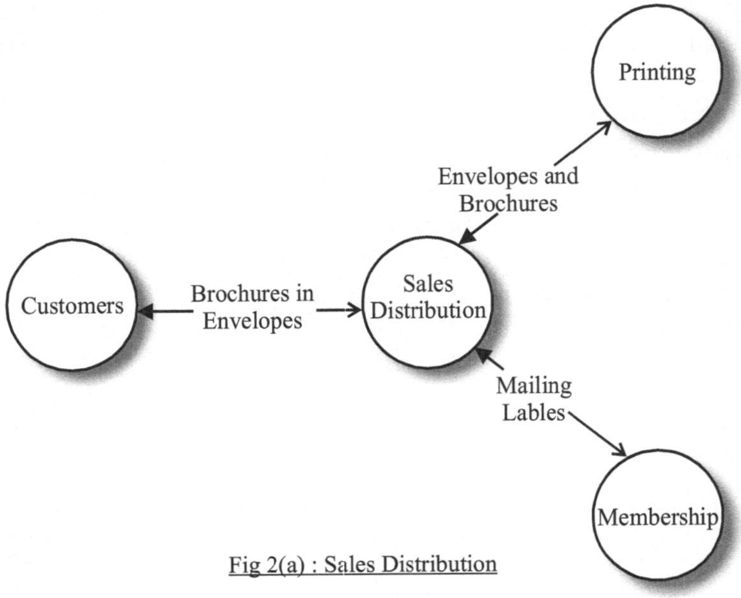


Fig 2(a) : Sales Distribution

Order Filling claims **(see fig 2a)** to send book requisitions to Inventory and to receive books in return, while Inventory claims **(see fig 2d)** that it receives book requisitions from Sales that it responds to with books. This is only a minor discrepancy; Sales is really only an aggregate organization that includes both Sales Distribution and Order Filling (**see fig 1**). This is resolved by updating fig 2d to the shown in fig 3.

According to Sales Distribution (see fig 2a), mailing labels are received by them directly from Membership. However, according to Membership (see fig 2e), it does not create mailing labels at all but instead sends mailing lists to Printing, which in turn generates mailing labels. Printing corroborates this latter view in fig 2h. One of the primary purposes of SRD is to uncover misunderstandings in how an organization behaves; therefore, these types of discrepancies are to be expected. Since there can be only one easily, we know that the issue can be resolved. In this case, Sales Distribution was mistaken. We correct fig 2a with fig 4.

When SRD is performed on real companies, functional and support organizational perspective tend not to be complementary. This is primarily due to the fact that when a functional organization is asked what it does, it tends to stress its primary functional purpose rather than its interface to support organizations. Thus many of the information flows reported by personnel (see fig 2f) and Accounting (see fig 2g) do not appear on other DFDs. These should be resolved by either deleting those support information flows (if there is no plan to automate them ) or adding them to all functional organizations' DFDs (to achieve consistency). In this case, we have chosen to delete them.

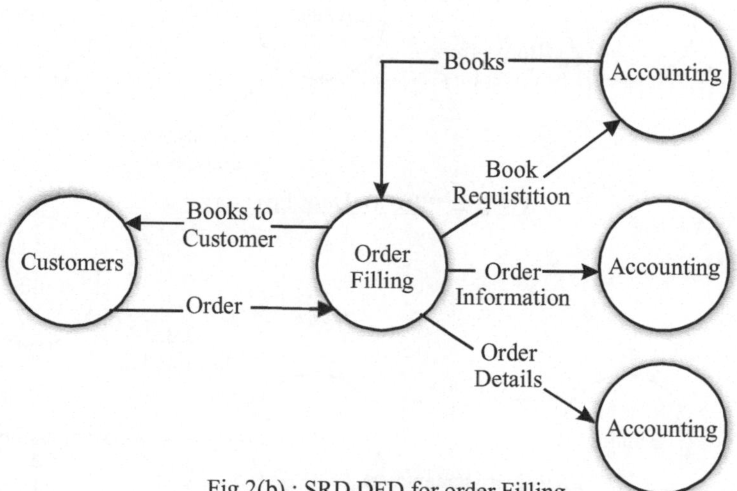


Fig 2(b) : SRD DFD for order Filling

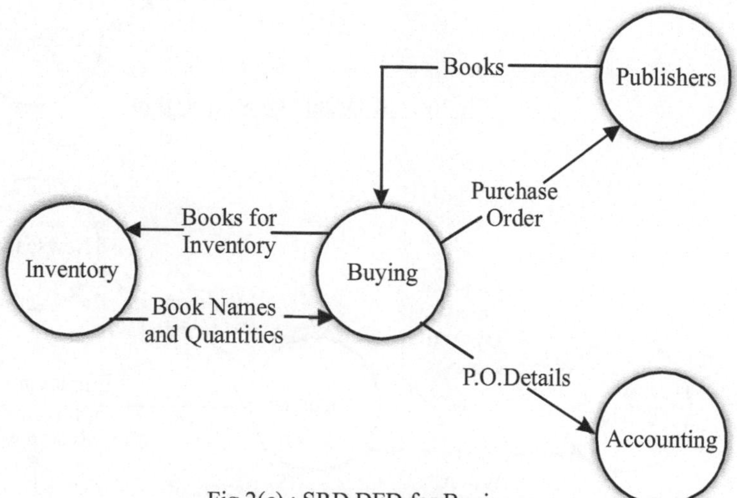


Fig 2(c) : SRD DFD for Buying

Once the preceding issues are resolved, we can easily merge the individual DFDs into one consistent DFD, as shown in fig 5. It now

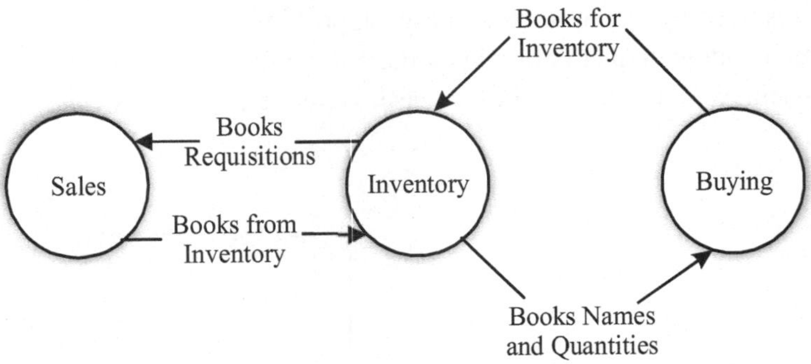


Fig 2(d) : SRD DFD for Inventory

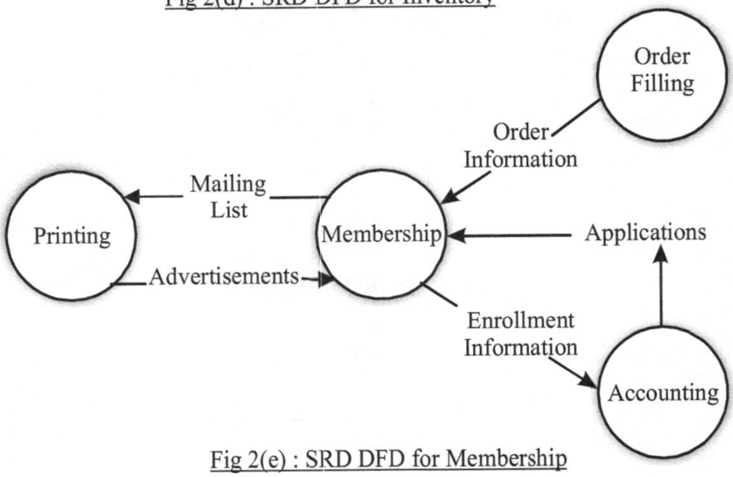


Fig 2(e) : SRD DFD for Membership

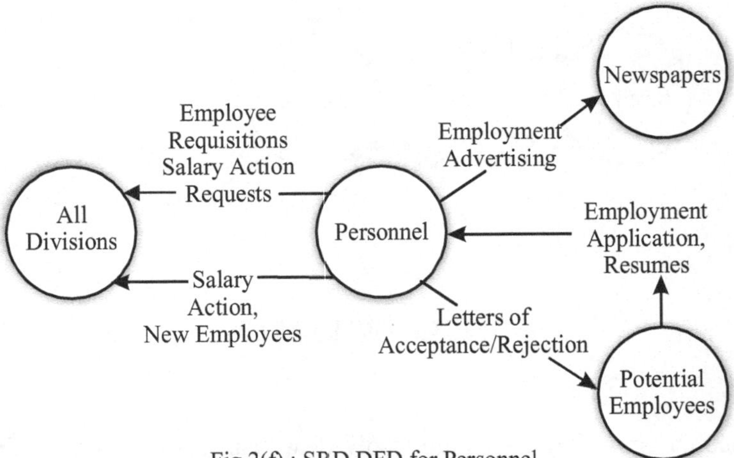


Fig 2(f) : SRD DFD for Personnel

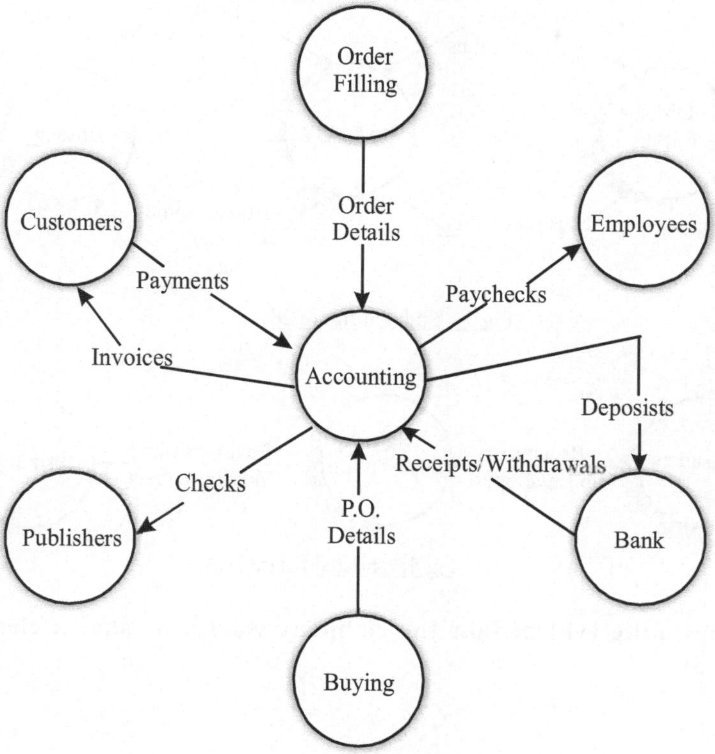


Fig 2(g) : SRD DFD for Acconting

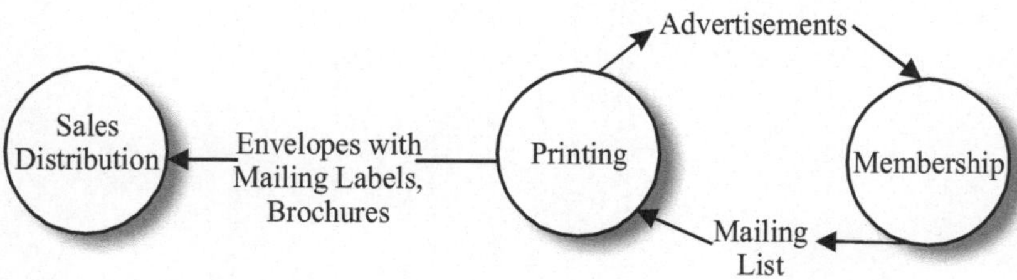


Fig 2(h) : SRD DFD for Printing

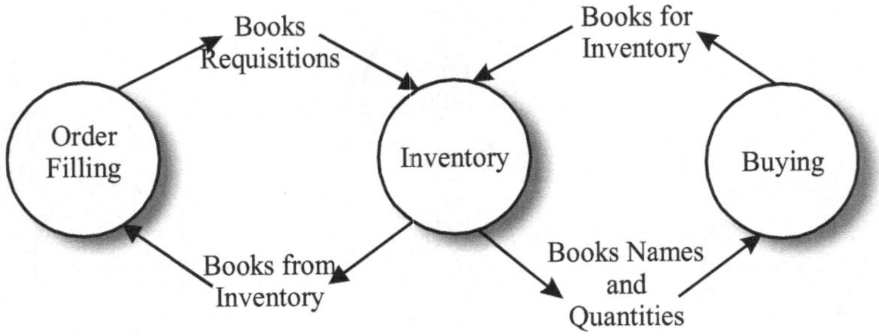


Fig 3 : Updated figure 2d

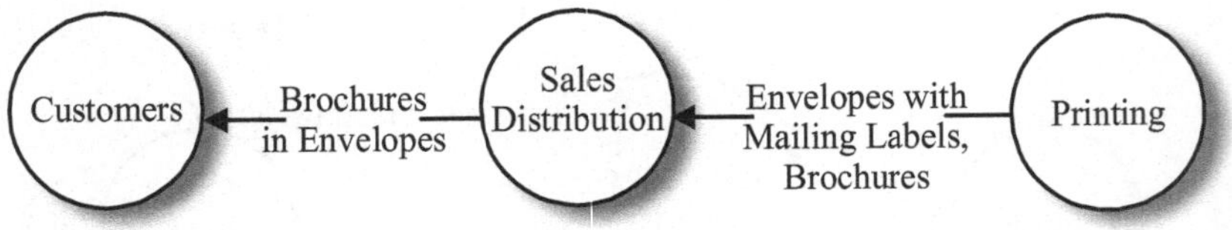


Fig 4: Updated figure 2(a)

**becomes quite evident how the company works. As shown clearly in figure 5:**

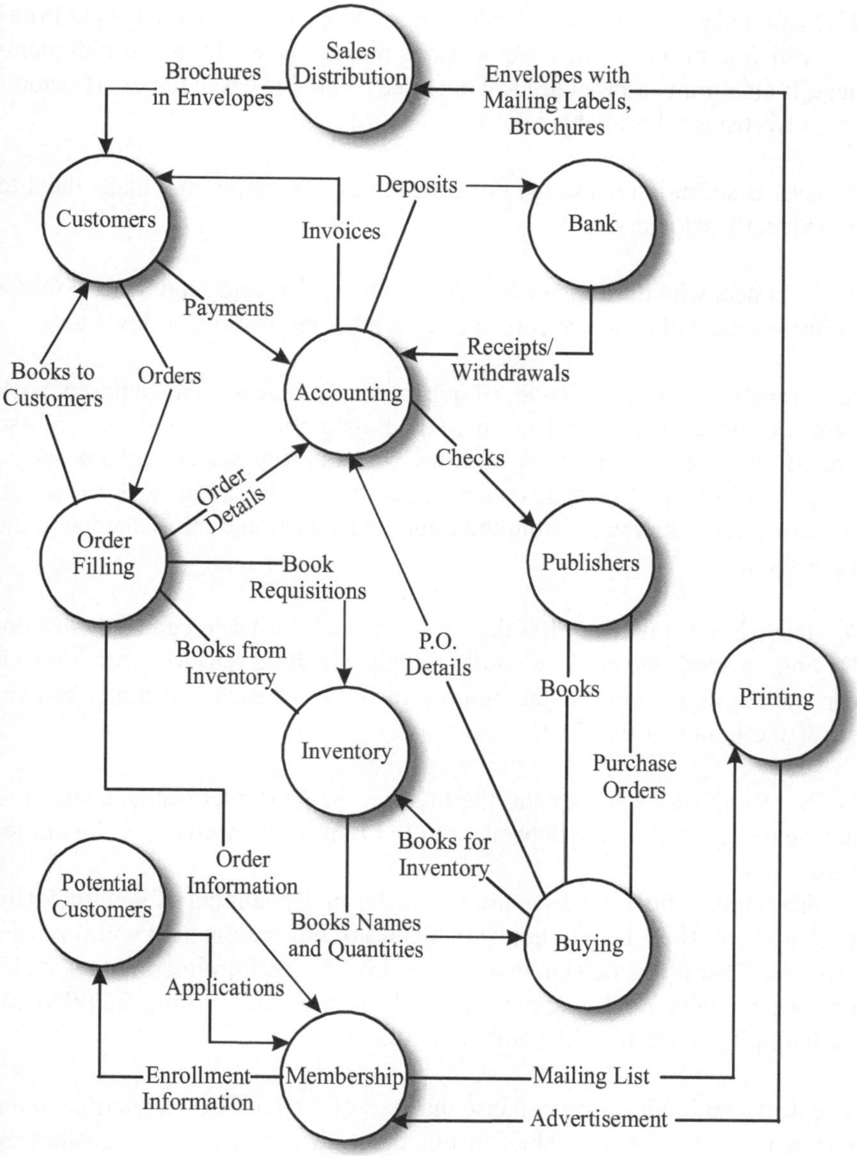


Fig 5: DFD for LOCS

**1.** Printing prints advertisements to join the book club. Membership sends this enrollment information to potential Customers. Some of those people respond with applications to join the book club.

**2.** On a regular (e.g., monthly basis, Membership sends mailing lists to Printing, which in turn runs off envelopes and mailing labels for all current members. It also prints a brochure to be mailed to all current members (Customers) advertising all available books.

**3.** Sales Distribution packs the brochures in the envelopes and mails them to all current Customers.

**4.** Customers who desire to order books, place orders and send them to Order Filling. Order Filling sends corresponding book requisitions to Inventory.

**5.** If Inventory does not have a book in stock, it sends the required book names & quantities needed to buy, which assembles and sends a purchase order to Publishers, who sends back the books to Buy, which replenishes the Inventory. Buying also sends copies of purchase order details to Accounting, which makes withdrawals from the Bank (via check) and mails cheque to the Publishers.

**6.** Meanwhile if Inventory has the books in stock (or has received them from Buying), it sends the books to Order Filling, which (a) tells Membership so it can update its records for the number of books to each Customer, and (b) sends the books to the Customers.

**7.** On receipt of the books and the invoice, the Customer sends payment to Accounting, which make deposits into the Bank and receives receipts in return.

At this point of time, we have a much better understanding of how the company operates (i.e., the problem ) but no idea of how automation will solve the problem. That is a good sign that we are correctly performing problem analysis - we are neither defining the external behaviour (i.e., writing the SRS) nor designing the internal of the software system.

The next step in SRD is to collapse that part of the DFD corresponding to the company into just one bubble. In this case, all bubbles except Customers, Potential Customers, Bank, and Publishers comprise the company. When we collapse these into one bubble, preserving all its external interfaces, we arrive at fig 6. Furthermore at our current level of increased understanding of the company, we can now isolate three major functions of LOCS: A-soliciting new customers, B-selling books, and C-buying books. The next step in using SRD is to define these functions in terms of the information flows defined in **fig6.**

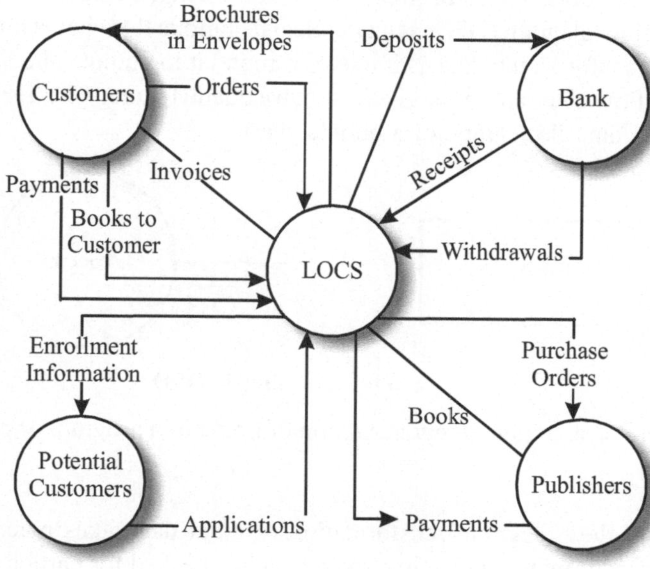


Fig 6: Collapsed DFD for LOCS

Using the notation Ai, Bi, and Ci to denote the ith step in function A, B, and C, respectively, to label the arcs, we arrive at **fig 7.**

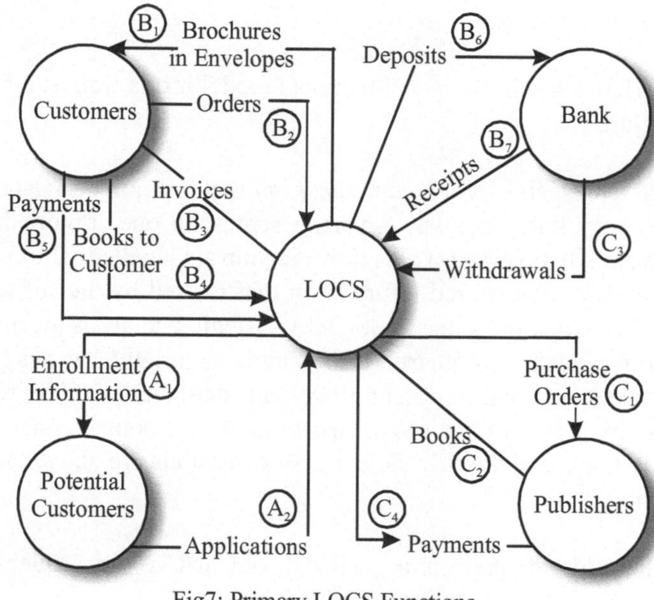


Fig7: Primary LOCS Functions

**Q11. List the differences between Data Flow Diagram and Flowchart.**

(i) A data flow diagram (DFD) is a graphical technique that shows information flow and transforms the data as it move from input to output. The basic form of a data flow diagram is as given in subsequent Figure. The DFD is also known as a data flow graph or a bubble chart.

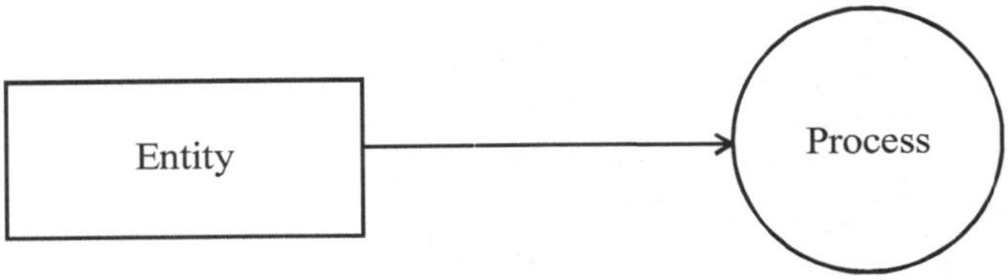


**Zero level or simple DFD**

A flow chart is a graphical representation of Logic of a program or procedural design.

**(ii)** In Data flow diagram transformation of input data takes place. In flow chart no transformation occur only data may be checked for particular validation.

**(iii)** The data flow diagram is used to represent a system or software at any level of abstraction. DFDs may be partitioned into levels that represent increasing information flow and functional detail.
Not an issue in flow chart.

**(iv)** DFD offers a mechanism for functional modelling as well as information flow modelling.

**(v)** A circle represents a *process* or *transform* that is applied to data (or control) and changes it in some way. An arrow represents one or more data items or data objects. All arrows on a data flow diagram are labelled. The double line represents a *data store*-stored information that is used by the software. The simplicity DFD notation is one reason why structured analysis techniques are the most widely used. Flow chart is quite simple pictorially. Various entities in flow chart are boxes that represent processing step, diamond box represents logical condition and arrows show flow of control. Loops e.g. do-while, do until can be represented easily. Select case extensions are shown as if-then-else construct.

**(vi)** The data flow diagram is a graphical tool that is very valuable during software requirements analysis.

**(vii)** However, the diagram can be misinterpreted if its function is confused with the flowchart. A data flow diagram depicts information flow without explicit representation of procedural logic (*e.g.,* conditions or loops). It is not a flowchart.

In flow chart additional complications of all logical tests leads to difficult situations to control software flow, increases possibility of error and have negative effect on readability and maintainability.

## TESTABILITY, UNDERSTANDABILITY & MODIFIABILITY

Testability, understandability and modifiability are closely related. It is very difficult in an SRS to quantify their required levels in a final product. This is unfortunate because these are among the most important contributors to full life cycle cost of software. Specifying required levels of cohesion and coupling in the design is probably the best the industry has to offer at this point. Cohesion should be expressed as minimally acceptable for any one module and a minimally acceptable average for all modules in the design. Coupling should be expressed as maximally acceptable for any pair of modules and a maximally acceptable average for all pairs of modules in the design.

Certain languages are also inherently more understandable and thus more maintainable and flexible. There is certainly a great deal of controversy concerning which languages fits into which categories, but most people agree that in general, the higher the language, the easier it is to understand. Operations, control structures and data types are closer to the application and further from the underlying machine. In addition some languages enable us easily to construct abstractions from available primitive elements and thus raise the effective level of the language.

CHAPTER-5

# MODULARITY

Design is a meaningful engineering representation of something that is to be built. It can be traced to a customer's requirements and at the same time assessed for quality against a set of predefined criteria for "good" design.

## ANALYSIS MODEL & DESIGN MODEL MAPPING

Each of the elements of the analysis model provides information that is necessary to create the four design models required for a complete specification of design. The flow of information during software design is illustrated in following Figure

The data design transforms the information domain model created during analysis into the data structures that will be required to implement the software. The data objects and relationships defined in the entity relationship diagram and the detailed data content depicted in the data dictionary provide the basis for the data design activity.

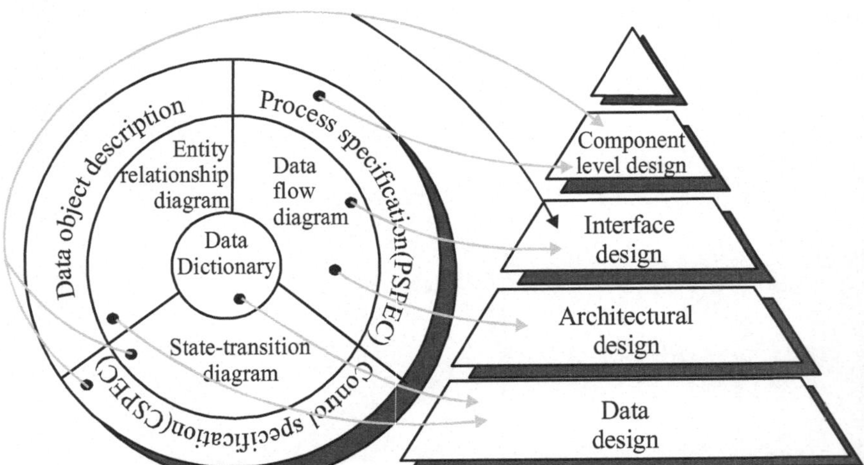

The architectural design defines the relationship between major structural elements of the software, the "design patterns" that can be used to achieve the requirements that have been defined for the system and the constraints that affect the way in which architectural design patterns can be applied.
The interface design describes how the software communicates within itself, with systems that inter-operate with it and with humans who use it.
The component-level design transforms structural elements of the software architecture into a procedural description of software components.

## DESIGN CONCEPTS

### MODULARITY

**Q1. Write briefly about modularity.**

The concept of modularity in computer software has been used for almost five decades. Software architecture embodies modularity; that is, software is divided into separately named and addressable components, often called modules, that are integrated to satisfy problem requirements.

Let C(x) be a function that defines the perceived complexity of a problem x, and E(x) be a function that defines the effort (in time) required to solve a problem x. For two problems, $p_1$ and $p_2$, if

$C(p_1) > C(p_2)$.................(1)

it follows that

$E(p_1) > E(p_2)$...........(2)

As a general case, this result is intuitively obvious. It does take more time to solve a difficult problem.
Another interesting characteristics has been uncovered through experimentation in human problem solving. That is

$C(p_1 + p_2) > C(p_1) + C(p_2)$................(3)

Expression (3) implies that the perceived complexity of a problem that combines $p_1$ and $p_2$ is greater than the perceived complexity when each problem is considered separately. Considering (3) and the condition implied by Expressions(1 & 2), it follows that

$E(p1 + p2) > E(p1) + E(p2)$ .....................(4)

This leads to a "divide and conquer" conclusion – it's easier to solve a complex problem when you break it into manageable pieces.

## COUPLING

**Q2. What is module coupling ?**

**#Define module coupling & cohesion.**

Coupling is a measure of interconnection among modules in a software structure. Coupling depends on the interface complexity between modules, the point at which entry or reference is made to a module and what data pass across the interface.

As long as a simple argument list is present (i.e. simple data are passed; a one-to-one correspondence of items exists), low coupling (called data coupling) is exhibited in this portion of structure. A variation of data coupling, called stamp coupling, is found when a portion of a data structure (rather than simple arguments) is passed via a module interface.

Control coupling is very common in most software designs where a "control flag" (a variable that controls decisions in a subordinate or super-ordinate module) is passed between modules.

Modules access a data item in a global data area (e.g., a disk file or a globally accessible memory area.

The highest degree of coupling, content coupling, occurs when one module makes use of data or control information maintained within the boundary of another module.

## COHESION

Cohesion is a natural extension of the information-hiding concept. A cohesive module performs a single task within a software procedure, requiring little interaction with procedures being performed in other parts of a program. Stated simply, a cohesive module should (ideally) do just one thing.

At the low (undesirable) end of the spectrum, we encounter a module that performs a set of tasks that relate to each other loosely, if at all. Such modules are termed coincidentally cohesive. A module that performs tasks that are related logically (e.g., a module that produces all output regardless of type) is logically cohesive. When a module contains tasks that are related by the fact that all must be executed with the same span of time, the module exhibits temporal cohesion.

When processing elements of a module are related and must be executed in a specific order, procedural cohesion exists. When all the processing elements concentrate on one area of a data structure, communicational cohesion is present.

**Q3. When will you say that a module is coincidentally cohesive, logically cohesive or temporarily cohesive? Explain with appropriate examples.**

**[JUNE02, Q4(b)]**

Cohesion is a measure of the relative functional strength of a module and is also a natural extension of information hiding concept. When a module performs a set of tasks that relate to each other loosely, is said to be coincidentally cohesive and when a module performs tasks that are related logically is said to be logically cohesive and when a module contains tasks that are related by the fact that all must be executed within the same span of time, then it is said to be temporal cohesive.

For example, consider a module that performs error processing for engineering analysis package. The module is called when the computed data exceeds prespecified bounds. The module performs the following tasks :

**(1)** Stores computer based supplementary data on original computed data.
**(2)** It produces an error report on the user's workstation.
**(3)** It performs follow-up calculations requested by the user.
**(4)** It updates a database.
**(5)** It provides menu selection for subsequent processing.

Although the preceding tasks are loosely related, each is an independent functional unit or entity that might be performed best as a separate module. Combining the functions into a single module will increase the error propagation at time when modifications are to be made to any one of the processing tasks given above.

**Q4. Explain, using an example, how coupling and cohesion are related, Also give two examples to illustrate different levels of coupling and cohesion. [DEC04, Q4(a)]**

**Coupling & Cohesion are related as given in example :**

Coupling increases as number of calls between modules increases, or amount of shared data increases but at the same time cohesion decreases. If there had been reduced number of calls, coupling would have decreased & cohesion had increased. Module interaction is the point where cohesion & coupling are distinguished.

**Different Levels of Coupling**

A good design will have low coupling. Thus, interfaces should be carefully specified in order to keep low value of coupling.

| | |
|---|---|
| Data Coupling | (Best) |
| Stamp Coupling | ↑ |
| Control Coupling | |
| External Coupling | |
| Common Coupling | |
| Content Coupling | (Worst) |

**Figure :** The types of module coupling.

**Example 1 :** Some types of coupling are less desirable than others. The least desirable occurs when one module actually modifies another. Then the modified module is completely dependent on the modifying one. We call this content coupling and occur when one module modifies local data values or instructions in another module, or when one module branches into middle of another module. In figure (a), module B branches into D, even though D is supposed to be under the control of C.

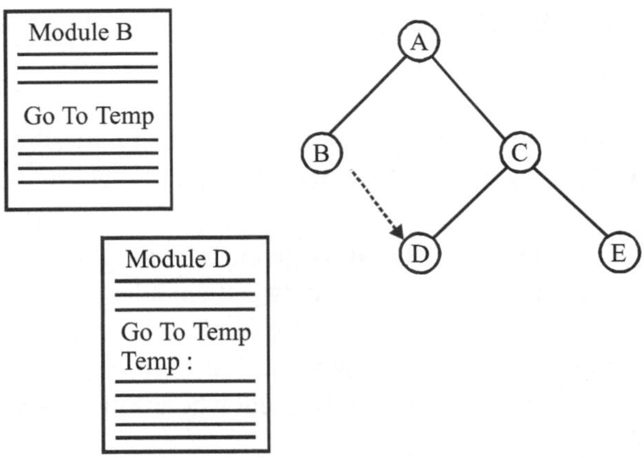


**Figure (a) : Example of content coupling.**

**Example 2 :** We can reduce the amount of coupling somewhat by organizing our design so that data are accessible from a common data store. However, dependency still exists, since making a change to the common data means tracing back to all modules that access that data to evaluate the effect of that change. This kind of dependence is called common coupling. With common coupling, it can be difficult to determine which module is responsible for having set a variable to a particular value. Figure (b) shows how common coupling works.

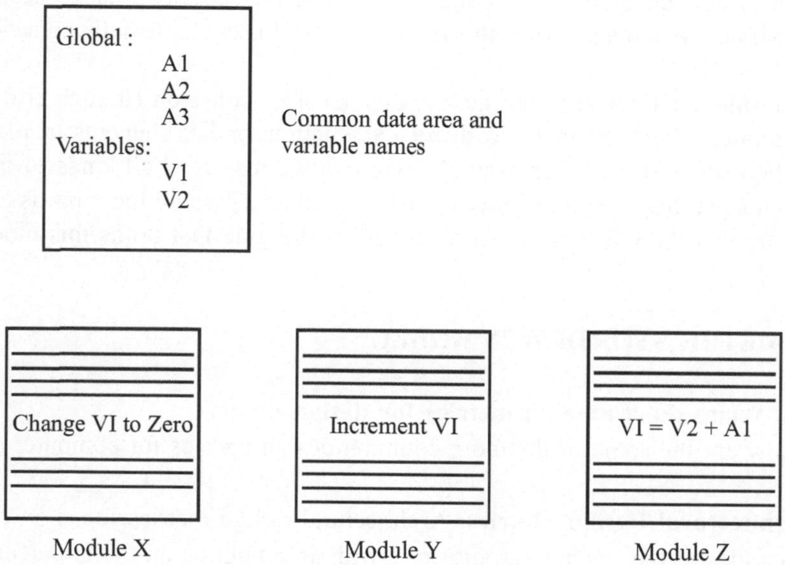


**Figure(b) : Example of common coupling**

**Different Levels of Cohesion**

| Cohesion type | Level |
|---|---|
| Functional Cohesion | Best (high) |
| Sequential Cohesion | ↑ |
| Communicational Cohesion | |
| Procedural Cohesion | |
| Temporal Cohesion | |
| Logical Cohesion | |
| Coincidental Cohesion | Worst (low) |

**Figure :** Types of module cohesion

**Example 1 :** The worst degree of cohesion, coincidental is found in a module whose elements have no apparent relationship to one another. In this case, unrelated functions, processes or data are found in the same module for reasons of convenience. For example, a module that checks a user's security classification and also prints this month's payroll is coincidentally cohesion.

**Example 2 :** Logical is the next higher level of cohesion (though still not desirable), where several logically related functions or data elements are placed in the same module. For example, one module may read all kinds of input (from tape, disk, communication port), regardless of where the input is coming from or how it will be used; "input" is the glue that holds this module together.

## METRICS FOR DESIGN MODEL

**Q5. Write short note on metrics for design model.**

Below are the some of the more common design metrics for computer software.

**Architectural Design Metrics:** Architectural design metrics focus on characteristics of the program architecture with an emphasis on the architectural structure and the effectiveness of modules. These metrics are black box in the box in the sense that they do not require any knowledge of the inner workings of a particular software component.

**Component-level Design Metrics:** Component-level design metrics on internal characteristics of software component and include measures of the "three Cs"-module cohesion, coupling and complexity. These measures can help a software engineer to judge the quality of a component-level design.

The metrics presented in this section are glass box in the sense that they require knowledge of the inner working of the module under consideration. Component-level design metrics may be applied once a procedural design has been developed. Alter natively, they may be delayed until source code is available.

**Cohesion Metrics :** The metrics are defined in terms of five concepts and measures.

*Data slice.* Stated simply, a data slice is a backward walk through a module that looks for data values that affect the module location at which the walk began.

*Data tokens.* The variables defined for a module can be defined as data tokens for the module.
*Glue tokens.* This set of Data tokens lies on one or more data slice.
*Superglue tokens.* These data tokens are common to every data slice in a module.
*Stickiness.* The relative stickiness of a glue token is directly proportional to the number of data slices that it binds.

**Coupling Metrics :** A metric for module coupling is one that encompasses data and control flow coupling, global coupling, and environmental coupling.

**Complexity Metrics :** The most widely used (and debated) complexity metric for computer software is cyclomatic complexity.
The metric provides a quantitative measure of testing difficulty and an indication of ultimate reliability.

**Interface Design Metrics**
*Layout appropriateness* (LA) is a worthwhile design metric for human/computer interfaces. A typical GUI uses *layout entities*-graphic icons, text, menus, windows, and the like-to assist the user in completing tasks.
For a specific layout (i.e., a specific GUI design), cost can be assigned to each sequence of actions according to the following relationship :
cost=3 [frequency of transition($k$) X cost of transition($k$)]
Where $k$ is a specific transition from one layout entity to the next as a specific task is accomplished.

**Q6. What are the five components of a design method ? Take any method which you know and describe its components. [JUNE01, Q6(a)]**
The five components of a design method are as follows :
**(i)** Data Flow Diagram
**(ii)** Data Dictionary
**(iii)** Entity Relationship Diagram
**(iv)** PERT Chart
**(v)** HIPO Diagram

**Data flow diagrams (DFDs)** have been used for many years prior to the advent of computers. DFDs show the flow of data through a system. The system may be a company, an organization, a set of procedures, a computer hardware system, a software system or any combination of the proceeding. The DFD is also known as a data flow graph or a bubble chart.

The following observations about DFDs are important :

**1.** All names should be unique. This makes it easier to refer to items of the DFD.

**2.** Remember that a DFD is now a flow chart. Arrows in a flow chart represent the order of events; arrows in DFD represent flowing data. A DFD does not imply any order of events.

**3.** Suppress logical decisions. If we ever have the urge to draw a diamond-shaped box in a DFD, suppress that urge! A diamond –shaped box is used in flow charts to represent decision points with multiple exit paths of which only one is taken. This implies an ordering of events, which makes no sense in a DFD.

**4.** Do not become bogged down with details. Defer error conditions and error handling until the end of the analysis.

| Symbol | Name | Function |
|---|---|---|
|  | Data Flow | Used to connect processes to each other, to sources or sinks; the arrowhead indicates direction of data flow. |
| 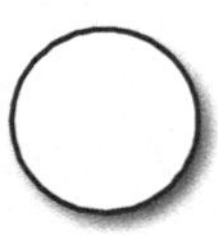 | Process | Perform some transformation of input data to yield output data. |
|  | Source or Sink (External Entity) | A source of system inputs or sink of system outputs. |
| 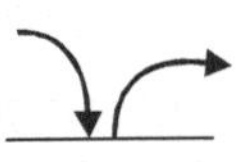 | Data Store | A repository of data; the arrowheads indicate net inputs and net outputs to store. |

Fig : Symbols for data flow diagrams

# CHAPTER-6

# SOFTWARE TESTING

**Q1. Why should we test ?**

Although software testing is itself an expensive activity, yet launching of software without testing may lead to cost potentially much higher than that of testing, especially in system where human safety is involved. In most system, however, it is the cost factor, which place a major role. It is both the driving force and the limiting factor as well. The most damaging error are those, which are not discovered during the testing process and therefore remain when the system 'goes live'. It is not possible to test the software for all possible combination of input cases. No software would ever be released by its creators if they were asked to certify that it was totally free of all error.

**Q2. What do you know about various types of special system tests ? Explain them briefly.** **[JUNE01, Q2(c)]**

Various types of special tests are as follows :

**1) Peak load test :**

During this test a stress test and performance test are applied aggregately to know the effect. For example special test may generate 10 interrupt where on average only 2 interrupts per second are being generated - input data rates may be increased abnormally maximum amount of memory may be examined when it is equipped with performance test it enable to show result about resource sharing (e.g. processors cycles) etc.

**2) Recovery testing :**

In some cases fault is fluorescent i.e. the system does not cease down. But in another cases the system fault may cause economic danger if it is not corrected within a specified time. A system test that forces the software to get fail in a variety of ways and verifies that the recovery is done in proper form is known as recovery testing.

**3) Security Testing :**

Security testing verifies that the protection mechanism built into a system will protect the system from improper penetrations into the system because any system that manages sensitive information is a target of improper penetration. The illegal penetration can be done by the hackers who are penetrating the system for playing games or by dishonest employees who want to take revenge from the employer can also try to penetrate the system or some individuals who are penetrating the system for their personal interests.

In security testing the tester plays the role of a person who is desiring to penetrate the system or may try to break down the protective measures; may cause system errors; may try to find the key for the system security.

**4) Stress Testing :**

Stress tests are designed to take the programs within abnormal situations by providing abnormal stress on the system. The stress testing may demand resources in abnormal quantity, frequency or volume.

A variation of stress testing is a technique called sensitivity testing. Sensitivity testing attempts to uncover data combinations within valid input classes that may cause instability or improper processing.

**5) Performance testing :**

This type of testing is done to test the performance of a software within a system. Rather performance testing occurs throughout all the steps in the testing process. At the unit level also we are conducting white box testing. Performance testing is often compelled with stress testing & always requires hardware & software for testing. By this a tester can uncover situations that lead to the degradation of a system or even system failure.

## 🗁TESTABILITY

**Q3. Explain testability & its characteristics.**

In ideal circumstances, a software engineer designs a computer program, a system or a product with "testability" in mind. Software testability is simply how easily (a computer program) can be tested.

A set of characteristics that lead to testable software are :

**Operability** – "The better it works, the more efficiently it can be tested."

**Observability** – "What you see is what you test."

**Controllability** – "The better we can control the software, the more the testing can be automated and optimized.

**Decomposability** – "By controlling the scope of testing, we can more quickly isolate problems and perform smarter retesting.

**Simplicity** – "The less there is to test, the more quickly we can test it."
**Stability** – "The fewer the changes, the fewer the disruptions to testing."
**Understandability** – "The more information we have, the smarter we will test."

## TESTING TYPES

Any engineered product (and most other things) can be tested in one of two ways:
**1.** Knowing the specified function that a product has been designed to perform, tests can be conducted that demonstrate each function is fully operational while at the same time searching for errors in each function;
**2.** Knowing the internal workings of a product, tests can be conducted to ensure that "all gears mesh," that is, internal operations are performed according to specifications and all internal components have been adequately exercised.

### BLOCK BOX TESTING

**Q4. Write short note on Black Box testing.**

Black-box testing, also called behavioral testing, focuses on the functional requirements of the software. That is, black-box testing enables the software engineer to derive set of input conditions that will fully exercise all functional requirements for a program. Black-box testing is not an alternative to white-box techniques. Rather, it is a complimentary approach that is likely to uncover a class of errors than white-box methods.

Black-box testing attempts to find errors in the following categories:
**(1)** incorrect or missing functions,
**(2)** interface errors,
**(3)** errors in data structures or external database access,
**(4)** behavior or performance errors, and
**(5)** initialization and termination errors.

### WHITE BOX TESTING

**Q5. Explain white box testing method.**

White box testing is a test case design method that uses the control structure of the procedural design to derive test cases. Using white box testing methods, the software engineer can derive test cases that

**(1)** guarantee that all independent paths within a module have been exercised at least once
**(2)** exercise all logical decisions on their true and false sides
**(3)** execute all loops at their boundaries and within their operational bounds, and
**(4)** exercise internal data structures to ensure their validity.

The white box testing is useful for finding following type of software errors:
- Logical errors and incorrect assumptions are inversely proportional to the probability that a program path will be executed. Errors tend to creep into our work when we design and implement function, conditions, or control that are out of the mainstream.
- We often believe that a logical path is not likely to be executed when, in fact, it may be executed on a regular basis.
- Typographical errors are random. When a program is translated into programming language source code, it is likely that some typing errors will occur.

## BASIC PATH TESTING

Basis path testing is a white-box testing technique. The basis path method enables the test case designer to derive a logical complexity measure of a procedural design and use this measure as a guide for defining a basis set of execution paths.

### CYCLOMATIC COMPLEXITY

**Q6. Explain McCabe's Cyclomatic Number.**

Cyclomatic complexity is a software metric that provides a quantitative measure of the logical complexity of a program. When used in the context of the basis path testing method, the value computed for cyclomatic complexity defines the number of independent paths in the basis set of a program and provides us with an upper bound for the number of tests that must be conducted to ensure that all statements have been executed at least once.
Cyclomatic complexity has a foundation in graph theory and provides us with an extremely useful software metric. Complexity is computed in one of the three ways:
**1.** The number of regions of the flow graph correspond to the cyclomatic complexity.
**2.** Cyclomatic complexity, V(G), for a flow graph, G, is defined as
$V(G)=E-N+2$
Where $E$ is the number of flow graph edges, $N$ is the number of flow graph nodes.

**3.** Cyclomatic complexity, *V(G),* for a flow graph, *G,* is also defined as $V(G)=P+1$

Where *P* is the number of predicate nodes contained in the flow graph G.

**Advantages of McCabe Cyclomatic Complexity :**

- It can be used as a ease of maintenance metric.
- Used as a quality metric, gives relative complexity of various designs.
- It can be computed early in life cycle than of Halstead's metrics.
- Measures the minimum effort and best areas of concentration for testing.
- It guides the testing process by limiting the program logic during development.
- Is easy to apply.

**Drawbacks of McCabe Cyclomatic Complexity :**

The cyclomatic complexity is a measure of the program's control complexity and not the data complexity the same weight is placed on nested and non-nested loops. However, deeply nested conditional structures are harder to understand than non-nested structures. It may give a misleading figure with regard to a lot of simple comparisons and decision structures. Whereas the fan-in fan-out method would probably be more applicable as it can track the data flow.

## BLACK BOX METHODS

### Q7. Explain Boundary value analysis & equivalence partitioning.

**BOUNDARY VALUE ANALYSIS**

It has been observed that if the specific test cases are designed to check the boundaries of the input domain, probability of detecting an error increases. Consider a function F with two input variables x and y. These input variables will have some boundaries:

$a \leq x \leq b$

$a \leq y \leq d$

Hence input x and y are bounded by two intervals [a,b] and [c,d] respectively. For input x, we may design test cases with values a and b, just above a and b and also just below a and b. These test cases will have more chances to detect an error.

**EQUIVALENCE PARTITIONING**

Equivalence partitioning is a black-box testing method that divides the input domain of a program into classes of data from which test cases can be derived. An ideal test case single-handedly uncovers a class of errors (e.g., incorrect processing of all character data) that might otherwise require many cases to be executed before the general error is observed. Equivalence partitioning strives to define a test case that uncovers classes of errors, thereby reducing the total number of test cases that must be developed.

Equivalence classes may be defined according to the following guidelines:
**1.** If an input condition specifies a range, one valid and two invalid equivalence classes are defined.
**2.** If an input condition requires a specific value, one valid and two invalid equivalence classes are defined.
**3.** If an input condition specifies a member of a set, one valid and one invalid equivalence class are defined.
**4.** If an input condition is Boolean, one valid and one invalid class are defined.

## TESTING ACTIVITIES

During testing, the major activities are centered around the examination and modification of source code. We proceed in levels from individual modules to the entire software system. At one end, we attempt to test modules in all possible ways so as to detect any error. From there, we combine and aggregate the modules and test their detailed structure and functions. At the end, we may ignore the internal structure of the software and concentrate on how it responds to the typical kind of operations that will be requested by the user. These three phases of testing are usually referred to as unit testing, integration testing, and system testing.
Generally, system testing is functional rather than structural.

### UNIT TESTING

**Q8. Write short note on Unit Testing. [JUNE01, Q6(b)(i)]**

Unit testing is the process of taking a module and running it in isolation from the rest of the software product by using prepared test cases and comparing the actual results with the results predicated by the specifications and design of the module. One purpose of testing is to find (and remove) as many error in the software as practical. There are number of reasons in support of unit testing than testing the entire product.
**1.** The size of a single module is small enough that we can locate an error fairly
easily.
**2.** The module is small enough that we can attempt to test it in some demonstrably
exhaustive fashion.

**3.** Confusing interactions of multiple error in widely different parts of the software are eliminated.

## INTEGRATION TESTING

**Q9. Write short note on Integration Testing. [JUNE99]**

The purpose of unit testing is to determine that each independent module is correctly implemented. This gives little chance to determine that the interface between modules is also correct, and for this reason integration testing must be performed. One specific target of integration testing is the interface: whether parameters match on both sides as to type, permissible ranges, meaning and utilization.

Top down – integration produced down the invocation hierarchy, adding one module at a time until an entire tree level is integrated; and thus it eliminates the need for drivers. The bottom up strategy works similarly from the bottom and has no need of stubs. A sandwich strategy runs from top and bottom concurrently, meeting somewhere in the middle.

Integration should follow the lines of first putting together those subsystem that are of great concern. This prioritization might dictate top-down integration if control and the user interface were the most worrisome or complex part of software. This can occur, for instance, if the customer is anxious to see a running program early in the testing phase. In another situation, the machine interface and performance might be of special interest, and then bottom-up integration would be dictated. With bottom-up integration we stand better chance of experiencing a high degree of concurrency during our integration. It has also been said that top-down integration is an exercise in faith that everything will work out well, whereas bottom-up integration shows that things really do work.

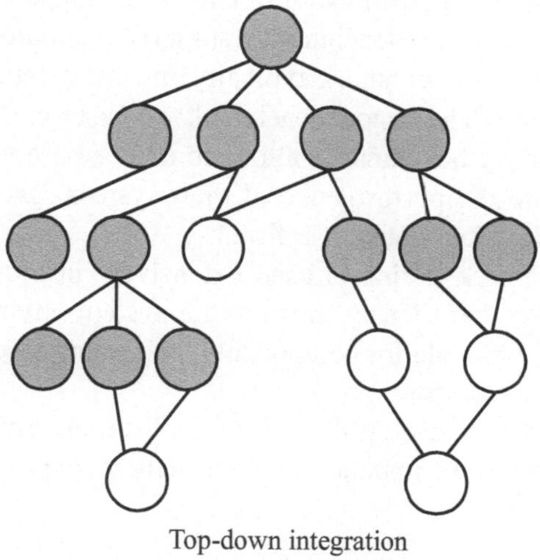

Top-down integration

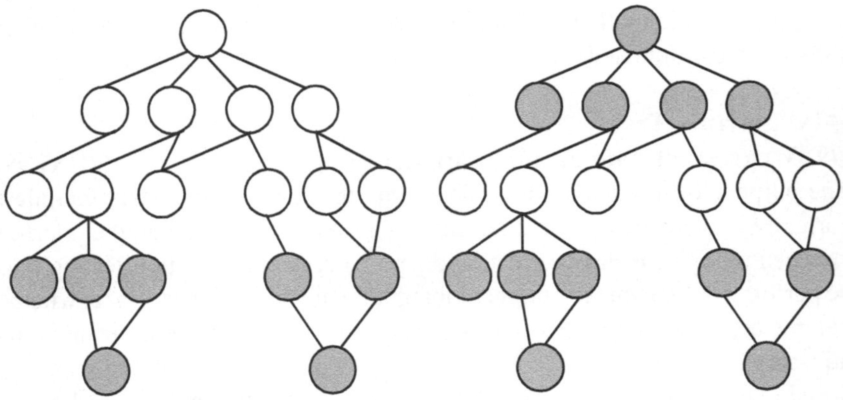


**Fig : Three different integration approaches**

## BENCHMARK TESTING

**Q10. Write a short note on "Benchmark Testing". [JAN01, Q5(c)]**

A benchmark is a test used by computer hardware, software and application vendors to test the performance of a system. Benchmark are designed so that the same test can be executed on a variety of hardware and software platforms. Because the same tests can be run on a variety of systems, the results can be compared to give a relative indication of performance.

Benchmarks usually test a specific function, as they can give only an indication of the system performance in that area. In practice we may find a system performs extremely well in OLTP(Online Transaction Processing) system benchmark but does not perform well in a decision support environment.

There are two categories of Benchmark testing (i) Standard and (ii) Custom. The industry standard benchmark typically run by computer hardware or software manufacturer. The custom benchmark is done by end user of integrator. The industry standard benchmarks allow computer hardware and software venders to compare the performance of their system against other system. These tests provide a fair status of a firm.

The custom benchmark testing is used extensively in industry to compare systems with a test that closely mirror's the system environment. Custom benchmark is also available for component level testing to know deficiencies and can make improvements.

Custom benchmark are also applicable to application software on different modules and functions. A comparative statement helps in product improvement process.

**Q11. What is system testing & during system testing which attributes of software are Vital to the user?**

Of the three levels of testing, the system level is closest to everyday experience. We test many things; a used car before we buy it, an on-line cable network service before we subscribe, and so on. A common pattern in these familiar forms is that we evaluate a product in terms of our expectations; not with respect to a specification or a standard. Consequently, goal is not to find faults, but to demonstrate performance. Because of this we tend to approach system testing from a functional standpoint rather than form a structural one. Since it is so intuitively familiar, system testing in practice tends to be less formal than it might be, and is compounded by the reduced testing that usually remains before a delivery deadline.

As we know, software is one component of a large computer based system. Ultimately, software is incorporated with other system components (e.g. new hardware, information), and thus, a series of special tests are to be conducted. Many times, software products are designed to run on a variety of hardware configurations. The software should actually be tested on many different hardware set-ups, although the full usage of memory, processor, operating system, and peripheral possibilities may be too large for complete testing.

There are many types of specifications, and we should be aware of those as we perform system testing. For instance, there may be a specified level of performance required from the software. This may involve measurement of response time under various loads and operating conditions. It may also require measurement of main and disk memory usage. Software reliability should also be measured during all other tests of the integrated product. If minimum and average up-time behaviour of the product were specified, then these should be met. The time and effort needed to recover from failures should also be recorded & compared with specifications. These specifications should represent customer's wants & needs, and during system testing, we can try to see if the requirements & specifications really do coincide.

Petschenik gives some guidelines for choosing test cases during system testing. The first is that testing the system's capabilities is more important than testing its components. This implies that failures that are catastrophic should be looked for whereas failures that are merely annoying need not worry us. The idea is that a user can deal with a badly formatted report, but probably cannot deal with unavailability of the report.

Petschenik's second rule is that testing the usual is more important than testing the exotic. This can be accomplished by subjecting the software to the kind of use that is representative of actual use, as described in the operational profile. The user may be able to help with this kind testing. In fact, software engineers may exhibit blind spots that cause them to notice exotic problems; while they ignore problems that user would spot immediately.

Third, if we are testing after modification of an existing product, we should test old capabilities rather than new ones. The rationale here is that the user is not depending on the new functions of the software, and would not be paralysed if these were not right. But a failure in the old functionality could do just that- paralyse the user's entire operation.

The rationale for Petschenik's testing priorities is that exhaustive testing of functional capabilities is incomplete with the kind of short update cycle imposed on many software products. Just s dependability is more important to the user than the total correctness, the basic and existing functionality also weigh much more heavily than total functionality. Foremost we should avoid disrupting current usage by introducing a new release of the product that would not support current functions.

During system testing, we should evaluate a number of attribute of the software that are vital to the user and are listed in Table.

| | |
|---|---|
| Usable | Is the product convenient, clear, and predictable? |
| Secure | Is access to sensitive data restricted to those with authorization? |
| Compatible | Will the product work correctly in conjunction with existing data, software, and procedures? |
| Dependable | Do adequate safeguard against failure and methods for recovery exist in the product? |
| Documented | Are manuals complete, correct, and understandable? |

These represent the operational correctness of the product and may be part of the software specifications.

**Q12. What is the Overall Strategy for Software testing.**

A strategy for software testing may also be viewed in the context of the spiral unit testing where testing begins at the vortex of the spiral and concentrates on each unit ( i.e., component ) of the software as implemented in source code. Testing progresses by moving outward along the spiral to integration testing, where the focus is on design and the construction of the software architecture. Taking another turn outward on the spiral, we encounter validation testing, where requirements established as part of software requirements analysis are validated against the software that has been constructed. Finally, we arrive at system testing, where the software and other system elements are tested as a whole. To test computer software, we spiral out along streamlines that broaden the scope of testing with each turn.

Considering the process from a procedural point of view, testing within the context of software engineering is actually a series of four steps that are implemented sequentially. The steps are shown in Figure.

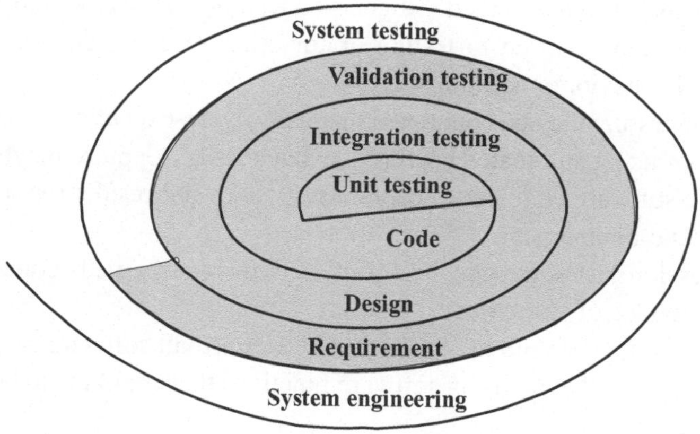


Figure: Testing Strategy

Initially, tests focus on each component individually, ensuring that it functions properly as a unit. Hence, the name unit tests. Unit testing makes heavy use of white-box testing techniques, exercising specific paths in module's control structure to ensure complete coverage and maximum error detection. Next, components must be assembled or integrated to form the complete software package. Integration testing addresses the issues associated with the dual problems of verification and program construction. Black-box test case design techniques are the most prevalent during integration, although a limited amount of white-box testing may be used to ensure coverage of major control paths. After the software has been integrated (constructed), during requirement analysis) must be tested. Validation testing provides final assurance that software meets all function, behavioral, and performance requirements. Black-box testing techniques are used exclusively during validation.

**Q13. Write short notes on :**

**a) Regression Testing :** Each time a new module is added as part of integration testing, the software changes. New data flow paths are established, new I/O may occur, and new control logic is invoked. These changes may cause problems with functions that previously wired flawlessly. In the context of an integration test strategy, regression testing is the re-execution of some subset of tests that have already been conducted to ensure that changes have not propagated unintended side effects.

In a broader context, successful tests (of any kind) result in the discovery of errors, sand errors must be corrected. Whenever software is corrected, some aspect of the software configuration ( the program, its documentation, or the data that support it) is changed. Regression testing is the activity that helps to ensure that changes (due to testing or for other reasons) do not introduce unintended behavior or additional errors.

Regression testing may be conducted manually, by re-executing a subset of all test cases or using automated capture/playback tools. Capture/playback tools enable the software engineer to capture test cases and results for subsequent playback and comparison.

The regression test suite (the subset of tests to be executed) contains three different classes of test cases:

- A representative sample of tests that will exercise all software functions.
- Additional tests that focus on software functions that are likely to be affected by the change.
- Tests that focus on the software components that have changed.

**b) Smoke testing :** Smoke testing is an integration testing approach that is commonly used when "shrink wrapped" software products are being developed. It is designed as a pacing mechanism for time-critical projects, allowing the software team to assess its project on a frequent basis. In essence, the smoke testing approach encompasses the following activities:

**1.** Software components that have been translated into code are integrated into a "built." A build includes all data files, libraries, reusable modules, and engineered components that are required to implement one or more product functions.

**2.** A series of tests if designed to expose errors that will keep the build from properly performing its function. The intent should be to uncover "show stopper" errors that have the highest likelihood of throwing the software project behind schedule.

**3.** The build is integrated with other builds and the entire product (in the current form) is smoking tested daily. The integration approach may be top down or bottom up.

**c) Alpha & Beta testing :** **[JUNE01, Q1(f)]**

A customer conducts the alpha test at the developer's sites. The software is used in natural setting with the developer "looking over the shoulder" of the user and recording errors and usage problems. Alpha tests are conducted in a controlled environment / conditions.

The beta test is conducted at one or more customer sites by the end-user of the software. Unlike alpha testing, the developer is generally not present. Therefore, the beta test is a "live" application of the software in an environment that cannot be controlled by the developer. The customer records all problems (real or imagined) that are encountered during beta testing and reports these to the developer at regular intervals. As a result of problems reported during beta tests, software engineers make modifications and then prepare for release of the software product to the entire customer base.

**d) Stress testing :** Stress tests are designed to confront programs with abnormal situations. In essence, the tester who performs stress testing asks: "How high can we crank this up before it fails?"

Stress testing executes a system in a manner that demands resources in a abnormal quantity, frequency, or volume. *For example,*

**(1)** Special tests may be designed that generate ten interrupts per second, when one or two is the average rate.

**(2)** Input data rates may be increased by an order of magnitude to determine how input functions will respond.

**(3)** Test cases that require maximum memory or other resources are executed.

**(4)** Test cases that may cause thrashing in a virtual operating system are designed.

**(5)** Test cases that may cause excessive hunting for disk-resident data are created. Essentially, the tester attempts to break the program.

A variation of stress testing is a technique called sensitivity testing. In some situations (the most common in mathematical algorithms), a very small ranges of data contained within the bounds of valid data for a program may cause extreme and even erroneous processing or profound performance degradation.

**Q14. Will exhaustive testing (even if it is possible for very small programs) guarantee that the program is 100 percent correct? Explain your answer.**

Software engineers some times refer to "exhaustive" testing when in fact they mean "exhausting" testing. Tests are almost never exhaustive. Having lots of tests which give the right results may be reassuring but it can never be convincing. Rather than relying on testing we should be relying in reasoning. We should be relying on arguments which can convince the reader using logic. However, exhaustive testing is impractical and infeasible, as even for small programs the number of elements in the input domain can be extremely large. No, the exhaustive testing does not guarantee that the program is 100% correct. It includes all the possible inputs to the program. It tells us whether output of the program is correct or not for all the possible input test cases. Although, the output is correct for all the input cases still there may be some error in the program. Exhaustive testing presents certain logistical problems. For even small programs, the number of possible logical paths can be very large. For example, consider 100 line program in C language. After some basic data declaration, the program contains two nested loops that execute from 1 to 20 times each, depending on conditions specified at input. Inside the interior loop, four-if-else constructs are required. There are approximately $10^{14}$ possible paths that may be executed in this program.

## DEBUGGING

The goal of testing is to identify errors (bugs) in the program. The process of testing gives symptoms and a program's failure is a clear symptom of the presence of an error. After getting a symptom, we begin an investigation to localize the error, i.e. to find out which module or interface is causing it. Then that section of the code is to be studied to determine the cause of the problem. This process is called debugging. Hence, debugging is the activity of locating and correcting errors. It can start once a failure has been detected. Unfortunately, going from the detection of a failure to correcting the error that is responsible, is far from trivial. It is one of the least understood activities in software development and is practiced with the least amount of discipline. It is often approached with much hope and little planning.

CHAPTER-7

# SOFTWARE RELIABILITY

## SOFTWARE RELIABILITY AND HARDWARE RELIABILITY

**Q1. Explain software reliability.**

The field of hardware reliability has been established for some time. Hence, one might ask how software reliability relates to it. In reality, the division between hardware and software reliability is somewhat artificial. Both may be defined in the same way. Therefore, one may combine hardware and software component reliabilities to get system reliability. Both depend on the environment. The source of failures in software is design faults, while the principal source in hardware has generally been physical deterioration. However, the concepts and theories developed for software reliability could really be applied to any design activity, including hardware design.

Once a software (design) defect is properly fixed, it is in general fixed for all time. Failure usually occurs only when a program (design) is exposed to an environment that it was not developed or tested for.

## FAILURE & FAULTS

**Q2. What are Failure & Faults ?**

Failure is something dynamic. The program has to be executed for a failure to occur. The term failure relates to the behavior of the program. This is the very general definition of failure. It can include such things as deficiency in performance attributes and excessive response time.

A fault is the defect in the program that, when executed under particular conditions, causes a failure. There can be different sets of conditions that cause failures, or the conditions can be repeated. Hence a fault can be the source of more than one failure. A fault is a property of the program rather than a property of its execution or behavior. It is what we are really referring to in general when we use the bug.

Reliability quantities have usually been defined with respect to time, although it would be possible to define them with respect to other variables. We are concerned with three kinds of time. The execution time for a program is the time that program, takes to execute. The second kind of time is calendar time.

It is the familiar time that we normally experience.

Sometimes the term clock time is used for a program. It represents the elapsed time from to end of program execution on a running computer. It includes wait time and the execution time of other programs.

### ENVIRONMENT

**Q3. Define environment and run type.**

The environment is described by the operational profile. We need to build up to the concept of the operational profile through several steps. It is possible to view the execution of a program as a single entity. The executive can last for months or even years for a real time system. However, it is more convenient to divide the execution into runs. The definition of run is somewhat arbitrary, but it is generally associated with some function that the program performs. Thus, it can conveniently describe the functional environment of the program. Runs that are identical repetitions of each other are said to form a run type. The proportion of runs of various types may vary, depending on the functional environment.

**Q4. Discuss the relationship between the human interface aspects of software and reliability.**

Interface design focuses on three areas of concern :

**(1)** The design of interfaces between software modules.

**(2)** The design of interfaces between the software and other non-human procedures and consumers of information.

**(3)** The design of interface between a human and the computer.

**Reliability :** The human interface of software and reliability are closely related. The software interface should be based on the following guidelines.

**1.** Consistent : Consistent format for menu; copy and input;

**2. Meaningful Feedback :** System should provide the user with visual and auditory feedbacks to ensure that two-way communication is established.

**3. Ask for Verification :** If a user requests the deletion of a file, ask for a confirmation "Are You Sure....?" Message should be displayed.

**4. Easy Reversal of most action : UNDO** functions should be available in every interactive application.

**5.** Reduce the amount of information that must be memorized between actions.

**6. Keystokes** should be **minimized**.

**7.** The system should protect itself from errors that might cause it to fail.

**8.** The **context sensitive help** must be available.

**9.** Display only that **information** that is **relevant** to the current context.
**10.** The **presentable formate** to enable the user to rapidly assimilate the information.
**11. Meaningful error message** must be displayed.
**12.** Use the available geography of the **display screen** and **use** it **efficiently.**
**13. Deactivate** commands and menus that are **inappropriate** in the context of current actions.
**14. Let** the **user control** the interactive flow interface must also consider the response time, error handling and help facility.

While End-User is not at Ease, operating the system, the utilization of the system would be greatly affected.

Estimates of the likelihood that a human error will occur in a human-machine system scenario are useful in both quantifying system reliability and in identifying better designs that reduce the potential for human errors.

**Q5. Explain the concept of Software Reliability, using an example. How can you conclude that a specific software is reliable ?**

**[JUNE04, Q4(b)]**

Reliability is the degree to which the system performs its intended functions over a time. In other words, reliability means that the information gathered is dependable enough to be used for making decisions about the system being studied. The term reliability is synonymous with dependability, consistency and accuracy. For example: If we administer the same questionnaire to the same subjects, will we get the same or similar results thus over here, in this example reliability is referred as stability, dependability and predictability.

We can conclude that a specific software is reliable only when the requirements are met by the software. The outputs come in same sequence as expected. The software should be friendly enough to expose its features and collect relevant information from user when situation arises. But new requirements become a big obstacle in reliability issue.

# CHAPTER-8

# RE-ENGINEERING & CASE

## RE-ENGINEERING

Consider any technology product that has served you well. You use it regularly, but it's getting old. It breaks too often, takes longer to repair than you'd like, and no longer represents the newest technology. What to do? If the product is hardware, you will likely throw it away and buy a newer model. But if it is custom-built software, that option may not be available. You will need to rebuild it. You will create a product with added functionality, better performance and reliability and improved maintainability. That is what we call re-engineering.

Software re-engineering is concerned with taking existing legacy systems and re-implementing them to make them more maintainable. As a part of this re-engineering process, the system may be redocumented or restructured. It may be translated to a more modern programming language, implemented on existing hardware technology. Thus, software re-engineering allows us to translate source code to a new language, restructure our old code, migrate to a new platform (such as client server), capture and then graphically display design information and redocument poorly documented systems.

## REVERSE ENGINEERING

Reverse Engineering is the process followed in order to understand different unknown and hidden information about a software system. It is becoming important, since several existing software products lack proper documentation, are highly unstructured, or there structure has degraded through a series of maintenance efforts. Maintenance activities cannot be performed without a complete understanding of the software system.

Apparently, understanding software looks a trivial task, but in the absence of any external documentation or clues, the task often becomes almost impossible.

## REVERSE ENGINEERING TOOLS

Reverse engineering is performed with the help of certain tools, otherwise doing the job manually would require enormous amount of time and labour, rendering the whole purpose of it not only useless but also expensive. Four basic components of a reverse engineering tool are :

**1.** The Restructure detects poorly structured code fragments and replaces them by equivalent structured code.

**2.** The Cross Referencer lists the places where each variable is defined and used.

**3.** The Static Analyzer detects anomalous constructs such as uninitialized variables and dead code.

**4.** The Text Editor and other simple tools support browsing and editing of the source code.

In addition to these, a reverse engineering tool may incorporate graphical user-interface and other visualization tools. **In the following subsections, we shall look at two reverse engineering tools.**

## CASE

The workshop for software engineering has been called an integrated project support environment (**discussed later in this chapter**) and the tools that fill the workshop are collectively called computer-aided software engineering.

CASE provides the software engineer with the ability to automate manual activities and to improve engineering insight. Like computer-aided engineering and design tools that are used by engineers in other disciplines, CASE tools help to ensure that quality is designed in before the product is built.

"environment" that encompasses tools, a database, people, hardware, a network, operating systems, standards and myriad other components.

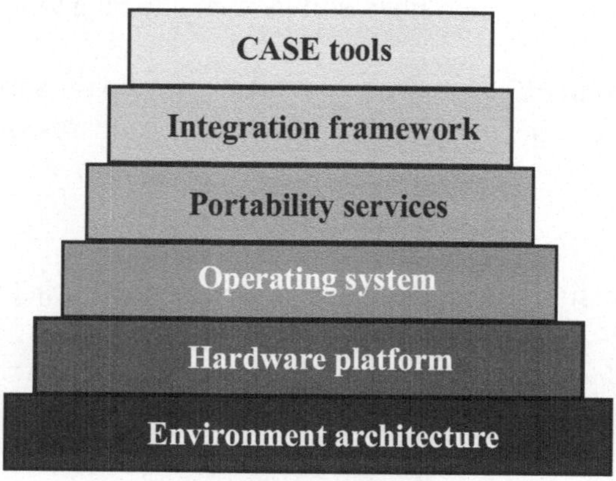

The environment architecture, composed of the hardware platform and system support (including networking software, database management, and object management services), lays the ground work for CASE. But the CASE environment itself demands other building blocks. A set of portability services provides a bridge between CASE tools and their integration framework and the environment architecture. The integration framework is a collection of specialized programs that enables individual CASE tools to communicate with one another, to create a project database, and to exhibit the same look and feel to the end-user (the software engineer). Portability services allow CASE tools and their integration framework to migrate across different hardware platforms and operating systems without significant adaptive maintenance.

**ADVANTAGES**

**1.** CASE tools assist in a particular software engineering activity (as analysis modeling).

**2.** CASE tools help to ensure that quality is designed before the product is built.

**Features that a future generation CASE tool should support :**

**1.** Assess global impact of a change; that is, how a change in one function effects requirements for other functions.

**2.** Improvement in reengineering tools that have wider range of programming languages.

**Q1. Explain the terms 'CASE tools' and 'CASE environment'. Give at least two advantages of using CASE tools. Describe two features that a future generation CASE tool should support. [DEC04, Q6(a)]**

**"CASE tools" :** the workshop for software engineering has been called an integrated project support environment and the tools that fill the workshop are collectively called computer-aided-software engineering tools.

**"CASE environment" :** "environment" that encompasses tools, a database, people, hardware, a network, operating systems, standards, and myriad other components.

**Advantages :**

**1)** CASE tools assign in a particular software engineering activity (as analysis modeling).

**2)** CASE tools help to ensure that quality is designed in before the product is built

**Features that a future generation CASE tool should support :**

**1)** Access global impact of a change; that is, how a change in one function affects requirements for outer functions.

**2)** Improvement in reengineering tools that have wider range of programming languages.

**Q2. State and explain the functionality of the various categories of CASE tools. [JUNE04, Q3(a)]**

CASE tools can be classified by function, by their role as instruments for managers or technical people, by their use in the various steps of the software engineering process, by the environment architecture (hardware and software) that supports them or even by their origin or cost.

**Business process engineering tools :** By modeling the strategic information requirements of an organization, business process engineering tools provide a "meta-model" from which specific information systems are derived. Rather than focusing on the requirements of a specific application, business information is modeled as it moves between various organizational entities within a company.

**Process modeling and management tools :** If an organization works to improve a business (or software) process, it must first understand it. Process modeling tools (also called process technology tools) are used to represent the key elements of a process so that it can be better understood.

**Project planning tools :** Tools in this category focus on two primary areas : software project effort and cost estimation and project scheduling.

**Risk analysis tools :** Identifying potential risks and developing a plan to mitigate, monitor and manage them is of paramount importance in large projects.

**Metrics and management tools :** Software metrics improve a manager's ability to control and coordinate the software engineering process and a practitioner's ability to improve the quality of the software that is produced.

**Quality assurance tools :** The majority of CASE tools that claim to focus on quality assurance are actually metrics tools that audit source code to determine compliance with language standards.

**Database management tools :** Database management software serves as a foundation for the establishment of a CASE database (repository) that we have called the project database.

**Software configuration management tools :** Software configuration management lies at the kernel of every CASE environment. Tools can assist in all five major SCM tasks - identification, version control, change control, auditing and status accounting.

**Analysis and design tools :** Analysis and design tools enable a software engineer to create models of the system to be built.

**Prototyping tools :** A variety of different prototyping tools can be used. More sophisticated CASE prototyping tools enable the creation of a data design, coupled with both screen and report layouts. Many analysis and design tools have extensions that provide a prototyping option.

**Integration and testing tools :** In their directory of software testing tools, Software Quality Engineering defines the following testing tools categories :

**1)** Data acquisition - tools that acquire data to be used during testing.

**2)** Static measurement - tools that analyze source code without executing test cases.

**3)** Dynamic measurement - tools that analyze source code during execution.

**4)** Simulation - tools that simulate function of hardware or other externals.

**5)** Test management - tools that assist in the planning, development and control of testing.

**6)** Cross-functional tools - tools that cross the bounds of the preceding categories.

**Test management tools :** Test management tools are used to control and coordinate software testing for each of the major testing steps.

**Reengineering tools :** Tools for legacy software address a set of maintenance activities that currently absorb a significant percentage of all software-related effort.

# Solved Papers
# CS-70

# CS-70 : INTRODUCTION TO SOFTWARE ENGINEERING
## JAN-2001

**Note:** *Question 1 is* ***compulsory****. Answer any* ***three*** *from the rest.*

**Q1(a). List any four important attributes, which all software products should have.** **[5]**

Refer to JUNE01, Q2(a), Page No.-178

**(b) Describe what is software process and what is software life cycle.** **[5]**

A software process is a common process framework that is established by defining a small number of framework activities that are applicable to all software projects, regardless of their size or complexity. A number of task sets-each a collection of software engineering work tasks, project milestones, work products, and quality assurance points-enable the framework activities to be adapted to the characteristics of the software project and the requirements of the project team. Finally, umbrella activities-such as software quality assurance, software configuration management, and measurement-overlay the process model. Umbrella activities are independent of any one framework activity and occur throughout the process.

Life cycle of software is a long term view that encompasses the activities that occurs before development begins and after the software goes into active use.

**Phases of software life cycle :** Software project passes through several stages while in development process. The major classified stages are described below :

**1. Initial study :** Under this stage the current system is thoroughly analyzed e.g. its working pattern etc.. Any flow or the limitations; if found are also found out, in next phase the alternative solutions are described, also the current systems functionality able to be documented in detail. To collect the information various tools like (a) Interview (b) Questionnaire (c) On-site observation (d) Record Inspection are available.

**2. Requirement Specification :** In this phase the requirements which are derived from current, existing system plus the new requirement which are gathered from user by using information gathering tools in step 1, plus the solutions to the problem, limitation stated in step 1, all these are specified in great detail, so that each and every aspect will be worked out.

**3. System Design :** This phase is used to give the logical design to the system various tools are available to use for system design. Data Flow Diagram (DFD), Decision Table, Decision Tree, Structure chart, Entity Relationship Diagram (ERD) are used to describe the new logical mode of the system. Input screen, output screen and report format are also drawn at this stage.

**4. System Coding :** The logical model is now converted to real system by means of writing programs to computerized the system using the appropriate operating system, front end software, back end software, the database.

**5. System Testing :** The code written in the previous phase are tested exhaustively. Several testing methodologies are available. This phase makes sure the quality of the software in making.

**6. System Implementation and Training :** This is the next logical stage after testing the system.

**7. System Modification/Evaluation :** Once user starts using the system, he may suggest some modification or new requirement might have come up so there is a need to modify the system, if possible and if there are major modifications/changes, then there are chances to evaluate the system and it might give chance to attempt it as new project.

**(c) What are the Software Engineering layers? Explain them briefly. [5]**

Refer to Study material, Q7, Page No.-6

**(d) Describe the differences between functional and non-functional requirements. [JUNE01,Q3(c)] [5]**

Refer to DEC02, Q4(b), Page No.-154

**(e) What is meant by project planning and control? Explain briefly. [5]**

The project planning has four steps :

**1.** Organizing the resources available for the project : Knowledge about all the available resources is must, then comes the stage where the estimation is required about the resources to be used in terms of cost, effort and people required, time required with the project, this is very crucial aspect and to estimate this requires the prior sound experience and expertise to make estimation. And to compare with the available resources and to schedule them.

**2.** Scheduling the events in the project : This step makes use of the tools available for the project scheduling activity, e.g. PERT chart, CPM chart, Gantt chart which are primarily used for making schedule of the project.

**3.** Evaluating progress : Once the estimation is made, schedule has been drawn with great precision, and the project works are under way, now the most important aspect arises is to evaluate the progress done and to document the progress done and make comparison of the progress done and the scheduled progress, if any discrepancy found the thorough investigation is required to know the exact reason, and to make sure the discrepancy eliminated of any sort. The evaluation is required to carry out at regular interval, which will give insight into how much progress been made and how much completion had been achieved and whether the project will be finished in time or not.

**4.** Establishing standards for the project : This is most important aspect, which suggests that the standards must be defined for all the aspects of the Project plan, standard describe the boundary the project process should meet with all steps of the project progress. To define the standard are not an easy task, as it requires the up-to-date knowledge about the system to be made, the available resources, the requirement from the project, and the quality criteria to follow for the system.

**(f) Describe risk management concepts and strategies to manage such risks.** **[5]**

Risk analysis and management are a series of steps that help a software team to understand and manage uncertainty. Many problems can plague a software project. A risk is a potential problem – it might happen, it might not.

2 Reactive Risk Strategy.

At best, a reactive strategy monitors the project for likely risks. Resources are set aside to deal with them, should they become actual problems. More commonly, the software team does nothing about risks until something goes wrong. Then, the team flies into action in an attempt to correct the problem rapidly.

2 Proactive Risk Strategy

A more intelligent strategy for risk management is to be proactive. A proactive strategy begins long before technical work is initiated. Potential risks are identified, their probability and impact are assessed, and they are ranked by importance. Then, the software team establishes a plan for managing risk. The primary objective is to avoid risk, but because not all risks can be avoided.

**Q2(a). Explain why the waterfall model of the software process is not an accurate reflection of software development activities. [5]**

Refer to JUNE04, Q1(a), Page No.-117

**(b) Give structure chart for Rail Reservation System showing data flow. [5]**

Refer to JUNE01, Q4(c), Page No.-183

**(c) What should be the structure of organization management, the "best" team? [5]**

Refer to Study material, Q5, Page No.-20

**Q3(a). What are the main factors to consider in project planning? [5]**

Main factors to be considered in project planning are :

**a.** Estimation techniques used; accuracy required
**b.** Lifecycle model, control functions, and reviews
**c.** Organizational structure
**d.** Level of formality in specifications, test plans
**e.** Level of verification and validation
**f.** Level of configuration management and quality assurance

**(b) Explain the following terms : [5]**
**(i) Portability**
**(ii) Reliability**
**(iii) Efficiency**
**(iv) Accuracy**
**(v) Correctness**

**1. Portability :**

It is the effort required to transfer the software from one hardware configuration to another i.e. software can run in different environment. Portability is an important issue with respect to different operating systems, processor, source language and object language. Further as the ratio of money spent on software and hardware increases it demands more portability.

As Unix is an operating system that has been ported to many hardware systems. The portability is required to reduce the effort of rewriting software from scratch as it requires months of work. Portability is preferable.

**2. Reliability :**

Software is reliable if the user can depend on it. Reliability can be defined in terms of probability that the software will operates as expected over a specified time interval.

Correctness is an absolute quality while reliability - if the incorrect software may still be reliable.

Reliability depends upon many factors. It can be measured, estimated; It invoke software safety and hazard analysis. Software reliability and software safety are closely related.

**3. Efficiency :**

The amount of computing resources and code required by a program to perform its function. Efficiency is a commendable goal. Further efficiency is a performance requirement and should be established in software requirement analysis. Next software should be as efficient as required with good design. Third code efficiency and code simplicity go hand in hand. Last clarity, readability or correctness can not be sacrificed for nonessential improvement in efficiency.

**4. Accuracy :**

The accuracy is one of the prerequisits of software. It is expected at every stage of development. Accurate software fetch more utilisation, make money and provide good results. The accuracy is also related to degree of acceptability of accuracy. If varies from application to application.

**5. Correctness :**

A program must operate correctly or it provides little value to its users. Correctness is the degree to which the software performs its required function. The most common measure for correctness is defects per KLOC where a defect is defined as a verified lack of conformance to requirements.

**(c) What is meant by "organizational paradigms" for Software Engineering teams? [5]**

There are four Organizational Paradigms for Software Engineering team:

**1. A closed paradigm :** A closed paradigm structures a team along a traditional hierarchy. Such teams can work well when producing software that is quite similar to past effort, but they will be less likely to be innovative when working within the closed paradigm.

**2. The random paradigm :** This paradigm structures a team loosely and depends on individual initiative of the team members. When innovation or technological break through is required, team following the random paradigm will excel. But such teams may struggle when "orderly performance" is required.

**3. The open paradigm :** This paradigm attempts to structure a team in a manner that achieves some of the controls associated with the closed paradigm but also much of the innovation that occurs when using the random paradigm. Work is performed collaboratively with heavy communication and consensus-based decision making. Open paradigm team structures are well suited to the solution of complex problems, but may not perform as efficiently as other teams.

**4. The synchronous paradigm :** This paradigm relies on the natural compartmentalization of a problem and organizes team members to work on pieces of the problem with little active communication among themselves.

**Q4(a). Define Data Flow Diagram. Give data flow diagram representing flow of work in an office. [6]**

Data flow diagrams (DFDs) have been used for many years prior to the advent of computers. DFDs show the flow of data through a system. The system may be a company, an organization, a set of procedures, a computer hardware system, a software system or any combination of the proceeding. The DFD is also known as a data flow graph or a bubble chart.

The following observations about DFDs are important :

**1.** All names should be unique. This makes it easier to refer to items of the DFD.

**2.** Remember that a DFD is now a flow chart. Arrows in a flow chart represent the order of events; arrows in DFD represent flowing data. A DFD does not imply any order of events.

**3.** Suppress logical decisions. If we ever have the urge to draw a diamond-shaped box in a DFD, suppress that urge! A diamond –shaped box is used in flow charts to represent decision points with multiple exit paths of which only one is taken. This implies an ordering of events, which makes no sense in a DFD.

**4.** Do not become bogged down with details. Defer error conditions and error handling until the end of the analysis.

| Symbol | Name | Function |
|---|---|---|
|  | Data Flow | Used to connect processes to each other, to sources or sinks; the arrowhead indicates direction of data flow. |
|  | Process | Perform some transformation of input data to yield output data. |
|  | Source or Sink (External Entity) | A source of system inputs or sink of system outputs. |
| 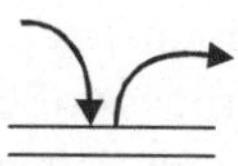 | Data Store | A repository of data; the arrowheads indicate net inputs and net outputs to store. |

Fig : Symbols for data flow diagrams

**DFD for work flow of an office :**

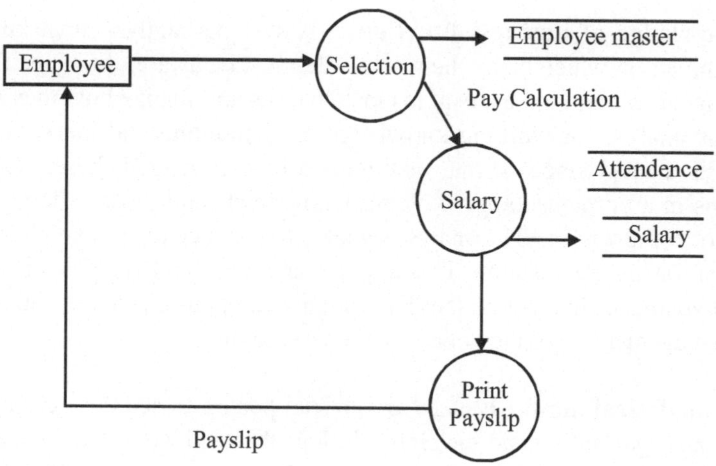

**(b) What is software crisis? In which major areas, can software crisis be broadly classified? [5]**

The crisis means the 'Turning point' in the course of anything. The software crisis is a term which refers to a set of problems that are encountered in the development of computer software. The problems are not limited to software that does not function properly. Rather, the problem encompasses problems associated with how we develop software, how we maintain a growing volume of existing software and how we can expect to keep pace with a growing demand for more software. In probable, all steps of software development life cycle(which encompasses, in broad terms, analysis, design, code, test), the crisis play its role.

**(c) What is System Analyst? What are the educational qualifications of a System Analyst? [4]**

System development generally consists of two major components : system analysis and system design. System analysis refers to the process of examining a business situation with the intent of improving it through better procedures and methods. System design is the process of planning a new business system of one to replace or complement an existing system.

System Analyst is a person, who analyzes the way the system works to identifies its problems. System analysts responsibilities vary among organizations. Below mentioned are the attributes of an analyst :

**1. Knowledge of business functions :** A systems analyst must know the environment in which he or she works. He must be aware of the peculiarities of management and the users at his installations and realize how they react to systems analyst. A working knowledge of accounting and marketing principles is a must since so many systems are built around these. Different sections in an organisation have conflicting needs and most systems are the result of compromise. The analyst's goal is to produce the system that will be the best for his organisation. This requires an open mind and flexibility in his ideas two areas. He must be familiar with his company's product and services and management's policies in areas concerning him.

**2. An analytical mind :** It takes an unusual person to see through problems facing an organisation and develop solutions that will work. Systems analysts often find themselves with more data than they can cope with. It requires an analytical mind to select pertinent data and concentrate on them in defining problems and forming solutions.

System Analyst must be having Master's Degree with atleast 5-10 years of experience as project Leader or a person having vast-experience from the industry but not having Master degree could also do, as knowledge about the system on hand is crucial about Analysis :

1. Experience with the same industry
2. Experience as a project degree could be said to be minimum set of educational qualification required from a person posting as System Analyst.

**Q5(a). What is meant by Project Modification? Is it exclusively due to poor planning or other factors also? [5]**

Software will undoubtedly undergo changes after it is delivered to the customer (a possible exception is embedded software). Changes also required to the existing product itself when some alteration required to the design, coding or may be to requirement also. Change will occur because errors have been encountered, because the software must be adopted to accommodate changes in its external environment or because the customer requires functional or performance enhancement. Software modification reapplies each of the preceding phases to an existing program rather than a new one.

There are several reasons, changes must be made to a software product. Requests for changes must be evaluated carefully, considering the following points :

* The impact of the changes to the existing product
* The impact on the available resources
* The cost
* The effect on the deadline

Project modification to the existing project may be because of the following reasons :

* **Obsolete** : The systems in an organization tend to become absolute quickly.
* **Poor follow-up** : The reasonability for follow up falls upon corporate executives instead of project leaders.
* **Inflexibility** : System become inflexible, so that minor modifications result in extensive program writing.
* **Lack of Documentation** : Procedure writing and documentation are, in general, neglected.

**(b) What are the typical Management Risks in Software Engineering? [5]**

Managers have the software responsibility. Much of the time they are under pressure of different fronts when dealing with person, technology or hardware or time schedule or quality assurance or costing. Some time they are pre occupied with myths. For example

We have the books with standard and procedure for building software, want that provide my people with every thing they need to know.

My people have state of art software development tools.

Such kind of myths are dangerous. While talking about risk then today and yesterday are beyond active concern. It is associated with future. In that connection if the actions today are managed they will reap good future.

Though change is our concern i.e. related to customer requirements, development techniques, target computers, time lines and quality.

In any tasks some kind of risk is always there - so it is futile to eliminate risk and it is questionable to try to minimize it. Rather approach should be to identify right risk to be taken.

The attitude towards risk is of high importance "Never worry about problems until they happened" such a attitude is dangerous. A proactive risk management is more preferable.

The management risk may be concerning to project risk. Technical Risk, Business risk or other known and unknown risk. Software Project Risk may be related to project schedule, cost of project, budgetary allocation, personnel, customer and requirement problems and their impact.

Technical Risk is associated with timeliness and quality of project. It include potential design, implementation interfacing, verification and maintenance problem beside ambiguity, technical uncertainty and technical obsolescence.

Business risk threatens the viability of software to built. Some of the business risk:

1. Building an excellent product that no one really want.
2. Building a product that no longer fit in business strategy of company.
3. Building a product that sales force do not understand how to sell it.
4. Losing support of senior management.

The above contents identify management risk in software engineering.

**(c) Write a short note on "Benchmark Testing". [5]**

A benchmark is a test used by computer hardware, software and application vendors to test the performance of a system. Benchmark are designed so that the same test can be executed on a variety of hardware and software platforms. Because the same tests can be run on a variety of systems, the results can be compared to give a relative indication of performance.

Benchmarks usually test a specific function, as they can give only an indication of the system performance in that area. In practice we may find a system performs extremely well in OLTP(Online Transaction Processing) system

benchmark but does not perform well in a decision support environment.
There are two categories of Benchmark testing (i) Standard and (ii) Custom. The industry standard benchmark typically run by computer hardware or software manufacturer. The custom benchmark is done by end user of integrator. The industry standard benchmarks allow computer hardware and software venders to compare the performance of their system against other system. These tests provide a fair status of a firm.

The custom benchmark testing is used extensively in industry to compare systems with a test that closely mirror's the system environment. Custom benchmark is also available for component level testing to know deficiencies and can make improvements.

Custom benchmark are also applicable to application software on different modules and functions. A comparative statement helps in product improvement process.

**Q6(a). Explain both Software Process Management and Human Resource Management. [6]**

**Software Process Management :** Software process management is about successfully managing the work processes associated with developing, maintaining, and supporting software products and software intensive systems. By successful management, we mean that the products and services produced by the processes conform fully to both internal and external customer requirements, and that they meet the business objectives of the organization responsible for producing the products. The concepts of process management is founded on the principles of statistical process control. These principles hold that by establishing and sustaining stable levels of variability.

**Human Resource Management :** A philosophy of people management based on the belief that human resources are uniquely important to sustained business success. An organization gains competitive advantage by using its people effectively, drawing on their expertise and ingenuity to meet clearly defined objectives. HRM is aimed at recruiting capable, flexible and committed people, managing and rewarding their performance and developing key competencies.

**(b) Discuss the differences between verification and validation and explain why validation is a particularly difficult process. [5]**

| Validation | Verification |
|---|---|
| Validation is the process of confirming the current activity or data to the standards defined. | Verification is the process of checking the authentication. |
| Validation are checked at the time of entering. | Verification are checked after validation done to check for authenticity. Verification could be carried out for the data entered and to test and check whether data stored in correct nature and form. |
| Example 1: While taking input of Age for admission to college, the minimum age defined as 18. So whatever data entered should be satisfying the validation clause, Otherwise the application would give an error message and prompt the user to enter the correct age.<br>Example 2. Student Id, while entering the student Id, if we have defined that the first character should be alphabet and next character could be anything. If user enters "2abc", then error message will be flashed, demanding albhabet to be entered by the user. | Example 1 : Verification carried out for the data which is stored in database. Some manipulation on age might have modified the age data and age might have become less than 18, Now since validation occurs at the time of data entry only, this changes in Age field validation can not take care of, But verification process will make sure that the data inside database are in a correct consistent manner, if the age data have become less than 18, the verification should flash error message accordingly.<br>Example 2 : Student Id, accepted, it follows the 1st character alphabet and next character could be anything. Like "A11" since it is accepted, now we need to search through our database to check whether this Student Id exists in our database or not |

Validation is difficult to process, because at the time of Data Entry one need to make sure of all possibility of the ways the data will be input and the possible error could occur and after assuming, one need to take care of avoiding it and for that the validation rule to be made for each and every field data-entry, that will be done. Moreover, validation testing run in the live environment using real data.

**(c) What is the distinction between alpha and beta testing? Explain why these forms of testing are particularly valuable. [4]**

Refer to JUNE01, Q1(f), Page No.-177

# CS-70 : INTRODUCTION TO SOFTWARE ENGINEERING
## JUNE-2001

---

**Note:** *Question 1 is* ***compulsory****. Answer any* ***three*** *from the rest.*

---

**Q1(a). What should be the structure of organization management the "best" team? [5]**

Refer to Study material, Q5, Page No.-20

**(b) What are the responsibilities and characteristics of a system analyst? [DEC02, Q3(a)]**

Following are the duties and attributes of system analyst :

**DUTIES**

**(a)** The first and perhaps most difficult task of systems analyst is problem definition. Business problems are quite difficult to define. It is also true, that problems cannot be solved until they are precisely and clearly defined.

**(b)** Initially a systems analyst does not know how to solve a specific problem. He must consult with managers, users and other data processing professionals in defining problems and developing solutions. He uses various methods for data gathering to get the correct solution of a problem.

**(c)** Having gathered the data relating to a problem, the systems analyst analyses them and thinks of plan to solve it. He may not come up personally with the best way of solving a problem but pulls together other people's ideas and refines them until a workable solution is achieved.

**(d)** Systems analysts coordinate the process of developing solutions. Since many problems have number of solutions, the systems analyst must evaluate the merit of such proposes solution before recommending one to the management.

**(e)** Systems analysts are often referred to as planners. A key part of the systems analyst's job is to develop a plan to meet the management's objectives.

**(f)** When the plan has been accepted, systems analyst is responsible for designing it so that management's goal could be achieved. Systems design is a time consuming, complex and precise task.

**(g )** Systems must be thoroughly tested. The systems analyst often coordinates the testing procedures and helps, in deciding whether or not the new system is meeting standards established in the planning phase.

**ATTRIBUTES**

**(a) Knowledge of Business functions :** A systems analyst must know the environment in which he or she works. He must be aware of the peculiarities of management and the users at his installation and realize how they react to systems analyst. A working knowledge of accounting and marketing principles is a must since so many systems are built around these two areas. He must be familiar with his company's product and services and management's policies in areas concerning him.

**(b) Knowledge of people :** Since a systems analyst works with others so closely, he or she must understand their needs and what motivates them to develop systems properly.

**(c) Knowledge of Data processing principles :** Most systems today are computer based. The systems analyst must fully aware about the potential and limitations of computers.

**(d) Ability to communicate :** As a coordinator, a systems analyst must communicate properly with people of different levels within an organisation. Systems analyst must listen carefully to what others say and integrate the thoughts of others into the systems development process.

**(e) Flexibility :** Systems analysts must be flexible in their thinking since they often do not get-their own way. Different factions in an organisation have conflicting needs and most systems are the result of compromise. The analyst's goal is to produce the system that will be the best for his organisation. This requires an open mind and flexibility in his ideas.

**(f) An analytical mind :** It takes an unusual person to see through problems facing an organisation and develop solutions that will work. Systems analysts often find themselves with more data than they can cope with. It requires an analytical mind to select pertinent data and concentrate on them in defining problems and forming solutions.

**(g) Well educated with sharp mind :** Systems analysts are called upon to work with people at all levels virtually in every aspect of business. They must know how to work with all of them and gain their confidence. Analysts must have sharp mind to learn quickly how people do their jobs.

**(c) Enumerate the goals of structured methodology of system analysis and design.** **[5]**

Refer to DEC02, Q3(b), Page No.-152

**(d) How are MIS and DSS related ? How do they differ from each other ?** **[5]**

Refer to DEC01,Q4(b), Page No.-171

**(e) Enumerate reasons which may cause system failure.** **[5]**

Below are the reasons which may cause system failure :

**a)** The user was not directly involved in the crucial phases of system development.

**b)** User requirements were not clearly understood or defined.

**c)** The analyst, programmer or both were in-experienced.

**d)** Everyone in the project team has conflicting objectives, so the project was bound to suffer.

**e)** User training was poor.

**f)** Existing hardware proved deficient to handle the new application.

**g)** The new system left features to be used in other departments which the old system was providing.

**h)** User changes requirements.

**i)** The new system was not user friendly.

**j)** Wrong Database Design : If normalization has not been carried well, the deficiency is the database design would guarantee the system failure.

**(f) What is the distinction between alpha and beta testing? Explain why these terms of testing are particularly valuable.** **[5]**

**Alpha Testing** : The alpha test is conducted at the developer's site by a customer. The software is used in a natural setting with the developer looking over the shoulder of the user and recording errors and usage problems. Alpha tests are conducted in a controlled environment.

**Beta Testing :** The beta test is conducted at one or more customer sites by the end user(s) of the software. Unlike alpha testing, the developer is generally not present. Therefore, the beta test is a live application of the software in an environment that cannot be controlled by the developer. The customer records all problems (real or imagined) that are encountered during beta testing and reports these to the developer at regular intervals. As a result of problems reported during beta test, the software developer makes modifications and then prepares for release of the software product to the entire customer base.

Hence Alpha Test and Beta Test lead to sure removal of any bugs which the software product might have. Alpha and beta test will give last chance or sort of platform from where the developer can make sure the software product is bug free/error free. Thus, these terms of testing are particularly valuable.

**Q2(a). What are four important attributes which all software products should have? Suggest four other attributes, which may be significant. [5]**

Below are the important attributes which all software products should have :

**1) Usability :** Software should have an appropriate user interface and documentation.

**2) Correctness :** A program is functionally correct if it behaves according to the specification of the functions it should provide.

**3) User Friendliness :** A software system is user friendly if its human users find it easy to use. This definition reflects the subjective nature of user friendliness. An application that is used by novice programmers qualifies as user friendly by virtue of different properties than an application that is used by expert programmers.

**4) Evolvability :** Software products are modified over time to provide new functions or to change existing functions. Indeed, the fact that the software is so malleable makes modifications extremely easy to apply to an implementation.

**Four other significant attributes are :**

**1) Understandability :** Some software systems are easier to understand than others. Of course, some tasks are inherently more complex than others. Given tasks of inherently similar difficulty, we can follow certain guidelines to produce more understandable programs. Understandability is an internal product quality, and it helps in achieving many of the other qualities such as evolvability and verifiability.

**2) Maintainability :** It should be possible for the software to evolve to meet changing requirements.

**3) Dependability :** The software should not cause physical or economic damage in the event of failure.

**4) Reliability :** Informally, software is reliable if the user can depend on it. The specialized literature on software reliability in term of statistical behavior- the probability that the software will operate as expected over a specified time interval.

**(b) Briefly explain the purpose of each of the sections in a software project plan. [5]**

The software project plan is a relatively brief documentation that is addressed to a diverse audience.

The sections for the software project plan are :

* **Introduction** :
- Purpose of Plan
- Project Scope and objectives
    * Statements of scope
    * Major functions
    * Performance issues
    * Management and technical constraints

* **Project Estimates**
- Historical data used for estimates
- Estimation techniques
- Estimates of effort, cost, duration
    * Risks management strategy
- Risk table
- Discussion of risks to be managed
    * Risk mitigation
    * Risk monitoring
    * Risk management (contingency plan)

* **Schedule**
- Project work breakdown structure
- Task network
- Timeline chart (Gantt Chart)
- Resource table

* **Project Resources**
- People
- Hardware and software
- Special resources

*** Staff organization**
- Team structure (if applicable)
- Management reporting

*** Tracking and control mechanisms**
- Quality assurance and control
- Change management and control

* Appendices

**(c) What do you know about various types of special system tests ? Explain them briefly. [5]**

Various types of special tests are as follows :

**1) Peak load test :**

During this test a stress test and performance test are applied aggregately to know the effect. For example special test may generate 10 interrupt where on average only 2 interrupts per second are being generated - input data rates may be increased abnormally maximum amount of memory may be examined when it is equipped with performance test it enable to show result about resource sharing (e.g. processors cycles) etc.

**2) Recovery testing :**

In some cases fault is fluorescent i.e. the system does not cease down. But in another cases the system fault may cause economic danger if it is not corrected within a specified time. A system test that forces the software to get fail in a variety of ways and verifies that the recovery is done in proper form is known as recovery testing.

**3) Security Testing :**

Security testing verifies that the protection mechanism built into a system will protect the system from improper penetrations into the system because any system that manages sensitive information is a target of improper penetration. The illegal penetration can be done by the hackers who are penetrating the system for playing games or by dishonest employees who want to take revenge from the employer can also try to penetrate the system or some individuals who are penetrating the system for their personal interests.

In security testing the tester plays the role of a person who is desiring to penetrate the system or may try to break down the protective measures; may cause system errors; may try to find the key for the system security.

**4) Stress Testing :**

Stress tests are designed to take the programs within abnormal situations by providing abnormal stress on the system. The stress testing may demand resources in abnormal quantity, frequency or volume.

A variation of stress testing is a technique called sensitivity testing. Sensitivity testing attempts to uncover data combinations within valid input classes that may cause instability or improper processing.

**5) Performance testing :**

This type of testing is done to test the performance of a software within a system. Rather performance testing occurs throughout all the steps in the testing process. At the unit level also we are conducting white box testing. Performance testing is often compelled with stress testing & always requires hardware & software for testing. By this a tester can uncover situations that lead to the degradation of a system or even system failure.

**Q3(a). Explain briefly the importance of system reliability. Can a system be hundred percent reliable? [5]**

It is very important for a system to be reliable because unlike many other quality factors can be measured, direct and estimated using historical data and development data. If the system is not reliable than the user can not trust the system because reliability means that we are getting accurate results.

A system can be hundred percent reliable in some specified environment that too for a specific period of time otherwise a system cannot be hundred percent reliable because there are certain conditions where the system is not in the control of the user. Like natural disaster can occur at any moment of time or the wire can break up at certain moment.

**(b) Explain why the intangibility of software systems poses special problems for the software project management. [5]**

Software by the nature is non-touchable, you can not touch it but one can feel the functionality. But just by looking of the software or the output or the input screen, one can not judge the ability of the software product. So, if any software which is onhand and if it is to be judged, one needs to operate it accordingly, it is like one does the testing, each and every module, program, conditions, scenarios should be checked and tested.

Until and unless, one follow the entire software path, no one can access the ability of the software product.

So, because of its intangibility aspect it is very difficult to understand the software product, unless one uses it thoroughly.

**(c) Describe the differences between functional and non-functional requirements. [JAN01,Q1(d);DEC02,Q4(b)] [5]**

In general, requirements are partitioned into **functional requirements** and **non-functional requirements**. Functional requirements are associated with specific functions, tasks or behaviours the system must support, while non-functional requirements are constraints on various attributes of these functions or tasks. In terms of the ISO quality characteristics for evaluation, the functional requirements address the quality characteristic of functionality while the other quality characteristics are concerned with various kinds of non-functional requirements. Because non-functional requirements tend to be stated in terms of **constraints** on the results of tasks which are given as functional requirements (e.g., constraints on the speed or efficiency of a given task), a task-based functional requirements statement is a useful skeleton upon which to construct a complete requirements statement. That is the approach taken in this work. It can be helpful to think of non-functional requirements as adverbially related to tasks or functional requirements: how fast, how efficiently, how safely, etc., is a particular task carried out by a particular system?

**Q4(a). Explain why the waterfall model of the software process is not an accurate reflection of software development activities. [5]**

Waterfall model is the oldest and widely used model for software engineering but it has some drawbacks as well, specially if we look at practical aspects of it.

**1)** It is often difficult for the customer to state all requirements explicitly. Thus natural uncertainty is not covered that exists at inception of projects.

**2)** Customer must have patience as working session of program is only available later in the project. That means if a major defect is detected after delivery, it becomes nearly impossible to correct.

**3)** Importantly, rear projects rarely follow the sequential flow that this model proposes. There is iteration, but it is indirect. Thus changes can cause confusion as project proceeds. A software development life cycle(SDLC) model that is better one and overcomes disadvantages mentioned above is incremental model.

Developers are often delayed unnecessarily. In an interesting analysis of actual projects, it is found that the linear nature of the classic life cycle leads to "blocking states" in which some project team members must wait for other members of the team to complete dependent tasks. In fact, the time spent waiting can exceed the time spent on productive work. The blocking states tends to be more prevalent at the beginning and end of a linear sequential process.

**(b) What are the differences between verification and validation? [5]**

| Validation | Verification |
|---|---|
| Validation is the process of confirming the current activity or data to the standards defined. | Verification is the process of checking the authentication. |
| Validation are checked at the time of entering. | Verification are checked after validation done to check for authenticity. Verification could be carried out for the data entered and to test and check whether data stored in correct nature and form. |
| Example 1: While taking input of Age for admission to college, the minimum age defined as 18. So whatever data entered should be satisfying the validation clause, Otherwise the application would give an error message and prompt the user to enter the correct age.<br>Example 2. Student Id, while entering the student Id, if we have defined that the first character should be alphabet and next character could be anything. If user enters "2abc", then error message will be flashed, demanding albhabet to be entered by the user. | Example 1 : Verification carried out for the data which is stored in database. Some manipulation on age might have modified the age data and age might have become less than 18, Now since validation occurs at the time of data entry only, this changes in Age field validation can not take care of, But verification process will make sure that the data inside database are in a correct consistent manner, if the age data have become less than 18, the verification should flash error message accordingly.<br>Example 2 : Student Id, accepted, it follows the $1^{st}$ character alphabet and next character could be anything. Like "A11" since it is accepted, now we need to search through our database to check whether this Student Id exists in our database or not |

**(c) Give structure chart for Rail Reservation System showing Data-flow. [5]**

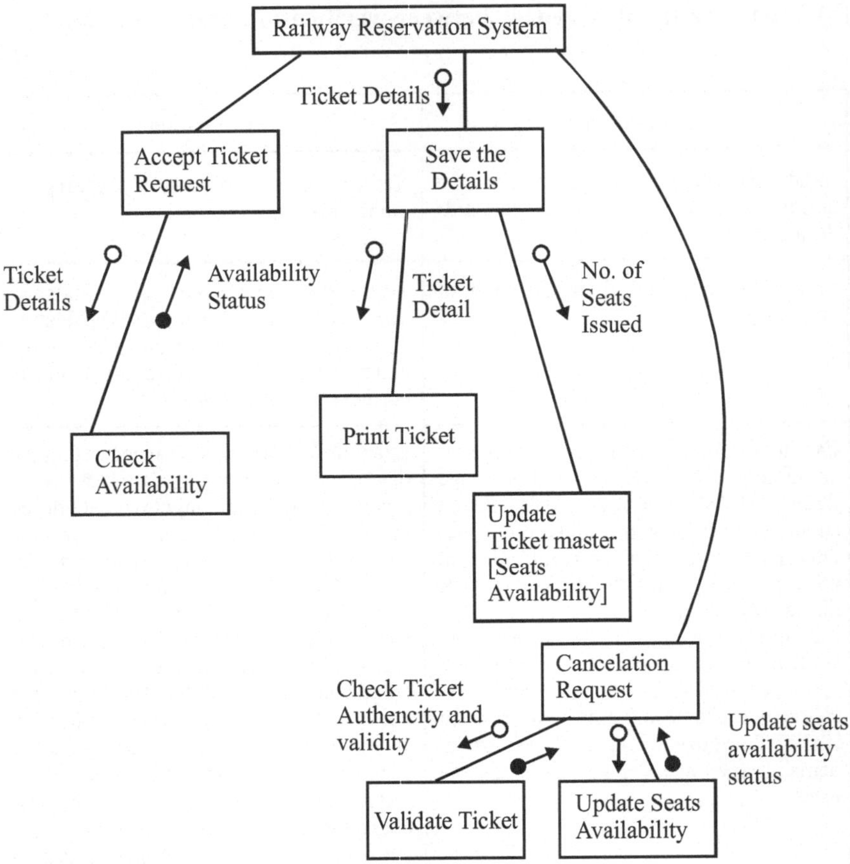


**NOTE :** In the above diagram, The Ticket details are accepted, Then seats availability is checked. On availability Ticket is issued and the Seats availability gets updated, and The Ticket is getting Printed.

On getting request for Ticket Cancellation, the ticket validity is checked, whether ticket is valid and ticket authenticity is checked whether travel date is greater than current date, if ticket is valid the available seats are updated.

**Symbols Used in Structures Chart :**

**1.** An arrow with Open Circle Shows Data Flows

**2.** An arrow with Closed Circle Shows Control Data Flows

Rectangle Explains Module [Information/Calculation]

**Q5(a). Give the attributes of an effective system analyst.** **[5]**

Refer to JUNE02, Q6(ii), Page No.-166

**(b) What are the important issues of Project Management ? [5]**

Project management is a people-intensive activity, and for this reason, competent practitioners often make poor team leaders. They simply don't have the right mix of people skills. And yet, as Edgemon states: Unfortunately all individuals just fall into a project manager role and become accidental project managers. In an excellent book of technical leadership, jerry Weinberg suggests a MOI model of leadership:

**Motivation**. The ability to encourage (by "push or pull") technical people to produce to their best ability.

**Organization**. The ability to mold existing processes (or invent new ones) that will enable the initial concepts to be translated into a final product.

**Ideas or innovation**. The ability to encourage people to create and feel creative even when they must work within bounds established for a particular software product or application.

Weinberg suggests that successful project leaders apply a problem solving management style. That is, a software project manager should concentrate on understanding the problem to be solved, managing the flow of ideas, and at the same time, letting everyone on the team know (by words and, far more important, by actions) that quality counts and will not be compromised.

Another view of the characteristics that define an effective project manager emphasizes four key traits:

**Problem solving.** An effective software project manager can diagnose the technical and organization issues that are most relevant, systematically structured solution or properly motivate other practitioners to develop the solution, apply lessons learned from past projects to new situations, and remain flexible enough to change direction if initial attempts at problem solution are fruitless.

**Managerial Identity**. A good project manager must take charge of the project. She must have the confidence to assume control when necessary and the assurance to allow good technical people to follow their instincts.

**Achievement.** To optimize the productivity of a project team, a manager must reward initiative and accomplishment and demonstrate through his own actions that controlled risk taking will not be punished.

**Influence and team building.** An effective project manager must be able to "read" people; she must be able to understand verbal and nonverbal signals and react to the needs of the people sending these signals. The manager must remain under control in high-stress situations.

**(c) Explain the various types of planning tools. [5]**

**Gantt Chart :**

The chart is first generation project planning tool. The Gantt chart uses horizontal bars to show the duration of the tasks or actions to be performed. The left hand side marks the beginning of the tasks and the right hand side marks its finish. The heavy horizontal bars are activities and the light horizontal bars are tasks. Broken horizontal bars show time delays. A task is a specific job that is assigned to a particular person to be done within the specific time. A group of tasks together makes an activity and group of activities make up milestone. The major drawback of the Gantt chart is that it does not show the relationships among the tasks & the milestones of the project. That is the interdependence of the task is not evident.

**Project Evaluation and Review Techniques (PERT Chart) :**

A PERT chart is valuable when a project is being planned. PERT Chart also makes use of the milestone charts to show its achievements but these are not the tasks. These are the terminal achievements called the events. Arrow are specified to represent tasks and circles represent the beginning or the end of the tasks. The PERT chart uses these paths and events to show the inter-relationship of project activities. Each task is limited by identifiable event. The Analyst has to bound by the duration, it simply tells that the activity has started or ended. Each task must have a beginning or end. Another task can be started only if the task on which it depends has been completed PERT does not allow tasks to return to starting tasks because in this case a task will never come to an end.

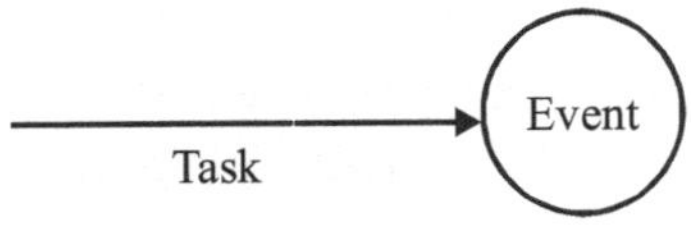


**Q6(a). What are the five components of a design method ? Take any method which you know and describe its components. [5]**

The five components of a design method are as follows :

**(i)** Data Flow Diagram

**(ii)** Data Dictionary

**(iii)** Entity Relationship Diagram
**(iv)** PERT Chart
**(v)** HIPO Diagram

**Data flow diagrams (DFDs)** have been used for many years prior to the advent of computers. DFDs show the flow of data through a system. The system may be a company, an organization, a set of procedures, a computer hardware system, a software system or any combination of the proceeding. The DFD is also known as a data flow graph or a bubble chart.

The following observations about DFDs are important :

**1.** All names should be unique. This makes it easier to refer to items of the DFD.

**2.** Remember that a DFD is now a flow chart. Arrows in a flow chart represent the order of events; arrows in DFD represent flowing data. A DFD does not imply any order of events.

**3.** Suppress logical decisions. If we ever have the urge to draw a diamond-shaped box in a DFD, suppress that urge! A diamond –shaped box is used in flow charts to represent decision points with multiple exit paths of which only one is taken. This implies an ordering of events, which makes no sense in a DFD.

**4.** Do not become bogged down with details. Defer error conditions and error handling until the end of the analysis.

| Symbol | Name | Function |
|---|---|---|
|  | Data Flow | Used to connect processes to each other, to sources or sinks; the arrowhead indicates direction of data flow. |
|  | Process | Perform some transformation of input data to yield output data. |
| 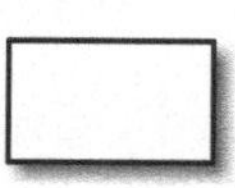 | Source or Sink (External Entity) | A source of system inputs or sink of system outputs. |
| 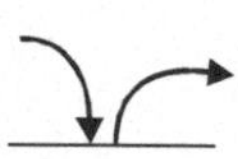 | Data Store | A repository of data; the arrowheads indicate net inputs and net outputs to store. |

Fig : Symbols for data flow diagrams

**(b) Explain : [5]**

**(i) Unit Testing [DEC03,Q6(a,iii)]**

Unit testing is the process of taking a module and running it in isolation from the rest of the software product by using prepared test cases and comparing the actual results with the results predicated by the specifications and design of the module. One purpose of testing is to find (and remove) as many error in the software as practical. There are number of reasons in support of unit testing than testing the entire product.

**1.** The size of a single module is small enough that we can locate an error fairly
easily.

**2.** The module is small enough that we can attempt to test it in some demonstrably
exhaustive fashion.

**3.** Confusing interactions of multiple error in widely different parts of the software
are eliminated.

**(ii) Module Testing**

Software system is divided in module, module comprises of different programs. While doing module testing each and every concerned program should be able to interact and should function smoothly to all input to the module, the database should not malfunction and output should have been given perfectly. For example : Bill generation is one module of Hotel Reservation System. When Bill Generation module testing carried out it is going to affect the Bill Transaction, Bill Master, Room-Master, Account related file. All functional aspects should be performed or checked thoroughly.

**(iii) System Testing**

Refer to JUNE02, Q6(i), Page No.-165

**(iv) α-Testing**

Refer to DEC02,Q6(i), Page No.-156

**(v) β-Testing**

Refer to DEC02,Q6(ii), Page No.-156

**(c) Suggest why data-flow diagrams are intuitive and easy-to-understand by non-technical staff. [5]**

DFD is the graphical representation of flow of data. Data is modified by a series of transformation, as data enters and goes through the software. DFD (Data Flow Diagram) is a graphical tool that shows flow of information from one place to another and the transformations that are applied as data move from input to output. The data flow diagram is used to represent a system of software at any level of abstraction.

Data flow diagrams are easy to understand by nontechnical staff also because there are a few symbols that are used in DFD. However DFD should not be confused with flow charts because in flowchart we do not show the flow of information but we use conditions or loops in flowcharts that can not be used within the DFD.

A DFD describes "what" data flow rather than "how" it flows. Thus it is often necessary to make sure that a complete documentation of the data flow is available for future reference.

# CS-70 : INTRODUCTION TO SOFTWARE ENGINEERING
## DEC-2001

**Note:** *Question 1 is* ***compulsory****. Answer any* ***three*** *from the rest.*

**Q1(a). Software is the differentiating characteristic in many computer based products and systems. Provide examples of two or three products and atleast one system in which software, not hardware, is the differentiating element. [DEC03,Q1(b)] [15]**

Refer to Study material, Q5, Page No.-4

**(b) You have been appointed as a project manager within an information system organization. Your job is to build an application that is quite similar to other that your team has built, although this one is larger and more complex. Requirements have been thoroughly documented by the customer. What team structure would you choose and why? [DEC03,Q3(a);DEC02,Q1(b);JUNE02,Q3(a)] [15]**

Refer to DEC03, Q3(a), Page No.-130

**Q2(a). "Unreasonable" deadlines are a fact of life in the software business. How should you proceed if you are faced with one? [8]**

Refer to DEC04, Q3(b), Page No.-107

**(b) Although adding people to a late software project can make it later, there are circumstances in which this is not true. Describe them. [7]**

* When experts are added to the late project.
* When experienced person (experience of the same kind of project) are added to the project.
* When appointed person are from the same organization and have worked for the similar kind of project
* When there are possibility of the next processes to be quickly over with added manpower so finally it won't look late.
* Or hiring people at the time of testing and implementation as not much technical skills are required.

**Q3(a). Describe five software application areas in which software safety and hazard analysis would be a major concern. [8]**

Refer to JUNE04, Q2(a), Page No.-118

**(b) Assume that you have been asked to develop a Library Information System. Make a list of risks that you would face as you begin this project. [7]**

A considerably more intelligent strategy for risk management is to be proactive. A proactive strategy begins long before technical work is initiated. The software team established a plan for managing risk. When risks are analysed, it is important to quantify the level of uncertainty and the degree of loss associated with each risk. The risks may be categorised as follows :

**(a) Project risks :**

If project risks become true, it is likely that the project schedule will go above and also the cost of the project will increase to a much larger scale.

**(b) Technical risks :**

These adversely effect the quality and timeliness of the software to be produced. Implementation may become impossible or difficult if these risks become true.

**(c) Business risks :**

These risks threaten the viability of the software to be built. The project or product becomes slow if business risks become true.

**(d) Known risks :**

These are those risks that can be uncovered after careful evaluation of the project plan.

**(e) Predictable risks :**

These risks are extrapolated from past project experience.

**(f) Unpredictable risks :**

These risks are extremely difficult to identify in advance.

**So, now below is the list of risks as per above discussion while developing a Library Information System :**

**(1)** If the team members are not able to complete the project within the specified time then cost of the project could be increased.

**(2)** If we are not able to develop the quality of the project this can also be a risk because the customer needs quality. Or he/she may reject the final product due to unsatisfactory quality.

**(3)** Changes incorporated in final stages of the project also increases the cost risk factor.

**(4)** If the leader of the project or the system analyst is an unexperienced person and if/she is not able to understand the requirements of the customer then a wrong product can be given to the customer.

With the above given risks there may be some known risks also. Those risks can be uncovered when we do the careful evaluation of the project. And lastly there may also be some risk in the project that cannot be seen but these may or may not occur.

**Q4(a). Several Organizations don't have their own software development divisions and they outsource the work of Software Development to External Software Development organizations. Is it justified to outsource all types of software projects or should the outsourcing be limited to only some categories? Explain your answer. [10]**

Software engineering activities are contracted to a third party who does the work at lower cost, and hopefully with higher quality. Software work conducted within a company is reduced to a contract management activity.

**Factors Negate the Favouring of Outsourcing :**

* The decision to outsource can be strategic or tactical. At a strategic level Managers consider whether a significant portion of all software work can be contracted to others. At the tactical level, a Project Manager determines whether part or all of a project can be best accomplished by sub-contracting some portion of the software work.

* The decision to outsource is often a financial one. A detailed discussion of the financial analysis of outsourcing is required. A brief review of the pros and cons of the decision is worthwhile.

* Company losses control over the software that it needs. A company runs the risks of putting the fate of its competitiveness into the hands of a third party.

**Factors favours the outsourcing :**

* Cost saving can usually be achieved by reducing the number of software people and the facilities.

System in hand should be evaluated by applying the above stated factors and if compromising the security and control aspect, crucial outsourcing is not to be adopted. If financial benefits are at front outsourcing must be adopted.

**(b) How are MIS and DSS related? How do they differ from each other? [JUNE01,Q1(d)] [5]**

It is viewed that DSS is an extension of MIS or can be defined as a second generation of MIS =>MIS is generated when we add predefined managerial reports that are span out of transaction processing, report generation and online inquiry capabilities - all integrated with a given functional area such as production or personnel MIS => DSS results from adding external data sources, accounting and statistical modules and interactive query capabilities, the outcome is system designed to survey all levels or management.

**Management level** **Information level System support**

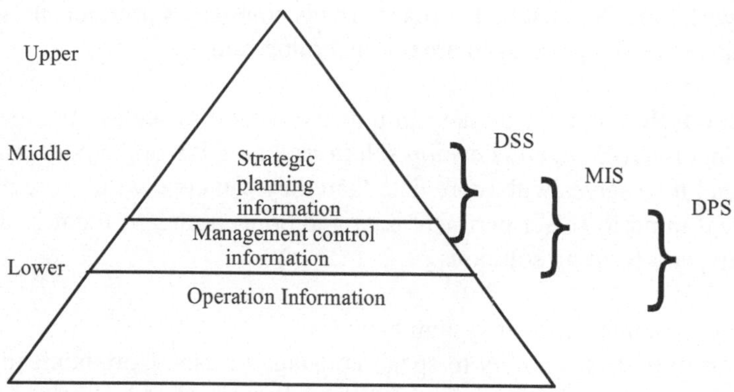


| | CATEGORY | CHARACTERISTICS |
|---|---|---|
| 1. | Management Information System | Provides input to be used in the managerial decision process. Deals with supporting well Structured decision situations. Typical Information requirements can be anticipated. |
| 2. | Decision Support System | Provides information to managers who must make judgements about particular situations. Support decision makers in situation that are not well-structured. |

**Q5(a). Discuss your perceptions of the ideal training and background for a System Analyst. [7]**

System development generally consists of two major components : system analysis and system design. System analysis refers to the process of examining a business situating with the intent of improving it through better procedures and methods. System design is the process of planning a new business system of one to replace or complement an existing system.

System Analyst is a person, who analyzes the way the system works to identifies its problems. System analysts responsibilities vary among organizations. Below mentioned are the perceptions of the ideal training and background for a System Analyst :

**1. Knowledge of business functions :** A systems analyst must know the environment in which he or she works. He must be aware of the peculiarities of management and the users at his installation and realize how they react to systems analyst. A working knowledge of accounting and marketing principles is a must since so many systems are built around these. Different sections in an organisation have conflicting needs and most systems are the result of compromise. The analyst's goal is to produce the system that will be the best for his organisation. This requires an open mind and flexibility in his ideas two areas. He must be familiar with his company's product and services and management's policies in areas concerning him.

**2. An analytical mind :** It takes an unusual person to see through problems facing an organisation and develop solutions that will work. Systems analysts often find themselves with more data than they can cope with. It requires an analytical mind to select pertinent data and concentrate on them in defining problems and forming solutions.

Two interpersonal skills of system analysis

**1) Communication :** ability to speak language of user. Communication not just means reports, interviews but fulfilling, listening and reacting to one another.

Closed communication is not ideal open communication is needed.

**2) Understanding :** i.e. identifying problems and having grasp of company goals and objectives and showing sensitivity to impact of system on people.

Two technical skills of System Analyst

**1) Creativity :** helping users model ideas into concrete plans and developing candidate system.

**2) Problem Solving :** Reducing problems to their elemental levels and developing alternate solutions.

Necessity of both skills depends upon stages of system development.

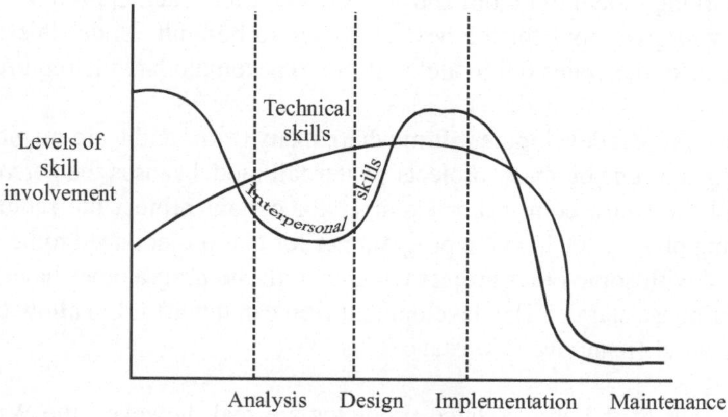


**During Analysis :** there is greater need of interpersonal skills - i.e. working with user to determine needs.

**During Design :** We need high technical skills even though interpersonal skills are required for user / analyst participation as a step to implementation.

**During Implementation :** Technical aspects focus on "proving" the software" Interpersonal aspects deal with "user training".

**During Maintenance :** Role of analyst drops off, except when an unanticipated problems appears.

**(b) Is application of water Fall Modal will be effective for all types of projects? Justify your answer with example. [8]**

Waterfall model is the oldest and widely used model for software engineering but it has some drawbacks as well, specially if we look at practical aspects of it.

**1)** It is often difficult for the customer to state all requirements explicitly. Thus natural uncertainty is not covered that exists at inception of projects.

**2)** Customer must have patience as working session of program is only available later in the project. That means if a major defect is detected after delivery, it becomes nearly impossible to correct.

**3)** Importantly, rear projects rarely follow the sequential flow that this model proposes. There is iteration, but it is indirect. Thus changes can cause confusion as project proceeds. A software development life cycle(SDLC) model that is better one and overcomes disadvantages mentioned above is incremental model.

*Project which requires to be build on prototype, where end user required the first working model to be out and be tested and feedback upon that working model will give input for the next prototype to be built. Under this circumstances also, the water fall model will fail to accommodate the requirement.

* For the project development firm where many teams and team members are working at a time on many projects, Water fall model causes the personnel to wait till their turn comes. For example for certain project the requirement gathering phase is ON, so the programmer for that project need to be accommodated with some other project OR rather all the programmer have to wait till their phase started. The development firm can not afford to allow this sort of personnel (manpower) wastage.

Since, each of the above stated problems are real, however, the Water fall model paradigm has a definite and important place in software engineering work. But well suited where the requirements are rigid and know before the development start. Waterfall model is well suited for in the development of embedded softwares, and Operating System etc.

**Q6. Write short notes on the following : [15]**
**(1) Human Resources Management**
Refer to JUNE02, Q6(iii), Page No.-167

**(2) Project Modifications**
Software project development activity is comprised of various sub activities, starting from formal discussion with customer to fix the requirement specification to software design, coding, testing, implementation and maintenance etc. After each sub stage or activity completion it is necessary to review the progress made that in terms of standards adopted their compliance and improve in Quality factor etc. At that stage the shortcoming force to carryout project modification. The software project may be in relation to schedules, performance, Quality and cost and compatibility with other product. Further this is true that in later stage modification in project are more serious and have deep impact as compared to early stage modification. Deep effect in later stages is seen when there is high coupling among the modules. Many times it is also desired under risk management to modify project to give a different dimension of progress.

**(3) Project Tracking**
Refer to DEC02, Q6(iii), Page No.-156

# CS-70 : INTRODUCTION TO SOFTWARE ENGINEERING
## JUNE-2002

**Note:** *Question 1 is* ***compulsory****. Answer any* ***three*** *from the rest.*

**Q1(a). List and explain the characteristics of software. How do these characteristics differ from hardware? [15]**

The following points explain characteristics of software and difference with hardware :

**i)** Software is developed or engineered, it is not manufactured in the classical sense. Although some similarities exists between software development and hardware manufacturing, the two activities are fundamentally different. In both activities, high quality is achieved through good design, but the manufacturing phase for hardware can introduce quality problems that are nonexistent (or easily corrected) for software.

**ii) Software does not "wear out."**

Following Figure depicts failure rate as a function of time for hardware. The relationship, often called the "bathtub curve," indicates that hardware exhibits relatively high failure rates early in its life (these failures are often attributable to design or manufacturing defects); defects are corrected and the failure rate drops to a steady state level (ideally, quite low) for some period of time. As time passes, however, the failure rate rises again as hardware components suffer from the cumulative affects of dust, vibration, abuse, temperature extremes and many other environmental maladies. Stated simply, the hardware beings to wear out.

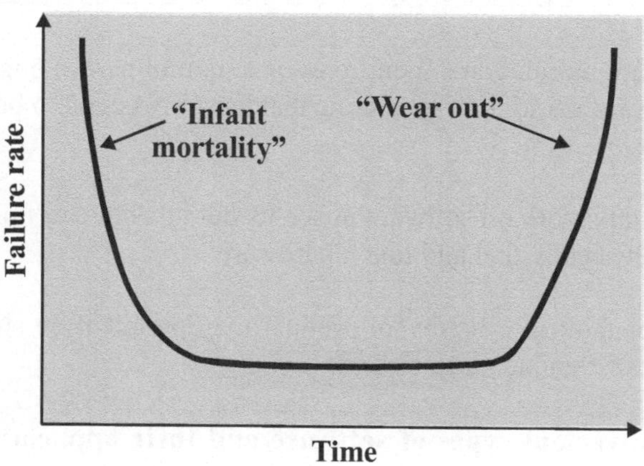

Software is not susceptible to the environmental maladies that cause hardware to wear out. In theory, therefore, the failure rate curve for software should take the form of the "idealized curve" shown in the following Figure. Undiscovered defects will cause high failure rates early in the life of a program. However, these are corrected (ideally, without introducing other errors) and the curve flattens as shown.

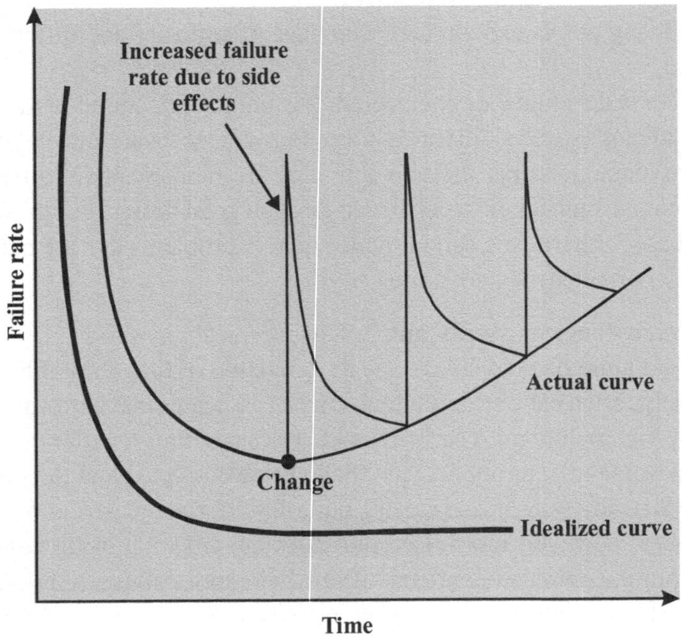


**Fig : Idealized and actual failure curves for software**

**iii)** In hardware world, component reuse is a natural part of engineering process. In software world, it is something that has only begun to be achieved on a broad scale.

**iv)** You can only work on software & see its outputs but can't physically feel it. You can physically feel and touch hardware.

**v)** Any minor fault in a hardware product may permit it be still usable but software doesn't enduce any errors.

**(b) Describe various types of software and their application domains, together with their special significance. [15]**

Software may be applied in any situation for which a pre-specified set of procedural steps (i.e., an algorithms) has been defined. Information content is important factor in determining the nature of a software application. Content refers to the meaning and form of incoming and outgoing information. For example, many business applications use highly structured input data (e.g. a database) and produce formatted "reports". Software that controls an automated machine (e.g. a numerical control) accepts discrete data items with limited structure and produces individual machine commands in rapid succession. Information determinancy refers to the predictability of the order and timing of information. An engineering analysis program accepts data that have a predefined order, executes the analysis algorithm(s) without interruption, and produces resultant data in report or graphical format. Such application are determinate. A multi-user operating system, on the other hand, accepts inputs that have varied content and arbitrarily timing, executes algorithm that can be interrupted by external conditions, and produces output that varies as a function of environment and time. Applications with these characteristics are indeterminate :-

**System Software :** System Software is a collection of programs and utilities for providing service to other programs. Other system application (e.g., operating system components, drivers, telecommunications processors) process largely indeterminate data. In either case, the system software area is characterized by heavy interaction with computer hardware; heavy usage by multiple users; concurrent operation that requires scheduling, resource sharing, and sophisticated process management; complex data structures; multiple external interfaces.

**Real-time software :** Software for the monitors/analyzes/controls real-world events as they occur is called real time. Elements of real-time software include a data-gathering component that collects and formats information from an external environment, an analysis component that transforms information as required by the application, a control/output component that responds to the external environment, and a monitoring component that coordinates all other components so that real-time response can be maintained.

Business Software : Business information processing is the largest single software application area. In a broad sense, business software is an integrated software and has many components related to a particular field of the business. Discrete "system" for example, payroll, accounts that accesses one or more large databases containing business information. Application in this area restructure existing data in a way that facilitates business operations or management decision-making. In addition to conventional data processing application, business software applications also encompass interactive computing.

**Engineering and scientific Software :** Engineering and scientific software have been characterized by "number crunching" algorithms. Applications range from astronomy to volcano logy, from automotive manufacturing. However, modern application within the engineering/scientific area are moving away from conventional numerical algorithms. Computer-aided design, system simulation, and other interactive applications have begun to take on real-time and even system software characteristics.

**Embedded software :** Embedded software resides in read-only memory and is used to control products and systems for the consumer and industrial markets. Embedded software can perform very limited and esoteric functions (e.g., digital functions in an automobile such as fuel control, dashboard displays, and braking systems)

**Artificial intelligence software :** Artificial intelligence (AI) software is the software, which thinks and behaves like a human. AI software makes use of non-numerical algorithms to solve complex problems that are not amenable to computation or straightforward analysis. Expert system, also called knowledge-based systems, pattern recognition (image and voice), artificial neural networks, theorem proving, and game playing are representative of application within this category.

**Q2(a). Provide five examples of Software Development Projects that would be amenable to prototyping. Explain your answer. [8]**

Refer to Study material, Q21, Page No.-18

**(b) Name three software applications that would be difficult for prototyping. Explain your answer. [7]**

Applications that are difficult to prototype include control and process control systems. Also all mission critical applications are difficult to apply prototyping :

1. Satellite launching
2. Weather forecasting
3. Space Shuttle Monitoring

Because under prototype model - The first version that comes one - having minimum core functionality and later subsequent versions get updated and finally the full-functional model comes into existence. As mission critical system can't work on partly functional models. These are highly sensitive to the inputs and may prove highly destructive if experimented with partly functional models.

**Q3(a). You have been appointed as a Project Manager for a major software products company. Your job is to manage the development of the next generation version of its widely used word-processing software. Because competition is intense, tight deadlines have been established and announced. What team structure would you choose and why?**
**[DEC02,Q1(b);DEC01,Q1(b)] [8]**

Refer to DEC03, Q3(a), Page No.-130

**(b) What software process models would you choose for the job mentioned in 3(a) and why? Explain, in brief. [7]**

* Since a project is a new version for the product already in the market, the requirements are properly documented. Need to just follow up with accommodating the certain new requirement which also had been properly defined.

*Because of tight deadlines, the work activity need to be focused and certainwork discipline need to be introduced so that the tight control is enforced.

The Prototype Model or the Spiral Model is required to follow. Below is the brief explanation of choosing prototype model :

* Already old version is out in the market, only new requirement need to be adjusted.

* Old product has already got the reviews from the customer and the customers are already familiar with the old product functionality.

* The customer feedback has been received with the old version, so can better the next version following the prototype model, which allow the project to rebuild around the old version.

Since, Spiral and Prototype Both follow the same methodology either of the method would be applicable. The point to remember is how the old version was built (using which paradigm), that can easily answer the question.

**Q4(a). A number of high-level programming languages support the internal procedure as a modular construct. How does this construct affect coupling? [8]**

Coupling is defined as the measure of interconnection among modules in a program structure. Coupling depends upon the interface complexity between modules, the point at which entry or reference is made to a module, and what data passes across the interfaces.

In software design we always need lowest coupling between the modules. Simple connectivity among the modules is always result in a software that is easier to understand and less prone to "ripple effect" which is caused when errors occur at one location and are spreaded through the system.

Internal procedure is a modular construct that is supported by a number of high level languages and produces common coupling. In this a number of module access global data which may cause errors and force the software to abort or stop its functioning. At moderate levels coupling is characterised by passage of control between different modules.

**(b) When will you say that a module is coincidentally cohesive, logically cohesive or temporarily cohesive? Explain with appropriate examples. [7]**

Cohesion is a measure of the relative functional strength of a module and is also a natural extension of information hiding concept. When a module performs a set of tasks that relate to each other loosely, is said to be coincidentally cohesive and when a module performs tasks that are related logically is said to be logically cohesive and when a module contains tasks that are related by the fact that all must be executed within the same span of time, then it is said to be temporal cohesive.

For example, consider a module that performs error processing for engineering analysis package. The module is called when the computed data exceeds prespecified bounds. The module performs the following tasks :

**(1)** Stores computer based supplementary data on original computed data.
**(2)** It produces an error report on the user's workstation.
**(3)** It performs follow-up calculations requested by the user.
**(4)** It updates a database.
**(5)** It provides menu selection for subsequent processing.

Although the preceding tasks are loosely related, each is an independent functional unit or entity that might be performed best as a separate module. Combining the functions into a single module will increase the error propagation at time when modifications are to be made to any one of the processing tasks given above.

**Q5(a). What are Risk components and Risk drivers? Describe the difference between them. [8]**

The risk drivers effect software risk components such as performance, cost, support and schedule. Thus, they are the root of cause as they drive the risk. Risk driver is a conceptual aspect whereas risk components are tangible entities.

The risk components are :

**(1) Performance :-** It is the degree of uncertainty that the product will meet its requirements and is fit for its intended use.

**(2) Cost :-** It is the degree of uncertainty that the products budget is maintained.

**(3) Support :-** It is the degree of uncertainty that the project will be easily corrected, adapted, and enhanced.

**(4) Schedule :-** It is the degree of uncertainty that the project schedule will be maintained and it will be delivered to customer on time.

The impact of each risk driver on the risk component is divided into one of the four categories i.e. negligible, marginal, critical, catastrophic.

**(1) Negligible :-** In this there is no reduction in technical performance. The software becomes easily supportable, possible budget is slow-run, and it has early achievable delivery date.

**(2) Marginal :-** In this there is minimal reduction in technical performance, the software has responsive support, it has sufficient financial support, and realistic, achievable schedule.

**(3) Critical :-** This category has some reduction in technical performance, there are minor delays in software modifications, there is some shortage of financial resources, and possible slippage in delivery date.

**(4) Catastrophic :-** This category has significant degradation to non-achievement of technical performance. It has non-responsive or unsupportable software, there are financial shortages is budgets and it has unachievable delivery date.

Risk drivers can be assessed on qualitative probability scale that has the following values : impossible, probable, and frequent.

**(b) How will you identify risks with your software? What are the risks associated with the overall size of the software? [7]**

Identification of risk is an outcome of analysing various factors associated with risk mentioned below :

**Dependencies**

Many risks arise due to dependencies of project on outside agencies or factors. Some typical dependency-related risk factors are:

- Availability of trained, experienced people.
- Inter-component or inter-group dependencies.
- Customer-furnished items or information.

**Requirement Issues**

Many projects face uncertainty and turmoil around the product's requirements. While some of this uncertainty is tolerable in early stages, but the threat to success increases if such issues are not resolved as the project progresses. Some typical factors are :

- Lack of clear product vision.
- Lack of agreement on product requirements.
- Un-prioritized requirements.

**Management issues**

Project Managers usually write the risk management plan and most people do not wish to air their weaknesses (assuming they even recognize them) in public. Some of these risk factors are :

- Inadequate planning and task identification
- nadequate visibility into actual project status
- Unclear project ownership and decision making
- Unrealistic commitments made, sometimes for the wrong reasons
- Managers or customers with unrealistic expectations.

**Lack of Knowledge**

The rapid rate of change of technologies and the increasing change of skilled staff, mean that our project teams may not have the skills we need to be successful

Some of the factors are :

- Inadequate training
- Poor understanding of methods, tools and techniques
- Inadequate application domain experience.

Following risks are associated with the overall size of the software written in terms of the item checklist for product size risks :

1. Estimate the size of the product.
2. Estimate the degree of confidence in estimated size.
3. Estimate the percentage of deviation in size of product.
4. Estimate the size of database created or used by the product.
5. Estimate the number of users of the product.

**Q6. Write short notes on the following : [15]**

**(i) System testing [JUNE01, Q6(b)(iii)]**

Of the three levels of testing, the system level is closest to everyday experience. We test many things; a used car before we buy it, an on-line cable network service before we subscribe, and so on. A common pattern in these familiar forms is that we evaluate a product in terms of our expectations; not with respect to a specification or a standard. Consequently, goal is not to find faults, but to demonstrate performance. Because of this we tend to approach system testing from a functional standpoint rather than form a structural one. Since it is so intuitively familiar, system testing in practice tends to be less formal than it might be, and is compounded by the reduced testing that usually remains before a delivery deadline.

**(ii) Attributes of a System Analyst** **[JUNE01, Q5(a)]**

**(a) Knowledge of Business functions :** A systems analyst must know the environment in which he or she works. He must be aware of the peculiarities of management and the users at his installation and realize how they react to systems analyst. A working knowledge of accounting and marketing principles is a must since so many systems are built around these. Different functions in an organisation have conflicting needs and most systems are the result of compromise. The analyst's gola is to produce the system that will be the best for his organisation. This requires an open mind and flexibility in his ideas.

**(b) Knowledge of people :** Since a system analyst works with others so closely, he or she must understand their needs and what motivates them to develop systems properly.

**(c) Knowledge of Data processing principles :** Most systems today are computer based. The systems analyst must fully aware about the potential and limitations of computers.

**(d) Ability to communicate :** As a coordinator, a system analyst must communicate properly with people of different levels within an organisation. System analyst must listen carefully to what others say and integrate the thoughts of others into the systems development process.

**(e) Flexibility :** Systems analysts must be flexible in their thinking since they often do not get.

**(f) An analytical mind :** It takes an unusual person to see through problems faced by an organisation and develop solutions that will work. System analyst often find himselves with more data than he can cope with. It requires an analytical mind to select relevant data and concentrate on them in defining problems and forming solutions.

**(g) Well educated with sharp mind :** System analyst is called upon to work with people at all levels virtually in every aspect of business. He must know how to work with all of them and gain their confidence. Analyst must possess sharp mind to learn quickly how people do their jobs.

**(iii) Human Resources Management** **[DEC01,Q6(i)]**

A philosophy of people management based on the belief that human resources are uniquely important to sustained business success. An organization gains competitive advantage by using its people effectively, drawing on their expertise and ingenuity to meet clearly defined objectives. HRM is aimed at recruiting capable, flexible and committed people, managing and rewarding their performance and developing key competencies.

## CS-70 : INTRODUCTION TO SOFTWARE ENGINEERING
## DEC-2002

**Note:** *Question 1 is* ***compulsory****. Answer any* ***three*** *from the rest.*

**Q1(a). List three important Software Engineering paradigms. Which of these paradigms do you think would be most effective and why? Justify with examples. [15]**

To solve problems in an industry, a software engineer must incorporate particular strategy. This process is often referred to as a process model or a software paradigm. A process model for software engineering is choosen based on the nature of the project and application, the methods and tools to be used.

Three important Software Engineering paradigms are given below :

**(i)** Most familiar model is the waterfall model, which is given in figure. This model has five phases; Requirements analysis and specification, design, implementation and unit testing, integration & system testing, and operation & maintenance.

**1. Requirement analysis and specification phase :** The goal of this phase is to understand the exact requirements of the customer and to document them properly. This activity is usually executed together with the customer, as the goal is to document all functions, performance and interfacing requirements for the software.

The resultant document is known as Software Requirement Specification (SRS) document.

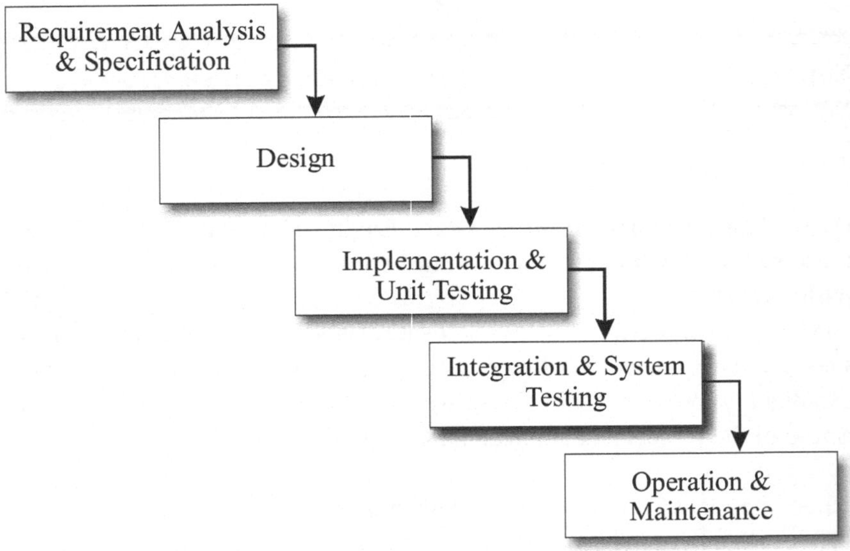


Fig : Waterfall model

**2. Design phase :** The SRS document is produced in the previous phase, which contains the exact requirements of the customer. The goal of this phase is to transform the requirement specification into a structure that is suitable for implementation in some programming language.

**3. Implementation and unit testing phase :** During this phase, design is implemented. If the SDD is complete, the implementation or coding phase proceeds smoothly, because all the information needed by the software engineers is contained in the SDD.

**4. Integration and system testing phase :** This is a very important phase. Effective testing will contribute to the delivery of higher quality software products, more satisfied users, lower maintenance costs, and more accurate and reliable results.

**5. Operation & maintenance phase :** Software maintenance is a task that every development group has to face, when the software is delivered to the customer's site, installed and is operational.

**(ii)** A disadvantage of waterfall model is that the working software is not available until late in the process, thus delaying the discovery of serious error. An alternative to this is to first develop a working prototype of the software instead of developing the actual software. The working prototype is developed as per current available requirements.

The developers use this prototype to refine the requirements and prepare the final specification document.

The developers should develop prototype as early as possible to speed up the software development process.

After the finalization of software requirement and specification (SRS) document, the prototype is discarded and actual system is then development using the waterfall approach. Thus, it is used as an input to waterfall model and produces maintainable and good quality software.

Prototyping can be problematic for the following reasons:

**1.** The customer sees what appears to be working version of the software, unaware that the prototyping is held together "with chewing gum and baling wire." Unaware that in the rush to get it working no one has considered over all software quality or long-term maintainability.

**2.** The developer often makes implementation compromises in order to get a prototype working quickly. An inappropriate operating system or programming language may be used simply because it is available and known; an inefficient algorithm may be implemented simply to demonstrate capability.

**(iii) The RAD Model**

RAD is "Rapid Application Development". It is a linear sequential software development process model. It emphasizes on an extremely short development cycle. If the requirements are well understood and the project goal is constrained i.e., these conditions are by no means guaranteed, the RAD process enables a development team to create a fully functional system within a short period of time. The RAD approach encompasses the following phases :

**1.** Business modelling
**2.** Data modelling
**3.** Process modelling
**4.** Application generation
**5.** Testing and turnover

The time constraints imposed on RAD project demand scalable scope.

From the above defined three paradigms we think that the prototype model is the best because waterfall model is the oldest and cannot work faster and

RAD requires sufficient human resources to create the right number of RAD terms. In prototype model the customer must have patience as the working version of the program will not be available until late in the project time span. Thus, in these situations the prototype model gives everything the "best".

**(b) You have been appointed as a Project Manager within an information systems organization. Your job is to build an application that is quite similar to the other that your team has built, although this one is larger and more complex. Requirements have been thoroughly documented by the customer. What team structure would you choose and why?**
**[DEC03,Q3(a);JUNE02,Q3(a);DEC01,Q1(b)] [15]**

The team structure depends on the management style of organization. The number of people who will populate the team and their skill levels, and the overall problem difficulty, three generic team organizations are :

**Democratic Decentralized (DD) :**
* This approach has No Permanent Leader
* Task Co-ordinators are appointed for short duration.
* Decisions on problems are appointed are made by group consensus.

**Controlled Decentralized (CD) :**
* Has defined leader, who coordinate the activity
* Problem solving remains a group activity

**Controlled Centralized (CC) :**
* Top level problem solving and internal team coordination are managed by a team leader.
* Communication between the leader and team members is vertical.

**Regarding the said project :**
* Since project is large more number of personnel will participate
* Since project is complex it will require the expert professionals
* Expert professional need to have freedom to work, they are just needed the deadlines to meet, should be having free hand to deal with, since they know their job on hand and have maturity and experience.

All of the above points advocate for the DD [Democratic Decentralized] team structure if the professionals involved with the project are from the organization itself.

**Q2. Discuss the way in which you would apply the problem solving loop to :**

**(i) understand requirements for a new word-processing product; and [7]**

* Collect features of the existing word processor
* Document their requirement
* Document their limitations
* Carry out survey, gather user's new requirement and expectations
* Improve the interface

**(ii) develop an advanced spelling checking component for the word processor. [8]**

* Collect details from different dictionary sources
* Provide easy interface for spell checking.
* Analyse the current word processor's spell checking and document its limitations and user's expectations from it.

**Q3(a). What are the duties of a Systems Analyst? What are his/her attributes, that may be desired as a professional? [JUNE01, Q1(b)] [8]**

Following are the duties and attributes of system analyst :

**DUTIES**

**(a)** The first and perhaps most difficult task of systems analyst is problem definition. Business problems are quite difficult to define. It is also true, that problems cannot be solved until they are precisely and clearly defined.

**(b)** Initially a systems analyst does not know how to solve a specific problem. He must consult with managers, users and other data processing professionals in defining problems and developing solutions. He uses various methods for data gathering to get the correct solution of a problem.

**(c)** Having gathered the data relating to a problem, the systems analyst analyses them and thinks of plan to solve it. He may not come up personally with the best way of solving a problem but pulls together other people's ideas and refines them until a workable solution is achieved.

**(d)** Systems analysts coordinate the process of developing solutions. Since many problems have number of solutions, the systems analyst must evaluate the merit of such proposes solution before recommending one to the management.

**(e)** Systems analysts are often referred to as planners. A key part of the systems analyst's job is to develop a plan to meet the management's objectives.

**(f)** When the plan has been accepted, systems analyst is responsible for designing it so that management's goal could be achieved. Systems design is a time consuming, complex and precise task.

**(g )** Systems must be thoroughly tested. The systems analyst often coordinates the testing procedures and helps, in deciding whether or not the new system is meeting standards established in the planning phase.

**ATTRIBUTES**

**(a) Knowledge of Business functions :** A systems analyst must know the environment in which he or she works. He must be aware of the peculiarities of management and the users at his installation and realize how they react to systems analyst. A working knowledge of accounting and marketing principles is a must since so many systems are built around these two areas. He must be familiar with his company's product and services and management's policies in areas concerning him.

**(b) Knowledge of people :** Since a systems analyst works with others so closely, he or she must understand their needs and what motivates them to develop systems properly.

**(c) Knowledge of Data processing principles :** Most systems today are computer based. The systems analyst must fully aware about the potential and limitations of computers.

**(d) Ability to communicate :** As a coordinator, a systems analyst must communicate properly with people of different levels within an organisation. Systems analyst must listen carefully to what others say and integrate the thoughts of others into the systems development process.

**(e) Flexibility :** Systems analysts must be flexible in their thinking since they often do not get-their own way. Different factions in an organisation have conflicting needs and most systems are the result of compromise. The analyst's goal is to produce the system that will be the best for his organisation. This requires an open mind and flexibility in his ideas.

**(f) An analytical mind :** It takes an unusual person to see through problems facing an organisation and develop solutions that will work. Systems analysts often find themselves with more data than they can cope with. It requires an analytical mind to select pertinent data and concentrate on them in defining problems and forming solutions.

**(g) Well educated with sharp mind :** Systems analysts are called upon to work with people at all levels virtually in every aspect of business. They must know how to work with all of them and gain their confidence. Analysts must have sharp mind to learn quickly how people do their jobs.

**(b) Enumerate the goals of structured methodology of system analysis and design. [JUNE 01, Q1(c)] [7]**

Structural analysis is a set of techniques & graphical tools that allow the analyst to develop a new kind of system specifications that are easily understood by the user. Structured analysis considers new goals & structured tools for analysis.

**The goals of structured methodology of system analysis & design are as follows :**

(i) Graphics should be used wherever it is possible to well communicate with the user & help the user also.
(ii) Differentiate between the logical & physical systems.
(iii) A logical system model should be build to familiarize the user with the system characteristics and inter-relationships before implementation.

**Q4(a). How will you identify risks to your project plan (estimates, schedule etc.)? What are the specific risks that are associated with the complexity of the system to be built and the "newness" of the technology that is packaged by the system? [10]**

Identification of risk is an outcome of analysing various factors associated with risk mentioned below :

**Dependencies**

Many risks arise due to dependencies of project on outside agencies or factors. Some typical dependency-related risk factors are:

- Availability of trained, experienced people.
- Inter-component or inter-group dependencies.
- Customer-furnished items or information.

**Requirement Issues**

Many projects face uncertainty and turmoil around the product's requirements. While some of this uncertainty is tolerable in early stages, but the threat to success increases if such issues are not resolved as the project progresses. Some typical factors are :

- Lack of clear product vision.
- Lack of agreement on product requirements.
- Un-prioritized requirements.

**Management issues**

Project Managers usually write the risk management plan and most people do not wish to air their weaknesses (assuming they even recognize them) in public. Some of these risk factors are :

- Inadequate planning and task identification
- nadequate visibility into actual project status
- Unclear project ownership and decision making
- Unrealistic commitments made, sometimes for the wrong reasons
- Managers or customers with unrealistic expectations.

**Lack of Knowledge**

The rapid rate of change of technologies and the increasing change of skilled staff, mean that our project teams may not have the skills we need to be successful

Some of the factors are :

- Inadequate training
- Poor understanding of methods, tools and techniques
- Inadequate application domain experience.

Following risks are associated with the complexity of the system to be built, written in terms of the item checklist for product complexity risks :

1. Estimate the size of the product.
2. Estimate the degree of confidence in estimated size.
3. Estimate the percentage of deviation in size of product.
4. Estimate the size of database created or used by the product.
5. Estimate the number of users of the product.

Risk associated with "newness" of the Technology :

The following check-list risks are associated with the newness of technology :

**1.** Is the technology to be built new to your organization.

**2.** Do the customers requirements demand the creation of new algorithms or input or output technology.

**3.** Does the software interface with new or unproven hardware.

**4.** Does the software to be built interface with a database system whose function and performance have not been proven in this application area.

**5.** Is a specialized user interface demanded by product requirements.

**6.** Do requirements demand the use of new analysis, design or testing methods.

**7.** Do requirements put excessive performance constraint on the product. If answer is 'Yes' further investigation is required.

**(b) Describe the differences between functional and non-functional requirements? [JAN01,Q1(d);JUNE01,Q3(c)] [5]**

In general, requirements are partitioned into **functional requirements** and **non-functional requirements**. Functional requirements are associated with specific functions, tasks or behaviours the system must support, while non-functional requirements are constraints on various attributes of these functions or tasks. In terms of the ISO quality characteristics for evaluation, the functional requirements address the quality characteristic of functionality while the other quality characteristics are concerned with various kinds of non-functional requirements. Because non-functional requirements tend to be stated in terms of **constraints** on the results of tasks which are given as functional requirements (e.g., constraints on the speed or efficiency of a given task), a task-based functional requirements statement is a useful skeleton upon which to construct a complete requirements statement. That is the approach taken in this work. It can be helpful to think of non-functional requirements as adverbially related to tasks or functional requirements: how fast, how efficiently, how safely, etc., is a particular task carried out by a particular system?

**Q5(a). Assume that you have been contracted by a university to develop an on-line course registration system. First, act as the student and specify the characteristics of a good system. [8]**

The aims or objectives of the registration system are as follows :

**(a)** The registration system offers details of various courses with names with eligibility criteria, duration and fee structure.

**(b)** A registration form is to be filled up by the candidate to register himself or herself.

**(c)** Different fee structure is defined for different courses.

**(d)** When the candidate is admitted to the course then Examination form is to be filled by the student.

As a student I think that the student who wants to get register himself/herself for a course in the university through an on-line course registration system, it should have the following facilities :

**(a)** Eligibility criteria for taking admission is to be provided for different courses.

**(b)** Provide information about various courses, the courses may be technical or non-technical.

**(c)** Details of each course are to be provided.

**(d)** Duration of different courses is to be provided.

**(e)** Fee structure of different courses is to be given.

**(f)** Examination pattern for each course is to be provided.

**(g)** Passing & grading criteria is also to be given.

**(h)** Syllabus of the various course is to given.

**(i)** One section with title "About University" is to given, which should contain all details about university achievements, recognitions, and industry profile of their ex-students.

Once the student go through all these information provided or information he/she needs, it will help him/her in taking decision about the admission / course. While, the goal of developer is to get all the requirements from the university and the student gets the desired output. In the on-line registration system it should be able to get all the information required by the university. Developer should consider the following things before developing the on-line course registration system :

**(1)** He should develop the data flow and the control diagram of the course registration system.

**(2)** He should describe the various types of courses that are being provided by the university.

**(3)** He should also provide the functional partitioning of the system.

**(4)** He should give the control and behavioural description of the system.

**(5)** He should provide the validation criteria of the course registration system.

**(b) For the Online Course Registration system mentioned in question 5(a), act as a developer and define parallel work activities during the project. [7]**

Gantt Chart showing parallel activities in the given problem :

| | | |
|---|---|---|
| 1. High level analysis | week 1 5 days | sequential |
| 2. Selection of hardware platform | week 1 1 day | sequential 1 |
| 3. Installation of hardware | week 3 2 weeks | parallel 2 |
| 4. Detailed analysis of core modules | week 1 2 weeks | sequential 1 |
| 5. Detailed analysis of supporting utilities | week 1 2 weeks | sequential 4 |
| 6. Programming of core modules | week 4 3 weeks | sequential 4 |
| 7. Programming of supporting modules | week 4 3 weeks | sequential 5 |
| 8. Quality assurance of core modules | week 5 1 week | sequential 6 |
| 9. Quality assurance of supporting modules | week 5 1 week | sequential 7 |
| 10. Core module training | week 7 1 day | parallel 6 |

| | | | |
|---|---|---|---|
| 11.Development of accounting reporting | week 6 | 1 week | parallel 5 |
| 12.Development of management reporting | week 6 | 1 week | parallel 5 |
| 13.Development of management analysis | week 6 | 2 weeks | sequential 5 |
| 14.Detailed training | week 7 | 1 week | sequential 1-13 |
| 15.Documentation | week 4 | 2 weeks | parallel 13 |

The various parallel activities in the given problem can be known from the above explanation.

**Q6. Write a short note on the following : [15]**

**(i) α-testing [JUNE01,Q6(b,iv)]**

A customer conducts the alpha test at the developer's sites. The software is used in natural setting with the developer "looking over the shoulder" of the user and recording errors and usage problems. Alpha tests are conducted in a controlled environment / conditions.

**(ii) β-testing [JUNE01,Q6(b,v)]**

The beta test is conducted at one or more customer sites by the end-user of the software. Unlike alpha testing, the developer is generally not present. Therefore, the beta test is a "live" application of the software in an environment that cannot be controlled by the developer. The customer records all problems (real or imagined) that are encountered during beta testing and reports these to the developer at regular intervals. As a result of problems reported during beta tests, software engineers make modifications and then prepare for release of the software product to the entire customer base.

**(iii) Project Tracking [DEC01,Q6(iii)]**

Project Tracking gives insight into the current status about project. Project Tracking is part of Project Management Activity - Project Management includes following activities :

**Activities :**

1. Project estimation
2. Project scheduling
3. Project execution
4. Project tracking
5. Project modification

Project Tracking activity compares the project progress made with the project schedule. Project Tracking gives insight into whether the project is on Schedule, behind the schedule or ahead of the schedule.

- If project progress is as per schedule - nothing serious or corrective measure is to be taken.
- If project progress is behind the schedule, the cause for the delay need to be worked out. This could give insight into wrong estimation, inefficiency or complexity of the project and the further schedule need to be worked out either by employing additional resources or further delaying a project, the cost benefit analysis and probability should be thoroughly checked in any, case.
- If project progress is ahead of project estimation.

The part of probe is why deadline is not accurate whether estimation was wrong, or the efficiency is compromised to furnish before schedule. This should be thoroughly checked.

# CS-70 : INTRODUCTION TO SOFTWARE ENGINEERING
## JUNE-2003

**Note:** *Question 1 is* ***compulsory****. Answer any* ***three*** *from the rest.*

**Q1(a). Propose a specific software project that would be amenable to the incremental model. Present a scenario for applying the model to the software.**

The incremental model combines elements of the linear sequential model (applied repetitively) with the iterative philosophy of prototyping. Referring to figure, the incremental model applies linear sequences in a staggered fashion as calendar time progresses. Each linear sequence produces a deliverable "increment" of the software.

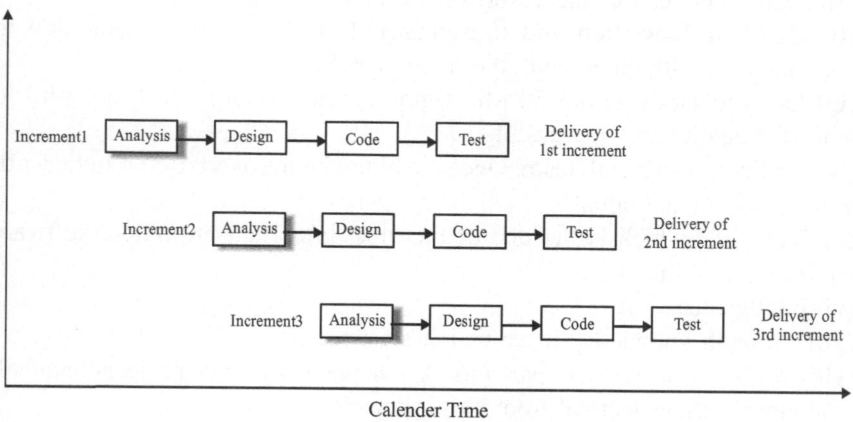


For example, word-processing software developed using the incremental paradigm might deliver basic file management, editing, and document production functions in the first increment; more sophisticated editing and document production capabilities in the second increment; spelling and grammar checking in the third increment; and advanced page layout capability in the fourth increment. It should be noted that the process flow for any increment can incorporate the prototyping paradigm.

- In word processing system, one core product is first developed.
- The rest of the product is built on this core.
- The project is actually divided into some modules which are generated in incremental steps.

- The word processing project has many features like Spelling checking, Editing, Coping and others.
- These all modules are divided between team members
- The team members generate them independently
- At last the integration of the module is done.
- Thus whole product is integrated.
- After first product has been deployed, the other features are added to the project and the second version of the product is deployed.

**(b) Make a list of 10 guidelines that will lead to software engineers who work to their full potential.**

These are the list of ten guidelines that leads to software engineers, although that software engineer can work with full potential :

**(i)** High analysis skills : One should possess high skills to analysis the given problem. As this is the core step in software development. If performed with efficiently then lead to successful software development.

**(ii)** Good oral, written and interpersonal skills are also demanded to communicate with client and other team members.

**(iii)** Skills to motivate others. Motivation is must to carry on team spirit to work for quality and successful.

**(iv)** Ability to work with team. One should not be introvert. Better to be work as team and an individual.

**(v)** Discipline which is the one of the most important attribute a software engineer should possess.

**(vi)** Intelligence.

**(vii)** Through knowledge of computer science.

**(viii)** Ability to learn from past mistakes happened in past projects handled. And apply lessons learned from those projects.

**(ix)** Remain in control under high-stress situation.

**(x)** Good programming abilities.

**Q2(a). The decision made by senior management can have a significant impact on the effectiveness of a software engineering team. Provide five examples to illustrate that this is true.**

Senior Manager is a person who defines the business issues that often have significant influence on the project. The whole project team follows the decision taken by senior management as well as the progress of the project depends on the decision of the senior management. Senior management gives all the practical and ethical decisions and guidelines.

Below are the five examples to illustrate that this is true :

**Example 1 :** Senior management should take decision to train and support process improvement and quality improvement training for the middle managers so they can pass it to the SET (Software Engineering Team), which will fetch a quality product. If the senior management will not take such decision then middle level management will also behaves as blocking factor in quality management or process improvement effort. The same will be passed to software engineering team. Thus, it will significantly effect the effectiveness of the SET(Software Engineering Team).

**Example 2 :** Decisions regarding budget by the senior management also impacts the effectiveness of a SET.

**Example 3 :** Decisions to introduce a new person in team by the senior management also results in impact on the effectiveness of SET, as new team member has to gain knowledge about the ongoing project then only he can start thinking over it.

**Example 4 :** Decision to make changes in senior management also puts influence on the effectiveness of a SET.

**Example 5 :** Suppose any software is developed and the work is going smoothly. In the later stages of development a problem encountered and the software engineering team is unable to solve the problem. In this situation senior management have the great impact. The quality and reliability issues are also guided by senior management.

Thus, it is true that the decisions made by senior management impact on the effectiveness of software engineering team.

**(b) Why should some software metrics be kept "private"? Provide examples of three metrics that should be private. Provide examples of three metrices that should be public.**

Private process data can serve as an important driver as the individual software engineer works to improve. Some process metrices are private to the software project team.

The personal software process (PSP) is a structured set of process description, measurements, and methods that can help engineers to improve their personal performance. It provides the scripts, and standards that help them to estimate and plan their work. It shows them how to define processes and how to measure their quality and productivity. A fundamental PSP principles is that everyone is different and a method that is effective for one engineer may not be suitable for another. The PSP thus helps engineers to measure and track their own work so they can find the methods that are best for them. Thats why some software metrices be kept private. Private metrices includes defect rates (by individual), defect rates (by module), and errors found during development. Defects reported for major software functions, errors found during formal technical reviews, and lines of code (LOC) or function points per module or function.

Examples of metrices that should be kept private :

**(i)** Technology

**(ii)** Process

**(iii)** Product

Examples of metrices that should be kept public :

**(i)** Product

**(ii)** People

**(iii)** Process

**Q3(a). You have been appointed a project manager for a small software products company. Your job is to build a break through product that combines virtual reality hardware with state of the art software. There is pressure to get the job done as soon as possible. What team structure would you choose and why?**

The problem is all regarding virtual reality hardware.

- Which requires more concentration and hard work.
- Centralised structure of the team completes tasks faster, it is most adoptable at handling simple problems.
- While decentralized structure of the team generates more and better solutions than individuals.
- Therefore, it has greater probability of success when working with difficult problem.
- Our problem is difficult too, so we should follow decentralised team structure for problem solving.
- In addition large projects can be handled easily by decentralized team.
- So for particular problem of virtual reality controlled decentralized (CD) Structure of the team is well suited.

**(b) What software process models would you choose for the job mentioned in 3(a) and why? Explain briefly.**

The software process model for this problem can be spiral model :

- Because this model is suitable for development of technically challenging software products.
- Spiral model is divided into number of frame work activities which are called task region.
- The different task regions are customer communication, planning, risk, analysis, engineering, construction and release and customer evaluation.
- The virtual reality hardware problem is really complex and challenging
- And it requires planning and construction at each stage.
- The task set of the spiral model gives the problem a realistic approach. Which is necessary for the given situation :
- The model will generate prototyping out any stage in the evaluation of product.
- It maintains systematic stepwise approach suggested by the classical life cycle.
- It cooperates the problem into an iterative framework that more realistically reflect the real world.

So, we can say the spiral model is well suited for the given situation.

**Q4(a). Present an argument against lines of code as a measure for software productivity. Will your case hold up when dozens or hundreds of projects are considered?**

**Some favourable points :**

- This is a direct approach for measurement.
- This is the simplest among all metrics available to estimate project size.

But, there are several shortcomings of LOC :

**1.** LOC gives a numerical value of problem size that can be vary widely with individual coding style - different programmers lay out their code in different ways.

**2.** A good problem size measure should consider the overall complexity of the problem and the effort needed to solve it, including design, code, test etc.

- LOC focuses on the coding activity alone.

**3.** LOC measure co-relates poorly with the quality and efficiency of the code.

- A longer code size does not necessarily imply better quality or higher efficiency.

**4.** It measures the lexical complexity of a program and does not address the more important logical and structural complexity.

Our case will hold up when dozens or hundreds of projects are considered as the LOC measure is even more difficult. We can use LOC to estimate complexity, efficiency etc. if we have small project but as the project grows in size LOC measure becomes a tedious task.

**(b) Cost and schedule estimates are developed during software project planning before detailed software requirement analysis or design has been conduced. Why do you think this is done? Are there circumstances when it should not be done.**

Refer to DEC04, Q2(a), Page No.-104

**Q5(a). What are "Known Risks" and " Predictable Risks"? List the difference between them.**

**Known Risks :** Known risks are those, that can be uncovered after careful evaluation of the project plan, the business and technical environment in which the project is being developed.

**Predictable Risks** : Predictable risks are extrapolated from past project experience, means the new team member can not predict that kind of risks.

**TABLE**

| Known Risks | Predictable Risk |
|---|---|
| • They are known to any team member of the project and can be uncovered after careful evaluation.<br>• They can be easily identified.<br>• Examples of known risks are unrealistic delivery date, lack of document requirements on software scope, poor development environment | • The predictable risks are not always known to each team member they could be uncovered only if they are predicted<br>• The team members only having some past experience can identify this kind of risk.<br>• Examples are staff turnover, poor communication with the customer, dilution of staff effort |

**(b) Describe five software application areas in which software safety and hazard analysis would be a concern.**

Following are the five application ares in which S/W safety and hazard analysis would be a major concern :

**1. Computer based control for automobile :** if significant hazards that can effect software for automobile are not identified & accessed then it may cause malfunctioning of automobile.

**2. Computer based system for nuclear reactions :** potential hazards related to reaction formation should be assessed in advance so as to ensure proper reactions taking place inside the reactor, otherwise loss of life may occur.

**3. Aircraft flight control :** safety analysis required to ensure that the software is capable of controlling the flight in all cases so as to be reliable & safe for humans.

**4. Weapons systems :** safety & hazard analysis is of utmost concern when weapon formation & automation is based on a software. We must make sure that all the latest modules & techniques are incorporated in software.

**5. Large scale industrial processes :** Industrial processes as iron and steel carrying, chemical works etc. need safety analysis for proper & efficient working of machines & tools that can prove to be of significant aid in human injury & life saving.

**Q6. Write short notes on the following :**

**(i) Scheduling of a software project.**

Software project scheduling is an activity that distributes estimated effort across the planned project duration by allocating the effort to specific software engineering tasks.

Scheduling of software project doesn't differ greatly from scheduling of any multitask engineering effort. Therefore, generalized project scheduling tools and techniques can be applied with little modification to software projects. Program Evaluation and Review Techniques (PERT) and Critical Path Method (CPM) are two project scheduling methods that can be applied to software development. Both techniques are driven by information already developed in project planning activities :

(i) Estimates of effort
(ii) A decomposition of the product function
(iii) The selection of the appropriate process model and task set
(iv) Decomposition of tasks

Both PERT and CPM provide quantitative tools that allow the software planner to:

(i) Determine the critical path
(ii) Establish "most likely" time estimates
(iii) Calculate "boundary times" that defines a time "window" for a particular task.

**(ii) S/W defects.**

Software defects are the anomaly left in the software product due to improper quality check or improper development of the software or due to any other reason.

The defect should be identified in testing and debugging. Normally the defect imply a quality problem that is discovered after the software has been released to client. The primary goal of the developer should be to detect errors in the project, so that they do not become defects after releasing it to the client. For detecting the error, the defect simplication model is used :

**(i)** The formal technical reviews are done to detect this kind of defects before their deployment.

**(ii)** Software Quality Assurance Activities are normally used to negate this kinds of defects.

**(iii)** SQA encompasses a quality management approach, effective software engineering technology, formal technical review, and multitiered testing strategy etc.

**(iii) Partitioning of a problem.**

Partitioning of problem, is an activity that sits at the core of software requirements. During the scoping activity no attempt is made to fully decompose the problem. Rather, partitioning is applied in two major areas :

**(a)** the functionality that must be delivered

**(b)** the process that will be used to deliver it

Stated simply, a complex problem is partitioned into smaller problems that are more manageable. This is the strategy that applies as project planning begins. Software functions, described in the statement of scope, are evaluated and refined to provide more detail prior to the beginning of estimation. Because both cost and schedule estimates are functionally oriented, some degree of decomposition is often useful.

# CS-70 : INTRODUCTION TO SOFTWARE ENGINEERING
## DEC-2003

**Note:** *Question 1 is* ***compulsory****. Answer any* ***three*** *from the rest.*

**Q1(a). Modify the Waterfall Model so that it can be used with small software projects that increase in complexity over time. Give a sketch of the new model. Also, list the documents that would evolve in the design process.**

Waterfall model is the oldest and widely used model for software engineering but it has some drawbacks as well, specially if we look at practical aspects of it.

**1)** It is often difficult for the customer to state all requirements explicitly. Thus natural uncertainty is not covered that exists at inception of projects.

**2)** Customer must have patience as working session of program is only available later in the project. That means if a major defect is detected after delivery, it becomes nearly impossible to correct.

**3)** Importantly, rear projects rarely follow the sequential flow that this model proposes. There is iteration, but it is indirect. Thus changes can cause confusion as project proceeds. A software development life cycle(SDLC) model that is better one and overcomes disadvantages mentioned above is incremental model.

The incremental model combines elements of the linear sequential model (applied repetitively) with the iterative philosophy of prototyping. Referring to Figure, the incremental model applies linear sequences in a staggered fashion as calendar time progresses. Each linear sequence produces a deliverable "increment" of the software.

When an incremental model is used, the first increment is often a core product. The core product is used by the customer (or undergoes detailed review). As a result of use and/or evaluation, a plan is developed for the next increment. The plan addresses the modification of the core product to better meet the needs of the customer and the delivery of additional features and functionality. This process is repeated following the delivery of each increment, until the complete product is produced.

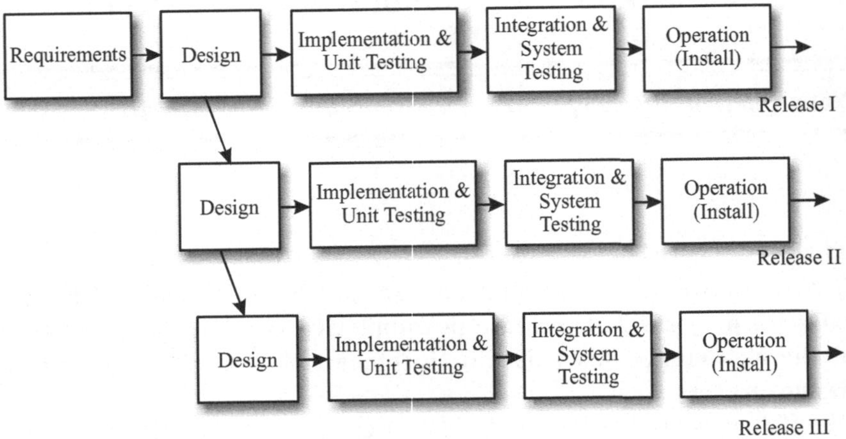


Fig : Iterative enhancement model.

Below mentioned is the list of the documents that would evolve in the design process :

**(i)** Requirement Analysis
**(ii)** Design Issues
**(iii)** System scope
**(iv)** System features

**(b) Software is the differentiating characteristic in many computer based products and systems. Provide examples of two or three products and atleast one system in which software, not hardware, is the differentiating element. [DEC01,Q1(a)]**

Refer to Study material, Q5, Page No.-4

**Q2(a). Develop a small application that analyzes each course offered by a university and reports the average grade obtained in the course for a given semester. Write a statement of scope that bounds this problem.**

The statement of scope that bounds the problem is as under :

The University consists of many courses. Each course have different number of subjects having different credit. In each course there are number of students, course co-ordinator. It is needed to maintain all these details about particular course as under :

**a)** Course
**b)** Course code
**c)** Course name
**d)** Course co-ordinator
**e)** Total number of subject

**f)** Total credit

**g)** Department

**h)** Number of semesters

Also the course can contain following fields :

Number of courses can be added to the application. For a particular code there would be one course co-ordinator that will guide in developing the course contents. There can be number of different subjects in particular course and each subject is having a specific grade. By analyzing student capacity and ability the grades are given. By averaging the grade with the total number of students in particular course for given semester the average grade can be obtained. Figure shows a diagram for a course module for any university. The system can be easily understood by the following diagram :

**A DFD representing application** :

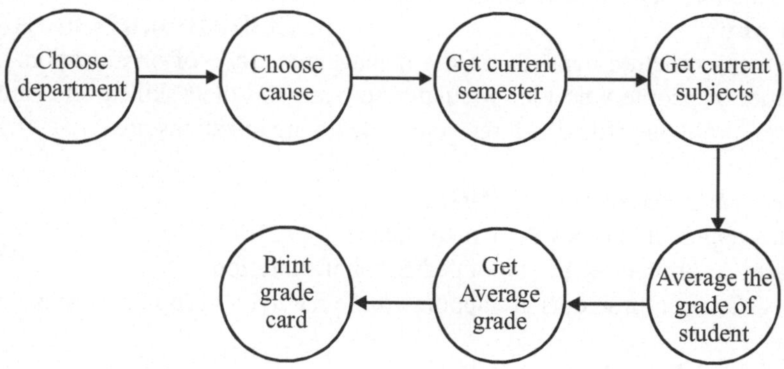


**(b) The software used to control an advanced machine require 32,000 lines of 'C' code and 4,500 lines of code of a specialized 4GL-like language. Estimate the number of functional points for the software.**

Count total $= 32{,}000 + 4{,}500$

$= 36{,}500$ line of code

$$\Sigma fi = \frac{32{,}00 + 4{,}500}{2}$$

$$= \frac{36{,}500}{2}$$

$$= 18{,}250$$

then, the function point for the software is

FP = count total *[0.65 + 0.01 * Σfi]

$$= 36{,}500 * [0.65 + 0.01 * 18{,}250]$$

$$= 36{,}500 * \left[\frac{65}{100} + \frac{18250}{100}\right]$$

$$= 36{,}500 * \left[\frac{65 + 18250}{100}\right]$$

$$= 36{,}500 * \frac{18250}{100}$$

$$= 365 * 18315$$

$$= 6684975$$

Total number of function point of the software = 66,84,975

**Q3(a). Assume that you have been appointed as Project Manager within an information systems organization. Your job is to build an application that is quite similar to others that your team has built, although this one is larger and more complex. Requirements have been thoroughly documented by the customer. What team structure would you choose and why? [DEC02,Q1(b);DEC01,Q1(b)]**

The team structure depends on the management style of organization. The number of people who will populate the team and their skill levels, and the overall problem difficulty, three generic team organizations are :

**Democratic Decentralized (DD)** :

* This approach has No Permanent Leader
* Task Co-ordinators are appointed for short duration.
* Decisions on problems are appointed are made by group consensus.

**Controlled Decentralized (CD)** :

* Has defined leader, who coordinate the activity
* Problem solving remains a group activity

**Controlled Centralized (CC)** :

* Top level problem solving and internal team coordination are managed by a team leader.
* Communication between the leader and team members is vertical.

**Regarding the said project** :

* Since project is large more number of personnel will participate
* Since project is complex it will require the expert professionals
* Expert professional need to have freedom to work, they are just needed the

deadlines to meet, should be having free hand to deal with, since they know their job on hand and have maturity and experience.

All of the above points advocate for the DD [Democratic Decentralized] team structure if the professionals involved with the project are from the organization itself.

**(b) What software process models would you choose for the job mentioned in 3(a) and why? Explain briefly.**

The project is little bit longer and more complex :

**1.** It requires proper requirement gathering

**2.** That is already properly documented

**3.** The project is going to be developed by experts

**4.** The increment model of the project should be followed

**5.** The increment model combines elements of the linear sequential model with prototyping. The incremental model combines elements of the linear sequential model with iterative philosophy of prototyping. The first increment is often a core product. i.e. the basic requirements are addressed, but many supplementary features remain undelivered. The core product is used by the customer, the PLAN addresses the modification of the core product to better meet the needs of the customer and the delivery of additional features and functionality. This process is repeated following the delivery of each increment, until the complete product is produced.

The incremental process is iterative/repetitive in nature. Incremental model is particularly useful when staffing is unavailable for a complete implementation by the business deadline that has been established for the project. Early increment can be implemented with fewer people. If the core product is well received, the additional staff can be added to implement the next increment.

**Q4(a). List the differences between Process and Project Metrics.**

| Process metrices | Project metrices |
|---|---|
| • Enable a software engg. organization to gain insight into the efficiency of an existing process<br>• Managers and practitioners can assess what works and what doesn't | • Enable to gain insight into the efficiency of the whole project.<br>• Managers can assess the status of an ongoing project track, potential risks, adjust work flow and tasks and evaluate the project teams ability. |
| • Process metrices are collected across all projects.<br>• They are collected over long period of time.<br>• Provide indicators that lead to long term software process improvement | • Project metrices is for particular project<br>• They are collected during each project.<br>• Provides indicators for short-term software process improvement. |

**(b) Develop a list of software characteristics (e.g.. : Graphical output etc.) that affect the complexity of a project. Prioritize the list.**

**Software characteristics are** :

**(i)** Graphical Output
**(ii)** User friendliness
**(iii)** Output after processing many tables
**(iv)** Getting complex reports
**(v)** Multiple looping and checking
**(vi)** Repeatability
**(vii)** Number of functionalities
**(viii)** Integration between different modules (high coupling and low cohesion)
**(ix)** Complex data calculation
**(x)** Requirements not gathered properly

**The above are some common characteristics that increase complexity of the system.**

To prioritize the list, it is necessary to understand the complexity of each characteristic

**1.** The most complex out of this is user friendliness, the system should always be user friendly, so that the user can easily operate it. To incorporate this functionality make the system complex.

**2.** The graphical output of the system makes complex calculation in code which also increases complexity.

**3.** If the requirements of the project is not properly known, then it will cause problems while creating project which makes the project complex.

**4.** If there is no mutual understanding between team members the project can't be developed easily.

**5.** If the project contains result that requires too many queries from the database to execute then it is also one kind of complexity.

**6.** The number of functionality added to the project also affect the complexity.

**7.** If there is so many number of looping and checking in the coding then it will increase code complexity.

**8.** Improper integration of modules OR high coupling among modules and low cohesion in modules is one of the main causes of project complexity.

**Q5(a). What are Process Risks? What are the Process and Technical issues that are related with Process Risks?**

Process risk is the degree to which the software process has been properly defined and is followed by development organization process risks typically impringe on the whole of the software development cycle as process forms the basis of development. Process risks may arise due to estimation problems, lack of proper analysis or choice of unsuitable process.

Some process risks are
**1)** Processes are not exactly identified.
**2)** Resources needed for process are not exactly met.
**3)** Ambiguity in the process.
**4)** Design does not suit actual concept.

Technical issues related to process risks.
**a)** If process is not technically implemented properly, implementation may be difficult or impossible.
**b)** Design may not be properly arrived at due to process risks.
**c)** Interface clarity becomes an overhead as well.
**d)** Maintenance is the biggest aspect that comes as an outcome of process risk.

**(b) How will you assess a risk? How can you manage it and make contingency planning?**
The following questions have derived from risk data obtained by surveying experienced software project managers. The questions are ordered by their relative importance to the success of a project and make contingency planning :

**(1)** Have top software and customer managers formally committed to support the project?
**(2)** Are end-users enthusiastically committed to the project and the system/ product to be built?
**(3)** are requirements fully understood by the software engineering team and their customers?
**(4)** Have customers been involved fully in the definition of requirements?
**(5)** Do end-users have realistic expectations?
**(6)** Is project scope stable?
**(7)** Does the software engineering team have the right mix of skills?
**(8)** Are project requirements stable?
**(9)** Does the project team have experience with the technology to be implemented?
**(10)** Is the number of people on the project team adequate to do the job?
The degree to which the project is at risk is directly proportional to the number of negatively responded questions given above. Thus, risk can be assessed by answering these questions.

A risk management strategy can be included in the software project plan or the risk management steps can be organized into a separate Risk Mitigation, Monitoring and Management Plan. The RMMM plan documents all work performed as part of risk analysis and is used by the project manager as part of the overall project plan.

Risk mitigation is a problem avoidance activity. Risk monitoring is a project tracking activity with three primary objectives : (1) to assess whether predicted risks do, in fact, occur; (2) to ensure that risk handling steps defined for the risk are being properly applied; and (3) to collect information that can be used for future risk analysis.

**Contingency Planning :**

It means managing risks to advice desired outcomes in the future. There we produce a plan for dealing with each significant and identifiable risk. We should monitor the project as development progresses, periodically reevaluating risks, their probability and their likely impact. We should write them in a way that communicates the nature and status of risks over the duration of the project.

**Q6(a). Write short notes on the following:**

**(i) Function Oriented Metrics**

Function-oriented software metrics use a measure of the functionally delivered by the application as a normalization value. Since 'functionality' cannot be measured directly, it must be derived indirectly using other direct measures.

Function points are derived using an empirical relationship based on countable (direct) measures of software's information domain and assessments of software complexity.

| | | | Weighting factor | | | |
|---|---|---|---|---|---|---|
| **Measurement parameter** | **Count** | | **Simple** | **Average** | **Complex** | |
| Number of user inputs | ☐ | × | 3 | 4 | 6 | = ☐ |
| Number of user outputs | ☐ | × | 4 | 5 | 7 | = ☐ |
| Number of user inquiries | ☐ | × | 3 | 4 | 6 | = ☐ |
| Number of files | ☐ | × | 7 | 10 | 15 | = ☐ |
| Number of external interfaces | ☐ | × | 5 | 7 | 10 | = ☐ |
| Count total --------→ | | | | | | ☐ |

**Number of user inputs** – Each user input that provides distinct application-oriented data to the software is counted.

**Number of user outputs** – Each user output that provides application-oriented information to the user is counted.

**Number of user inquiries** – An inquiry is defined as an on-line input that results in the generation of some immediate software response in the form of an on-line output.

**Number of files –** Each logical master file (i.e., a logical grouping of data that may be one part of a large database or a separate file) is counted.

**Number of external interfaces –** All machine readable interfaces (e.g., data files on storage media) that are used to transmit information to another system are counted.
To compute function points (FP), the following relationship is used:

$$FP = \text{count total} \times [0.65 + 0.01 \times \ (F_i)]$$

The $F_i$ (i = 1 to 14) are "complexity adjustment values"

**(ii) Spiral Model**
The spiral model, originally proposed by Boehm, is an evolutionary software process model that couples the iterative nature of prototyping with the controlled and systematic aspects of the linear sequential model. It provides the potential for rapid development of incremental versions of the software.

A spiral model is divided into a number of framework activities, also called task regions. Typically, there are between three and six task regions. Figure depicts a spiral model that contains six task regions:

- **Customer communication** – tasks required to establish effective communication between developer and customer.

- **Planning** – tasks required to define resources, timelines and other project related information.

- **Risk analysis** – tasks required to assess both technical and management risks.

- **Engineering** – tasks required to build one or more representations of the application.

- **Construction and release** – tasks required to construct, test, install and provide user support (e.g., documentation and training).

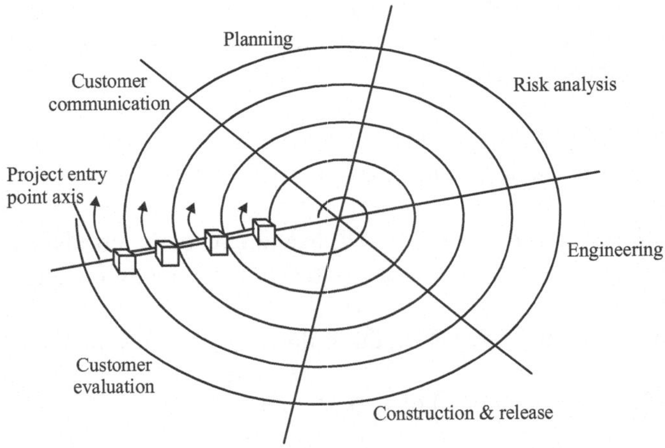


**Figure : A typical spiral model**

**Customer evaluation –** tasks required to obtain customer feedback based on evaluation of the software representations created during the engineering stage and implemented during the installation stage.

Each of the regions is populated by a set of work tasks, called a task set, that are adapted to the characteristics of the project to be undertaken. For small projects, the number of work tasks and their formality is low. For larger, more critical projects, each task region contains more work tasks that are defined to achieve a higher level of formality.

As this evolutionary process begins, the software engineering team moves around the spiral in a clockwise direction, beginning at the center. The first circuit around the spiral might result in the development of a product specification; subsequent passes around the spiral might be used to develop a prototype and then progressively more sophisticated versions of the software.

**(iii) Unit Testing [JUNE01,Q6(b,i)]**

Unit testing is the process of taking a module and running it in isolation from the rest of the software product by using prepared test cases and comparing the actual results with the results predicated by the specifications and design of the module. One purpose of testing is to find (and remove) as many error in the software as practical. There are number of reasons in support of unit testing than testing the entire product.

**1.** The size of a single module is small enough that we can locate an error fairly easily.

**2.** The module is small enough that we can attempt to test it in some demonstrably exhaustive fashion.

**3.** Confusing interactions of multiple error in widely different parts of the software are eliminated.

# CS-70 : INTRODUCTION TO SOFTWARE ENGINEERING
## JUNE-2004

**Note:** *Question 1 is* ***compulsory****. Answer any* ***three*** *from the rest.*

**Q1(a). What are the shortcomings of the Waterfall Model ? Propose a Software Development Life Cycle (SDLC) model which is a modified version of the Waterfall model but overcomes all the disadvantages of the Waterfall Model.** **15**

Waterfall model is the oldest and widely used model for software engineering but it has some drawbacks as well, specially if we look at practical aspects of it.

**1)** It is often difficult for the customer to state all requirements explicitly. Thus natural uncertainty is not covered that exists at inception of projects.

**2)** Customer must have patience as working session of program is only available later in the project. That means if a major defect is detected after delivery, it becomes nearly impossible to correct.

**3)** Importantly, rear projects rarely follow the sequential flow that this model proposes. There is iteration, but it is indirect. Thus changes can cause confusion as project proceeds. A software development life cycle(SDLC) model that is better one and overcomes disadvantages mentioned above is incremental model.

The incremental model combines elements of the linear sequential model (applied repetitively) with the iterative philosophy of prototyping. Referring to Figure, the incremental model applies linear sequences in a staggered fashion as calendar time progresses. Each linear sequence produces a deliverable "increment" of the software.

When an incremental model is used, the first increment is often a core product. The core product is used by the customer (or undergoes detailed review). As a result of use and/or evaluation, a plan is developed for the next increment. The plan addresses the modification of the core product to better meet the needs of the customer and the delivery of additional features and functionality. This process is repeated following the delivery of each increment, until the complete product is produced.

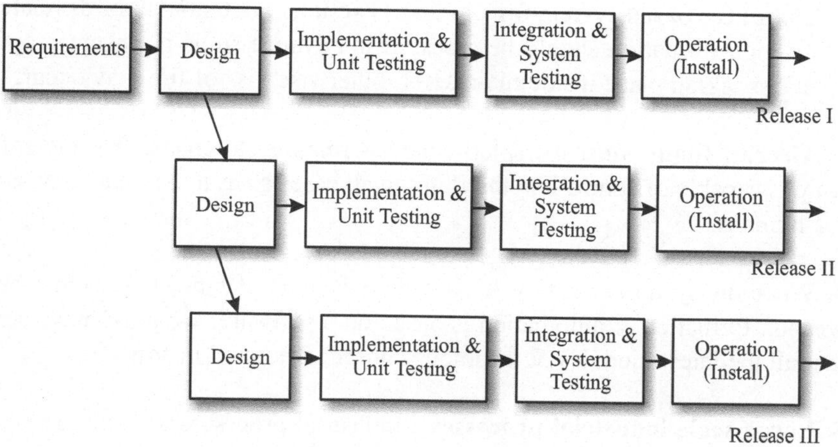


Fig : Iterative enhancement model.

**(b) Under what circumstances is product quality likely to be determined by the quality of the development team? Give at least two examples of the types of software products that are particularly dependent on individual talent and ability.** **15**

Product quality is determined by quality of development team when the demand is at a higher level. Some criterias are :

**1)** Problem is difficult so a better team is needed.

**2)** Required reliability of system to be build.

**3)** Rigidity of delivery date.

**4)** Size of resultant programs in lines of code.

**5)** Degree of sociability (communication) required for the project.

**6)** Time span of project because it effect time for which team will stay together.

Although, each and every software product is dependent on individual talent but some tend to have more stress on individual capability. Some examples are:

**i)** Software products where we have difficult customers.

**ii)** Software that uses a break through technology.

**Q2(a). Describe five software application areas in which safety and hazard analysis would be a major concern. Justify your answers.** **5**

**[DEC01, Q3(a)]**

Following are the five application areas in which S/W safety and hazard analysis would be a major concern :

**1. Computer based control for automobile :** If significant hazards that can effect software for automobile are not identified & accessed then it may cause malfunctioning of automobile.

**2. Computer based system for nuclear reactions :** potential hazards related to reaction formation should be assessed in advance so as to ensure proper reactions taking place inside the reactor, otherwise loss of life may occur.

**3. Aircraft flight control :** safety analysis required to ensure that the software is capable of controlling the flight in all cases so as to be reliable & safe for humans.

**4. Weapons systems :** safety & hazard analysis is of utmost concern when weapon formation & automation is based on a software. We must make sure that all the latest modules & techniques are incorporated in software.

**5. Large scale industrial processes :** Industrial processes as iron and steel carrying, chemical works etc. need safety analysis for proper & efficient working of machines & tools that can prove to be of significant aid in human injury & life saving.

**(b) (i) What are process risks? Give two examples of process risks.**

Process risk is the degree to which the software process has been properly defined and is followed by development organization process risks typically impinge on the whole of the software development cycle as process forms the basis of development. Process risks may arise due to estimation problems, lack of proper analysis or choice of unsuitable process.

Some process risks are

**1)** Processes are not exactly identified.

**2)** Resources needed for process are not exactly met.

**3)** Ambiguity in the process.

**4)** Design does not suit actual concept.

**(ii) Give four technical issues related to process risks. 10**

Four technical issues related to process risks.

**a)** If process is not technically implemented properly, implementation may be difficult or impossible.

**b)** Design may not be properly arrived at due to process risks.

**c)** Interface clarity becomes an overhead as well.

**d)** Maintenance is the biggest aspect that comes as an outcome of process risk.

**Q3(a). State and explain the functionality of the various categories of CASE tools. 8**

CASE tools can be classified by function, by their role as instruments for managers or technical people, by their use in the various steps of the software engineering process, by the environment architecture (hardware and software) that supports them or even by their origin or cost.

**Business process engineering tools :** By modeling the strategic information requirements of an organization, business process engineering tools provide a "meta-model" from which specific information systems are derived. Rather than focusing on the requirements of a specific application, business information is modeled as it moves between various organizational entities within a company.

**Process modeling and management tools :** If an organization works to improve a business (or software) process, it must first understand it. Process modeling tools (also called process technology tools) are used to represent the key elements of a process so that it can be better understood.

**Project planning tools :** Tools in this category focus on two primary areas : software project effort and cost estimation and project scheduling.

**Risk analysis tools :** Identifying potential risks and developing a plan to mitigate, monitor and manage them is of paramount importance in large projects.

**Metrics and management tools :** Software metrics improve a manager's ability to control and coordinate the software engineering process and a practitioner's ability to improve the quality of the software that is produced.

**Quality assurance tools :** The majority of CASE tools that claim to focus on quality assurance are actually metrics tools that audit source code to determine compliance with language standards.

**Database management tools :** Database management software serves as a foundation for the establishment of a CASE database (repository) that we have called the project database.

**Software configuration management tools :** Software configuration management lies at the kernel of every CASE environment. Tools can assist in all five major SCM tasks - identification, version control, change control, auditing and status accounting.

**Analysis and design tools :** Analysis and design tools enable a software engineer to create models of the system to be built.

**Prototyping tools :** A variety of different prototyping tools can be used. More sophisticated CASE prototyping tools enable the creation of a data design, coupled with both screen and report layouts. Many analysis and design tools have extensions that provide a prototyping option.

**Integration and testing tools :** In their directory of software testing tools, Software Quality Engineering defines the following testing tools categories :

**1)** Data acquisition - tools that acquire data to be used during testing.

**2)** Static measurement - tools that analyze source code without executing test cases.

**3)** Dynamic measurement - tools that analyze source code during execution.

**4)** Simulation - tools that simulate function of hardware or other externals.

**5)** Test management - tools that assist in the planning, development and control of testing.

**6)** Cross-functional tools - tools that cross the bounds of the preceding categories.

**Test management tools :** Test management tools are used to control and coordinate software testing for each of the major testing steps.

**Reengineering tools :** Tools for legacy software address a set of maintenance activities that currently absorb a significant percentage of all software-related effort.

**(b) When a project is behind schedule, what are the corrective steps that need to be taken ? 5**

If the team comes across a project that imposes unrealistic deadlines, may be due to external market pressures, following steps are recommended :

**1)** Perform a detailed estimate using historical data from past projects. Determine the estimated effort and duration for the project.

**2)** Using an incremental process model, develop a software engineering strategy that will deliver critical functionality by the imposed deadline, but delay other functionality until later. Document the plan.

**3)** Meet with the customer and (using the detailed estimate), explain why the imposed deadline is unrealistic.

**4)** Offer the incremental development strategy as an alternative

**5)** Form an optimal team structure to accomplish task.

**(c) "The testing of software is complete only when it is thrown away since whenever you are using it, you are indirectly testing it." Do you agree with this statement ? Justify your answer. 2**

I agree with the statement as it is true that you can remove errors from the software but not defects completely. We have the very famous model, the incremental model that is formed on the basis of previous feedback and then product is enhanced in the further releases. You can only try your level best with quality management and better techniques but user needs keep on changing with time.

**Q4(a). What is the job of a Systems Analyst ? What are two attributes of an effective System Analyst ? Explain them. 7**

System development generally consists of two major components : system analysis and system design. System analysis refers to the process of examining a business situation with the intent of improving it through better procedures and methods. System design is the process of planning a new business system of one to replace or complement an existing system.

System Analyst is a person, who analyzes the way the system works to identifies its problems. System analysts responsibilities vary among organizations. Below mentioned are the attributes of an analyst :

**1. Knowledge of business functions :** A systems analyst must know the environment in which he or she works. He must be aware of the peculiarities of management and the users at his installation and realize how they react to systems analyst. A working knowledge of accounting and marketing principles is a must since so many systems are built around these. Different sections in an organisation have conflicting needs and most systems are the result of compromise. The analyst's goal is to produce the system that will be the best for his organisation. This requires an open mind and flexibility in his ideas two areas. He must be familiar with his company's product and services and management's policies in areas concerning him.

**2. An analytical mind :** It takes an unusual person to see through problems facing an organisation and develop solutions that will work. Systems analysts often find themselves with more data than they can cope with. It requires an analytical mind to select pertinent data and concentrate on them in defining problems and forming solutions.

**(b) Explain the concept of Software Reliability, using an example. How can you conclude that a specific software is reliable ? 8**

Reliability is the degree to which the system performs its intended functions over a time. In other words, reliability means that the information gathered is dependable enough to be used for making decisions about the system being studied. The term reliability is synonymous with dependability, consistency and accuracy. For example: If we administer the same questionnaire to the same subjects, will we get the same or similar results thus over here, in this example reliability is referred as stability, dependability and predictability.

We can conclude that a specific software is reliable only when the requirements are met by the software. The outputs come in same sequence as expected. The software should be friendly enough to expose its features and collect relevant information from user when situation arises. But new requirements become a big obstacle in reliability issue.

**Q5(a). Give at least six developments that influence the way Software Development methodologies are being looked at. [DEC04, Q6(b)] 6**

Six developments that influence the way software development methodologies are being look at are :

**1)** Evolving role of computers in day to day life.
**2)** Drastic changes in hardware performance, computing architectures etc.
**3)** Replacement of a lone programmer with team of specialists.
**4)** Customization of products.
**5)** Component based construction.
**6)** Introduction of fourth generation (4GT) techniques.

**(b) What are the various software team organizations ? Also, give one example each, with justification, of a software project that fits for each type of team organization. 9**

The "best" team structure depends on the management style of your organization, the number of people who will populate the team and their skill levels, and the overall problem difficulty. Mantei suggests three generic team organizations :

**Democratic Decentralized (DD)** – This software engineering team has no permanent leader. Rather, "task coordinators are appointed for short durations and then replaced by others who may coordinate different tasks." Decisions on problems and approach are made by group consensus. Communication among team members is horizontal.

**Controlled Decentralized (CD)** – This software engineering team has a defined leader who coordinates specific tasks and secondary leaders that have responsibility for subtasks. Problem solving remains a group activity, but implementation of solutions is partitioned among subgroups by the team leader. Communication among subgroups and individual is horizontal. Vertical communication along the control hierarchy also occurs.

**Controlled Centralized (CC)** – Top-level problem solving and internal team coordination are managed by a team leader. Communication between the leader and team members is vertical.

Because a centralized structure completes tasks faster, it is the most adaptable in handling simple problems. Decentralized teams generate more and better solutions than individuals. Therefore such teams have a greater probability of success when working on difficult problems. Since the CD team is centralized for problem solving, either a CD or CC team structure can be successfully applied to simple problems. A DD structure is best for difficult problems.

e.g. DD

You have been appointed as a Project Manager within an information systems organisation. Your job is to build an application that is quite similar to the other that your team has built, although this one is larger and more complex. Requirement have been thoroughly documented by the customer.

Regarding the said project

- Since project is large more number of personnel will participate
- since project is complex, project will require the experts level professional.
- Expert professional need to have freedom to work, they are just needed the deadlines to meet, should be having free hand to deal with, since they know their job on hand and have maturity and experience.

All of the above scenario points advocate for the DD (Democratic Decentralized) team structure if the professionals involved with the project are from the organization itself.

e.g. CD

You have been appointed as a Project Manager within an information systems organisation. Your job is to build an application that is quite similar to the other that your team has built, although this one is larger and more complex. Requirement have been thoroughly documented by the customer.

Regarding the said project :

- Since project is large, more number of personnel will participate
- Since project is complex project will require the experts level professional
- All the requirements are thoroughly documented
- Already similar system had been built in past, basic guidelines are ready

All of the above points advocate for the **CD (Controlled Decentralized)** team structure if the professionals involved with the project are from the organization itself.

e.g. CC

You have been appointed as a Project Manager for a major software products company. Your job is to manage the development of the next generation version of its widely used word-processing software. Because competition is intense, tight deadlines have been established and announced.

Regarding the said project

- Since a project is a new version for the product already in the market, the requirements are properly documented. Need to just follow up with accommodating the certain new requirement which also had been properly defined.
- Because of tight deadlines, the work activity need to be focused and certain work discipline need to be introduced so that the tight control is enforced.
- Above point suggests that the personnel working on the project are from the organization only, so the understanding with each other and understanding of the software is also very good since right now new version is going to be developed, and tight deadlines enforced to have good leader who can motivate and control the project, which clearly suggest the Controlled Centralized team structure, where the top level problem solving and internal team coordination are managed by a team leader.

Communication between the leader and team members is vertical since requirements are already defined properly, no discussion and brain storming session are required with experts.

**Q6(a). What makes software design different from coding ? Your explanation should be built around at least 3 examples.** **8**

Software design is a meaningful engineering representation of something that is to be built. It can be traced to customer's requirements and assessed for quality.

Point of difference from coding

**1)** Design is an abstract view whereas coding is the written representation of each representation in design model.

E.g. the data design in design model comprises of E-R diagrams, Data Dictionary etc. These E-R diagrams and data dictionary are implemented in coding by RDBMS software.

If we look at the code itself, it doesn't reflect the clear picture of E-R diagrams and data dictionary as it is implemented at system level detail.

**2)** Design models lets us trace to user needs. We can analyse what went wrong in analysis phase. Thus a "good" design reflects the system. But a good coding (e.g. OOP) doesn't reflect the system as clearly to an abstract user that views the objects from a much simpler level of detail.

**3)** We can reorganize design to improve quality of software from a wider point of view. E.g. we can redefine Architectural design and interface design to better suit user needs which is far more difficult if we start from the coding itself.

**(b) Suppose you are part of a team that is developing a word-processing software. List seven risks associated with this project.** **7**

We can have two kinds of risks have

**1)** Generic risk

**2)** Product specific risk

**Seven risks arising out of above two categories are :**

**i)** Product Size : i.e. what is the memory space needed by word software.

**ii)** Business impact : i.e. constraints imposed by management or market place.

**iii)** Customer Characteristics : i.e. what type of customers will use the word application being developed.

**iv)** Process Definition : what process risks are there that have to be chosen for word.

**v)** Development Environment : what risks are associated with availability and quality of tools needed to build word.

**vi)** Technology : risk associated with "newness" of technology to be used for word application.

**vii)** Staff size and Experience : risk associated with overall technical and project experience of software engineers who will work on word application.

# CS-70 : INTRODUCTION TO SOFTWARE ENGINEERING
## DEC-2004

**Note:** *Question 1 is* ***compulsory****. Answer any* ***three*** *from the rest.*

**Q1(a). Software is the differentiating characteristic in many computer based products and systems. Provide examples of two products and at least one system in which software, not hardware, is the differentiating element. Explain your answers. [15]**

**[DEC03, Q1(b)][DEC01, Q1(a)]**

**System in which software is differentiating element :**

**ATM Machine :**

ATM Machine is a system from which a user can withdraw money.

**1.** The other functions of ATM are to view balance, deposits etc.

**2.** In this case the hardware is same.

**3.** The function of the S/W is integrated with S/W program installed on it.

**4.** The S/W program can be different for different bank ATMs.

**5.** Naturally ATMs of the same bank would have the same software, but the software may change bank by bank.

**6.** The functions implemented by software is for the deposits and withdraw of money as well as other options for types of account.

**7.** The S/W can be different for two different ATMs.

**8.** Thus in ATM the software is the differentiating element.

**Mobile Instrument :**

In this the hardware is instrument, but there can be number of different software to run that instrument

- There are no. of S/W available for mobile instrument.
- And the S/W can be changed and any new feature or item can be downloaded.

**Microprocessor chip :**

Here the S/W residing in the chip can change while the function of the chip remains same.

- Chip can be re-programmed and we can change the functions available.
- Once the chip has been written they can be modified in future for more enhancement.

**(b) What are software Libraries and software Toolkits? Give an example for each. What are software Modules? How will you reapply them? Also give an example of a S/W module. [15]**

Object-oriented technologies provide the technical framework for a component-based process model for software engineering.

The component-based development model composes applications from pre-packaged software components(called classes)

The engineering activity begins with the identification of candidate classes.

Once candidate classes are identified, the class library is searched to determine if these classes already exist. If they do, they are extracted from the library and reused. If a candidate class does not reside in the library, it is engineered using object-oriented methods. Thus library is a collection of classes from pre-established work e.g. iostream library in C++.

Currently, a software development environment that supports the 4GT paradigm includes some or all of the following tools: nonprocedural languages for database query, report generation, data manipulation, screen interaction and definition, code generation, high level graphics capability; spreadsheet capability and automated generation of HTML and similar languages used for Website creation using advanced software tools. These make up software tool kit e.g. abstract window tool kit.

Software is divided into separately named and addressable components, often called modules, that are integrated to satisfy problem requirements.

We can reapply software modules via. integration that can be top-down, bottom-up or sandwitched.

**Example of software module :**

We can have an application processing payroll for employees having many modules as transaction, entry, deletion, leaves etc. Transaction module here will typically show the status of employees i.e. date of joining, his post, his address and code etc. Our main focus is to isolate the module from other modules as much as possible.

**Q2(a). It seems odd that cost and schedule estimates are developed during software planning-before a detailed software requirement analysis or design has been conducted. Why do you think that this is done? Give at least four reasons. Are there circumstances when this should not be done? Give at least two such situations. [JUNE03, Q4(b)] [7]**

Cost and schedule estimates are developed during software project planning because

**1)** Cost and schedule estimates measure the uncertainty in the project.

**2)** They can measure the risk associated as an outcome of uncertainty then.

**3)** Cost and schedule are often formed out of historical information that strongly affects the project.

**4)** It leads to clear definitions of function, performance and interfaces.

Two situations where it should not be done are :

**i)** Where there is structural uncertainty i.e. requirements have not been clearly defined.

**ii)** Where project size is large i.e. larger the project more is the interdependency among various elements of software.

**(b) Is it possible to assess the quality of software if the customer keeps changing his/her mind about what it is supposed to do? Explain your answer with at least two examples. [8]**

It is not possible to assess quality of software if the customer keeps on changing his / her mind as all it leads to uncertainty that gives rise to risk in the project. It is very much required that in the analysis phase and system engineering phase, requirements are properly arrived at by discussion with customer else software hazards come up.

e.g.

**1)** Consider following project

It is demanded that a bank is computerized and a software product is needed for transaction. If the user initially states that for transaction he needs to have facility to process data of at most 3 customers at a time but later changes his mind to 5 customers, the application changes a lot and new modifications are to be made to design and code.

**2)** Consider a demand for a database management product where the initially stated demand was implicit locking of database, if not accessed frequently. Later it is demanded that such locking is not a need. Such changes can make the programmer's life stressful and dissatisfactory.

Both above examples show that quality is the outcome of good requirements statement.

**Q3(a). What are risks, and why should they be managed? Describe two typical risks in software Engineering and at least three corresponding techniques to manage them. [8]**

Risk concerns future happenings. Today and yesterday are beyond active concern, as we are already reaping what was previously sowed by our past

actions. The risk involves change, such as in changes of mind, opinion, actions or places. Risk involves choice and the uncertainty that choice itself entails.
Risk Analysis and control is a crucial factor for any software project and it is a topic of management.
Two typical risks in software engineering are :

**1) Technical risks**
Technical risks threaten the quality and timeliness of the software to be produced. If a technical risk becomes a reality, implementation may become difficult or impossible. Technical risks identify potential design, implementation, interface, verification and maintenance problems.

**2) Business risks**
Business risks threaten the viability of the software to be built. Business risks often jeopardize the project or the product. Candidates for the top five business risks are **(1)** building an excellent product or system that no one really want wants (market risk), **(2)** building a product that no longer fits into the overall business strategy for the company (strategic risk), **(3)** building a product that the sales force does not understand how to sell, **(4)** losing the support of senior management due to a change in focus or a change in people (management risk) and **(5)** losing budgetary or personnel commitment (budget risk).

Known risks are those that can be uncovered after careful evaluation of the project plan, the business and technical environment in which the project is being developed, and other reliable information sources.

Predictable risks are extrapolated from past project experience (e.g. staff turnover, poor communication with the customer, dilution of staff effort as ongoing maintenance requests are serviced.

**Three techniques to manage them :**
A risk management strategy can be included in the software project plan or the risk management steps can be organized into a separate Risk Mitigation, Monitoring and Management Plan.

The RMMM plan documents all work performed as part of risk analysis and is used by the project manager as part of the overall project plan.
Risk mitigation is a problem avoidance activity. Risk monitoring is a project tracking activity with three primary objectives: **(1)** to assess whether pre-

dicted risks do, in fact, occur; **(2)** to ensure that risk handling steps defined for the risk are being properly applied; and **(3)** to collect information that can be used for future risk analysis.

**(b) Unreasonable deadlines are a fact of life in software business. How would you proceed if you are faced with one? Example with two examples. [DEC01, Q2(a)] [7]**

The deadlines for the project has to be readied before project commences. To decide about a deadline is a part of Project Estimation activity. The Gantt Chart is used for scheduling the project work, and PERT chart is used to project the Maximum duration the project will take to finish. Since estimations are based on past experience, historical data, nature of the project work on hand, resources available, expertise required, complexity of the work. It is a fact for the software project that most of the project gets delayed, crosses the deadlines. The reasons for the delay could be as follows:

**1.** Complexity of the project
**2.** Man power shortage
**3.** Hardware failure
**4.** Electricity failure for long time
**5.** Unrealistic deadlines committed just to bag the order
**6.** End users are interrupting the project by adding new requirement every now and then.
**7.** Virus affection.
**8.** New technology has outdone the current work, now to develop project with the new technology.

If faced with the Unreasonable deadlines :
**1.** If the technology has outdated the current project, and new technology are just needed then it could be easy to convince the end user to approach the project with new technology. But this option requires the availability of knowledgeable expert.
**2.** If any resources shortage has been noticed, additional resources has to be added to the current project. (Resources could be manpower, hardware), this addition to new resources will cut the profit margin.
**3.** If resources are perfect still the deadlines is the problem. Project Manager need to reschedule the project Plan, project activity, the responsibilities of the personnel need to be reassigned. Team structure could be re-designed. This option may be having adverse effect, if the new team members are not experienced and not aware of the project nature, then deadline will be broken for sure.

**Q4(a). Explain, using an example, how coupling and cohesion are related, Also give two examples to illustrate different levels of coupling and cohesion.**

**Coupling & Cohesion are related as given in example :**

Coupling increases as number of calls between modules increases, or amount of shared data increases but at the same time cohesion decreases. If there had been reduced number of calls, coupling would have decreased & cohesion had increased. Module interaction is the point where cohesion & coupling are distinguished.

**Different Levels of Coupling**

A good design will have low coupling. Thus, interfaces should be carefully specified in order to keep low value of coupling.

| | |
|---|---|
| Data Coupling | (Best) |
| Stamp Coupling | ↑ |
| Control Coupling | |
| External Coupling | |
| Common Coupling | |
| Content Coupling | (Worst) |

**Figure :** The types of modules coupling.

**Example 1 :** Some types of coupling are less desirable than others. The least desirable occurs when one module actually modifies another. Then the modified module is completely dependent on the modifying one. We call this content coupling and occur when one module modifies local data values or instructions in another module, or when one module branches into middle of another module. In figure (a), module B branches into D, even though D is supposed to be under the control of C.

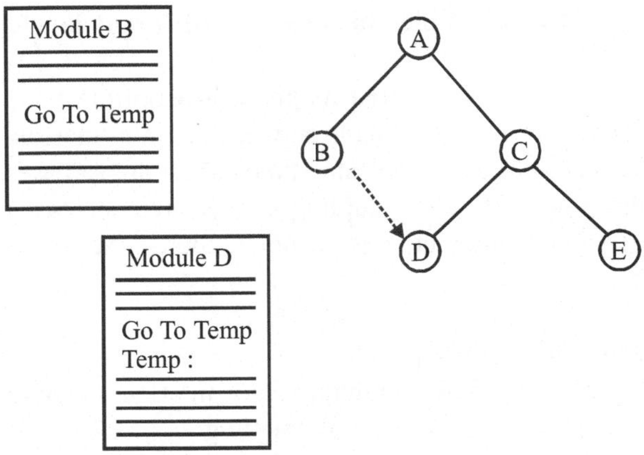


**Figure (a) : Example of content coupling.**

**Example 2 :** We can reduce the amount of coupling somewhat by organizing our design so that data are accessible from a common data store. However, dependency still exists, since making a change to the common data means tracing back to all modules that access that data to evaluate the effect of that change. This kind of dependence is called common coupling. With common coupling, it can be difficult to determine which module is responsible for having set a variable to a particular value. Figure (b) shows how common coupling works.

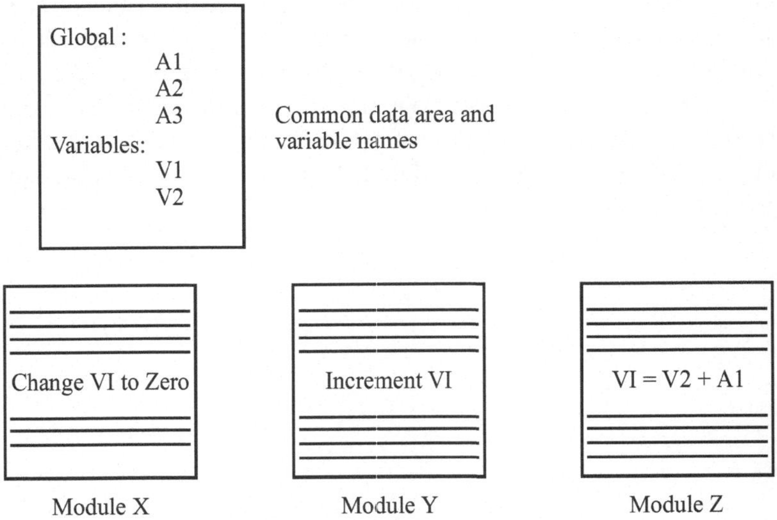


**Figure(b) :** Example of common coupling

**Different Levels of Cohesion**

| Levels of Cohesion | |
|---|---|
| Functional Cohesion | Best (high) |
| Sequential Cohesion | ↑ |
| Communicational Cohesion | |
| Procedural Cohesion | |
| Temporal Cohesion | |
| Logical Cohesion | |
| Coincidental Cohesion | Worst (low) |

**Figure :** Types of module cohesion

**Example 1 :** The worst degree of cohesion, coincidental is found in a module whose elements have no apparent relationship to one another. In this case, unrelated functions, processes or data are found in the same module for reasons of convenience. For example, a module that checks a user's security classification and also prints this month's payroll is coincidentally cohesion.

**Example 2 :** Logical is the next higher level of cohesion (though still not desirable), where several logically related functions or data elements are placed in the same module. For example, one module may read all kinds of input (from tape, disk, communications port), regardless of where the input is coming from or how it will be used; "input" is the glue that holds this module together.

**(b) Explain at least two technical and two interpersonal skills required for a System Analyst. When is one skill favoured over the other? Why? [7]**

Two interpersonal skills of system analysis

**1) Communication :** ability to speak language of user. Communication not just means reports, interviews but fulfilling, listening and reacting to one another.

Closed communication is not ideal open communication is needed.

**2) Understanding :** i.e. identifying problems and having grasp of company goals and objectives and showing sensitivity to impact of system on people.

Two technical skills of System Analyst

**1) Creativity :** helping users model ideas into concrete plans and developing candidate system.

**2) Problem Solving :** Reducing problems to their elemental levels and developing alternate solutions.

Necessity of both skills depends upon stages of system development.

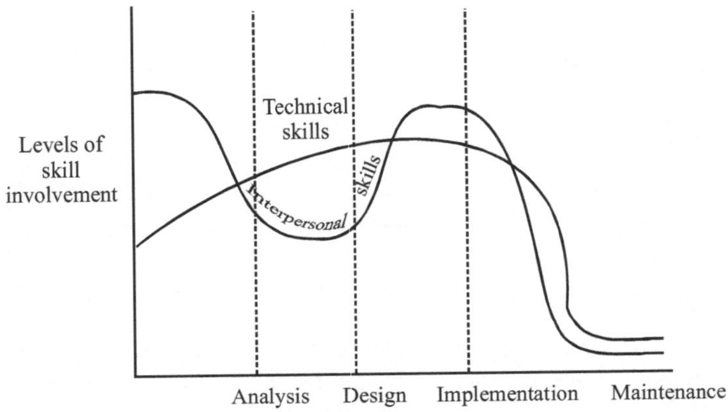


**During Analysis :** there is greater need of interpersonal skills - i.e. working with user to determine needs.

**During Design :** We need high technical skills even though interpersonal skills are required for user / analyst participation as a step to implementation.

**During Implementation :** Technical aspects focus on "proving" the software" Interpersonal aspects deal with "user training".

**During Maintenance :** Role of analyst drops off, except when an unanticipated problems appears.

**Q5(a). Complexity has been identified as an essential difficulty of software development. How does a requirements analysis help solve this problem? Explain with an example.** **[7]**

**Requirement Analysis :**

The success of any new software project is critically dependent on the initial "discovery" or "requirements analysis" phase of the project.

The software requirement analysis perform following steps to decrease the complexity of the system :

**1. Software requirement fundamental :** Software requirements analysis is a step that bridges the gap between system level software engineering and system design. Requirements analysis enables the system engineer to specify software function performance, indicate the software interface with other system elements and establish design constraints that the software must meet. The requirements analysis provides the software designer with a representation of information and function that can be translated to data, architectural and procedural design.

**2. Requirements definition - Analysis Tasks :** Software requirements analysis may be divided into five areas of effort :

**(a) Problem recognition -** The goal of the analyst is recognition of the basic problem elements as perceived by the user/customer.

**(b) Evaluation and synthesis -** The analyst must evaluate the flow and content of information, define and elaborate all software functions, understand software behaviour in context of the events that affect the system, establish system interface characteristics and design constraints;

**(c) Modeling -** The analyst should create models of the system which serves as a foundation for system design.

**(d) Specification -** The tasks associated with analysis and specification strive to provide a representation of software that can be reviewed and approved by the customer.

**(e) Review**

**3. Requirement Analysis Principles -**

The information domain of a problem must be represented and understood. The basic ingredients of every software are data and control, that is the data: numbers, characters, images, sound and the control events both reside in the information domain of a problem.

**4. Software Modeling - Prototyping :** Models created during software requirement analysis serve a number of important roles :

**(a)** The model aids the analyst in understanding the information, function and behaviour of the system under development.

**(b)** the model becomes the central focus point for review and, therefore, the key to a determination of completeness, consistency and accuracy of the specification.

**(c)** the model becomes the foundation for design, providing the designer with an essential representation of software that can be mapped into an implementation context.

**5. Development of a Software Requirements Specification :** The software specification may contain graphical and natural language descriptions of the software requirements.

As an example, consider a machine operator (a user) who interacts with the control computer for a manufacturing unit which is using a number of robots and numerically controlled machines. After careful review of requirements, the software for the control computer requires four different modes (roles) for interaction : programming mode, test mode, monitoring mode and troubleshooting mode. If suppose the requirement is not collected properly then it will effect the development at later stages of software life cycle by introduces changes, thus, increased complexity. Otherwise, when the requirements are known earlier then development will become smoother.

**(b) List four software development methodologies. For any one of these methodologies, give two problems that can be solved by it. Justify your choice of problems. [8]**

**(1) Sequential Model**

**System/information engineering and modeling :** Because software is always part of a larger system (or business), work begins by establishing requirement to software.

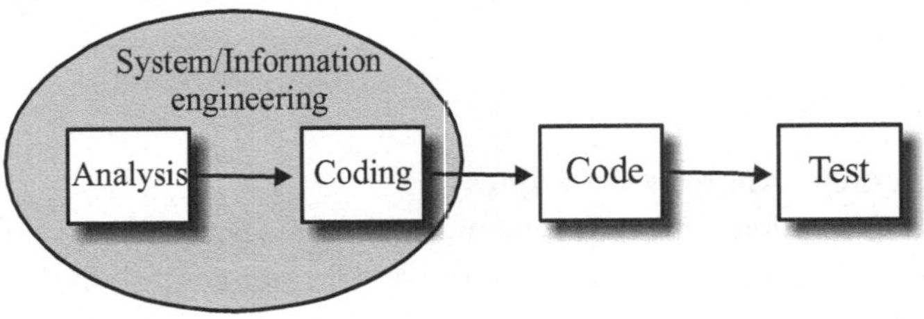


**Software requirements analysis**
**Design**
**Code Generation**
**Testing**
**Support**

**(2) Prototyping Model**

A disadvantage of waterfall model is that the working software is not available until late in the process, thus delaying the discovery of serious error. An alternative to this is to first develop a working prototype of the software instead of developing the actual software. The working prototype is developed as per current available requirements.

The developers use this prototype to refine the requirements and prepare the final specification document.

The developers should develop prototype as early as possible to speed up the software development process.

### (3) The Incremental Model

The incremental model combines elements of the liner sequential model (applied repetitively) with the iterative philosophy of prototyping. Referring to figure, the incremental model applies linear sequences in a staggered fashion as calendar time progresses. Each linear sequence produces a deliverable "increment" of the software.

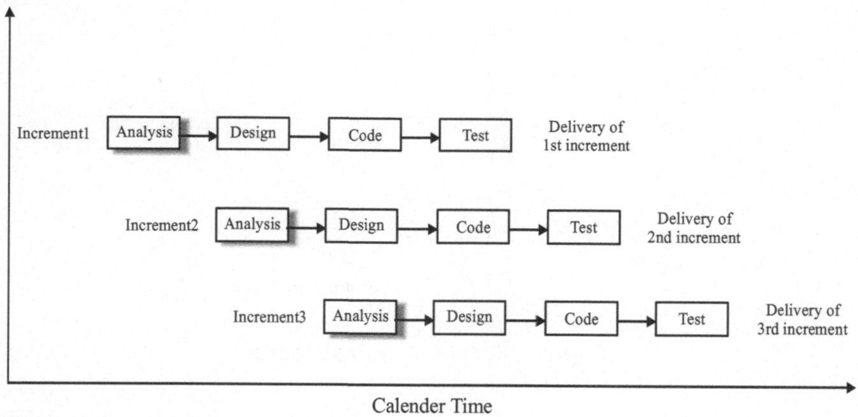


### (4) Spiral Model

The spiral model, originally proposed by Boehm, is an evolutionary software process model that couples the iterative nature of prototyping with the controlled and systematic aspects of the linear sequential model. It provides the potential for rapid development of incremental versions of the software.

A spiral model is divided into a number of framework activities, also called task regions. Typically, there are between three and six task regions. Figure depicts a spiral model that contains six task regions:

- **Customer communication** – tasks required to establish effective communication between developer and customer.

- **Planning** – tasks required to define resources, timelines and other project related information.

- **Risk analysis** – tasks required to assess both technical and management risks.

- **Engineering** – tasks required to build one or more representations of the application.

- **Construction and release** – tasks required to construct, test, install and provide user support (e.g., documentation and training).

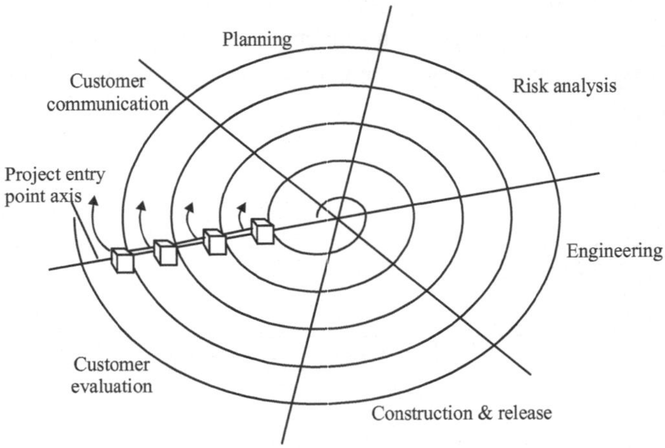


**Figure : A typical spiral model**

**Customer evaluation** – tasks required to obtain customer feedback based on evaluation of the software representations created during the engineering stage and implemented during the installation stage.

**Software Development Projects that would be amenable to prototyping**

Mathematical Algorithms

Subset of Command Driven Systems

Software applications that are relatively easy to prototype almost always involve human-machine interaction and/or heavy computer graphics. Other applications that are sometimes amenable to prototyping are certain classes of mathematical algorithms, subset of command driven systems and other applications where results can be easily examined without real-time interaction.

**Q6(a). Explain the terms 'CASE tools' and 'CASE environment'. Give at least two advantages of using CASE tools. Describe two features that a future generation CASE tool should support. [8]**

**"CASE tools" :** the workshop for software engineering has been called an integrated project support environment and the tools that fill the workshop are collectively called computer-aided-software engineering tools.

**"CASE environment" :** "environment" that encompasses tools, a database, people, hardware, a network, operating systems, standards, and myriad other components.

**Advantages :**

**1)** CASE tools assign in a particular software engineering activity (as analysis modeling).

**2)** CASE tools help to ensure that quality is designed in before the product is built

**Features that a future generation CASE tool should support :**

**1)** Access global impact of a change; that is, how a change in one function affects requirements for outer functions.

**2)** Improvement in reengineering tools that have wider range of programming languages.

**(b) List at least six factors that influence the software development methodologies. [JUNE04, Q5(a)]**

Six developments that influence the way software development methodologies are being look at are :

**1)** Evolving role of computers in day to day life.

**2)** Drastic changes in hardware performance, computing architectures etc.

**3)** Replacement of a lone programmer with team of specialists.

**4)** Customization of products.

**5)** Component based construction.

**6)** Introduction of fourth generation (4GT) techniques.

## CS-70 : INTRODUCTION TO SOFTWARE ENGINEERING
## JUNE - 2005

**Note:** *Questions no. 1 is* **Compulsory.** *Answer any* **three** *from the rest.*

**Q1(a). Explain the phases of software development life cycle. Draw the diagram of any one SDLC paradigm.**

**Following are the phases of software development life cycle :**

**1. Requirement analysis and specification phase:** The goal of this phase is to understand the exact requirements of the customer and to document them properly. This activity is usually executed together with the customer, as the goal is to document all functions, performance and interfacing requirements for the software.

The resultant document is known as software requirement specification (SRS) document.

**2. Design phase:** The SRS document is produced in the previous phase, which contains the exact requirements of the customer. The goal of this phase is to transform the requirements specification into a structure that is suitable for implementation in some programming language.

**3. Implementation and unit testing phase:** During this phase, design is implemented. If the SDD is complete, the implementation or coding phase proceeds smoothly, because all the information needed by the software engineers is contained in the SDD.

**4. Integration and system testing phase:** This is a very important phase. Effective testing will contribute to the delivery of higher quality software products, more satisfied users, lower maintenance costs, and more accurate and reliable results.

**5. Operation & maintenance phase:** Software maintenance is a task that every development group has to face, when the software is delivered to the customer's site, installed and is operational.

**Paradigm** has referred to a thought pattern in any scientific discipline. Here is the diagram of Waterfall model or paradigm of SDLC.

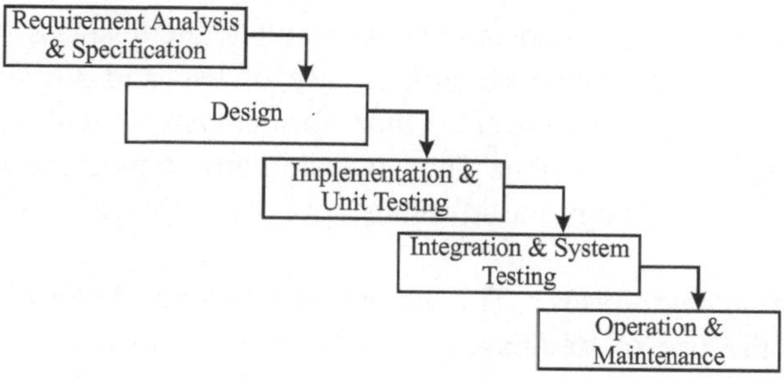


**(b) Explain the role of at least five associated development tools during software development.**

**Following are the five associated development tools during software development :**

**(i) GUI (Graphical User Interface) :** As the name indicates, it is an application environment that can work with graphical objects. Microsoft windows, a typical example, has the following components:

* Menus (including placement and name of options, and style such as pull down or popup)
* Icons (for identifying applications and resources)
* Titled windows (for view of multiple programs of data or for multiple views of a single program of data block)
* Dialog boxes for selecting files, options, and setting; when as options is selected, the one previously selected is turned off.
* Checklists from which the user can make multiple selections, as in specifying print of file attributes.

A GUI enforces consistency by restricting developers - they must support features for the program to run under the GUI. In addition, suggestions from the GUI's creators (such as the arrangement of menu options) often become defacto standards for applications.

**(ii) Emergence of CASE Tools :** As in other application areas, more and more work in system development is also being transferred to the computer itself, while human beings retain only the control element. Computer Aided Software Engineering tools are based on the above philosophy and some of their feature are : Diagramming support, screen painting, data dictionary maintenance, documentation support, etc. Certain CASE tools provide methodology specific support and many of them are multi-user tools.

**(iii) Using Prototyping and 4GL tools :** Prototype can be useful starting in developing a model of the proposed system, help in establishing the requirements more clearly. They may be constructed to simulate the business functionality of the system, its scope of coverage, ease of use and suitability to the organisation's way of working, etc. A more formal systems analysis and design can refine the prototype further. Thus, by using prototyping as a complement to the use of a methodology, the advantages of both approaches can be retained.

**(iv) Relational Databases :** The advent of relational database technology opened up the use of databases directly by the end user with minimal programming skills. Today there are many RDBMS available under different group of hardware platforms.

**(v) Object Oriented Programming :** As the sophistication and capabilities of new computer hardware have grown by leaps and bound, it has evident that new software development techniques are needed.

**(c) What is a software crisis? Explain two types of problems that cause a software crisis, each for the user point of view as well as form the programmer's point of view.**

The software crisis was a term used in the early days of software engineering, before it was a well-established subject. For the last several decades, tens of thousands of people, usually very intelligent and talented have been involved in the building of computer systems. The translation of a familiarity with computer hardware and software into the development of useful commercial or business information systems is not a straightforward or intuitive task. It is now well-known that the rate at which the hardware has been more and more accessible and at lower and lower prices, has created a matching demand for development of software in a similar scale. In essence, it refers to the difficulty of writing correct, understandable and verifiable computer programs. The roots of the software crisis are complexity, expectations, and change.

*Software crisis can be broadly classified in the following major areas :*

**From Programmer's Point of View :**

- Problem of compatibility
- Problem of portability
- Problem in documentation
- Problem in coordination of work of different people where a team is initiating to develop software.
- Problems that arise during actual run time in the organisation. Sometime the errors are not detected during sample run.
- Problem of piracy of software.
- Customers normally expand their specifications after program design and

implementation has taken place.

- Problem of maintenance in proper manner.

**From User's Point Of View :**

- Problem of different versions of software (user as well as operating system).
- Security problem for protected data in software.
- The customized software generally does not meet his total requirements
- Problem of virus
- Problem of software bugs, which comes to knowledge of customer after considerable data entry
- Certain software run only on specific operating system environment
- The problem of compatibility for user may be because of different size and density of floppy diskettes.
- Problem in learning all the facilities provided by the software because companies give only selective information in manual
- Certain software run and create files which expand their used memory spaces and create problem of disk management.
- Software crisis develops when system memory requirement of software is more than the existing requirements and/or availability.

**Available approaches and practices to cope with the issue :** Solving the software crisis was paramount to researchers and companies producing software tools. Software crises can be cope by using tools, discipline, formal methods, process, and professionalism.

**Q2(a). Explain at least five qualities of a software product.**

**1.Correctness**

❑ Software is correct if it satisfies the functional requirements specifications – assuming that specification exists.

❑ If specifications are formal, since programs are formal objects, correctness can be defined formally – It can be proven as a theorem or disproved by counter examples (testing).

**2. Reliability**

❑ Informally, user can rely on it.

❑ Can be defined mathematically as 'probability of absence of failure for a certain time period'.

❑ If specs are correct all correct software is reliable, but not vice-versa (in practice, however, specs can be incorrect…)

**3. Robustness**

❑ Software behaves "reasonably" even in unforeseen circumstances (e.g., incorrect input, hardware failure)

**4. Performance**

❑ Efficient use of resources – memory, processing time, communication
❑ Can be verified
❑ Complexity analysis
❑ Performance evaluation (on a model, via simulation)
❑ Performance can affect scalability
❑ A solution that work on a small local network may not work on a large intranet

**5. Usability**

Expected users find the system easy to use
❑ Other term: user-friendliness
Rather subjective, difficult to evaluate
❑ Affected mostly by *use interface*
(e.g., visual vs. textual)

**6. Verifiability**

❑ How easy it is to verify properties.
❑ Mostly an internal quality
❑ Can be external as well (e.g., security critical application)

**7.Reusability**

❑ Existing product (or components) used (with minor modifications) to build another product
❑ (Similar to evolvability)
❑ Also applies to process
❑ Reuse of standard parts measure of maturity of the field.

**8. Portability**

❑ Software can run on different h/w platforms or s/w environments
❑ Remains relevant as new platforms and environments are introduced (e.g., digital assistance)
❑ Relevant when downloading software in a heterogeneous network environment

**9. Understandability**

❑ Ease of understanding software
❑ Program modification requires program understanding

**10. Interoperability**

- ❑ Ability of a system to coexist and cooperate with other systems
- ❑ e.g., word processor and spreadsheet

**(b) List atleast seven major duties of System Analysis as performed during software development. Also list two attributes of an effective System Analyst.**

Following are the duties and attributes of system analyst :

**DUTIES**

**(a)** The first and perhaps most difficult task of systems analyst is problem definition. Business problems are quite difficult to define. It is also true, that problems cannot be solved until they are precisely and clearly defined.

**(b)** Initially a systems analyst does not know how to solve a specific problem. He must consult with managers, users and other data processing professionals in defining problems and developing solutions. He uses various methods for data gathering to get the correct solution of a problem.

**(c)** Having gathered the data relating to a problem, the systems analyst analyses them and thinks of plan to solve it. He may not come up personally with the best way of solving a problem but pulls together other people's ideas and refines them until a workable solution is achieved.

**(d)** Systems analysts coordinate the process of developing solutions. Since many problems have number of solutions, the systems analyst must evaluate the merit of such proposes solution before recommending one to the management.

**(e)** Systems analysts are often referred to as planners. A key part of the systems analyst's job is to develop a plan to meet the management's objectives.

**(f)** When the plan has been accepted, systems analyst is responsible for designing it so that management's goal could be achieved. Systems design is a time consuming, complex and precise task.

**(g)** Systems must be thoroughly tested. The systems analyst often coordinates the testing procedures and helps, in deciding whether or not the new system is meeting standards established in the planning phase.

**ATTRIBUTES:**

**(a)** Knowledge of Business functions: A systems analyst must know the environment in which he or she works. He must be aware of the peculiarities of management and the users at his installation and realize how they react to systems analyst. A working knowledge of accounting and marketing principles is a must since so many systems are built around these two areas. He must be familiar with his company's product and services and management's policies in areas concerning him.

**(b)** Knowledge of people: Since a systems analyst works with others so closely, he or she must understand their needs and what motivates them to develop systems properly.

**(c)** Knowledge of Data processing principles: Most systems today are computer based. The systems analyst must be fully aware about the potential and limitations of computers.

**(d)** Ability to communicate: As a coordinator, a systems analyst must communicate properly with people of different levels within an organisation. Systems analyst must listen carefully to what others say and integrate the thoughts of others into the systems development process.

**(e)** Flexibility: Systems analysts must be flexible in their thinking since they often do not get-their own way. Different sections in an organisation have conflicting needs and most systems are the result of compromise. The analyst's goal is to produce the system that will be the best for his organisation. This requires an open mind and flexibility in his ideas.

**(f)** An analytical mind: It takes an unusual person to see through problems facing an organisation and develop solutions that will work. Systems analysts often find themselves with more data than they can cope with. It requires an analytical mind to select pertinent data and concentrate on them in defining problems and forming solutions.

**(g)** Well educated with sharp mind: Systems analysts are called upon to work with people at all levels virtually in every aspect of business. They must know how to work with all of them and gain their confidence. Analysts must have sharp mind to learn quickly how people do their jobs.

**Q3(a). What is risk management? Explain atleast six risks in software engineering, along with corresponding risk management techniques.**

Risk management is the process of measuring, or assessing risk and then developing strategies to manage the risk. In strategies employed include transferring the risk to another party, avoiding the risk, reducing the negatives effect of the risk and accepting some or all of the consequences of a particular risk. Traditional risk management, focuses on risks stemming from physical or legal causes (e.g., natural disasters for fires, accidents, dead and lawsuits). Financial risk management, on the other hand, focuses on risks that can be managed using traded financial instruments. Regardless of the type of risk management, all large corporations have risk management teams and small groups and corporations practice informal, if not formal, risk management.

**Refer to June06, Q-5(a).**

**(b) What is a 4GL? List at least four advantage and three limitations of 4GLs.**

**A fourth-generation programming language** (abbreviated **4GL**) is a programming language designed with a specific purpose in mind, such as the development of commercial business software. Such languages arose after the introduction of modem, block-structured third-generation programming languages, which improved the process of software development.

**Four advantages :**

**(i)** A specification language made up of non-procedural instruction sets.
**(ii)** No programming task is required, the necessary code will be generated directly from the specifications.
**(iii)** They can be easily learn since there are relatively few commands, functions and structures. Programs written in a 4GL can be written very quickly (in comparison with the time taken to develop and write a program in a 3GL). Each statement written may generate a large amount of code containing a high level of functionality and productivity.
**(iv)** Make applications easy and quick to change, hence reducing maintenance cost.

**Three Limitations :**

**(i)** It can only address a small and very highly specialized area of development.
**(ii)** In a complex system can be developed, a number of different types of fourth generation languages must be integrated, and further procedural programming facilities must be provided.
**(iii)** It requires algorithm to solve the problem.

**Q4(a). You've been asked to build a software to support a 'LOW COST VIDEO EDITING SYSTEM'. The system accepts video tape as input, stores video on a disk, and then allows the user to do a wide range of edits to digitized video, and the result is output to tape. Explain technical risks (at least 5) that you may face as you begin a project of this type.**
**Risk concerns future happenings i.e. the things that can happen unknowingly.**

A considerably more intelligent strategy for risk management is to be proactive. A proactive strategy begins long before technical work is initiated. The software team establishes a plan for managing risk. When risks are analyzed, it is important to get the level of uncertainly and the degree of loss associated with each risk. The risks may be categorized as follow:

**1. Project risks:** There threaten the plan i.e. if project risks become true, it is likely that the project schedule will go above and also the cost of the project will increase to a much larger scale.

**2. Technical risks:** There threaten the quality and timeless of the software to be produced. Implementation may become impossible difficult if these risks become true.

**3. Business risks:** These risks threaten the viability of the software to be built. The project or product becomes slow if business risks becomes true.

**4. Known risks:** These are those risks that can be uncovered after careful evaluation of the project plan.

**5. Predictable risks:** These risks are extrapolated from past project experience.

**6. Unpredictable risks:** These risks may or not occur best these risks are extremely difficult to identify in advance.

So according to the above given categories the risks that would be faced in developing a video editing system are as follows:

**1.** The project should be given a last date and the risk after this can be if the team members are not able to complete the project within the specified time then cost of the project could be increased.

**2.** If we are not able to develop the quality of the project this can also be a risk because the customer needs quality.

**3**. If we have to make changes in the project after making it then it is also a cost increasing risk factor.

**4.** If the leader of the project or the system analyst is an inexperienced person and if he/she is not able to understand the needs of the customer then a wrong product can be given to the customer.

With the above given risks there may be some known risks also. Those risks can be uncovered when we do the careful evaluation of the project. And lastly there may also be some risk in the project that cannot be seen but these may or may not occur.

**(b). Define "Known risks" and "Predictable risks", with an example for each.**

**Known Risk :** These are those risks that can be uncovered after careful evaluation of the project plan. The business is being developed after the careful assess of business and technical environment and other sources of philanthropic information (e.g. not showing as realistic delivery date, lack of documented requirements or scopes of the software, and developing the environment is poor).

**Predictable Risk :** Predictable risks are those risks to make conclusion about a different past project experience (e.g. turnover of staff, communication with the customer is poor, weaker of staff effort as ongoing maintenance requests are serviced.)

**Q5(a). Describe the three generic types of team organization. How can the best team structure for a software project be determined. Explain with an example.**

**There generic team organizations are:**

The "best" team structure depends on the management style of your organization, the number of people who will populate the team and their skill levels, and the overall problem difficulty. Mantei suggests three generic team organizations :

**(i) Democratic Decentralized (DD)** – This software engineering team has no permanent leader. Rather, "task coordinators are appointed for short durations and then replaced by others who may coordinate different tasks." Decisions on problems and approach are made by group consensus. Communication among team members is horizontal.

**(ii) Controlled Decentralized (CD)** – This software engineering team has a defined leader who coordinates specific tasks and secondary leaders that have responsibility for subtasks. Problem solving remains a group activity, but implementation of solutions is partitioned among subgroups by the team leader. Communication among subgroups and individual is horizontal. Vertical communication along the control hierarchy also occurs.

**(iii) Controlled Centralized (CC)** – Top-level problem solving and internal team coordination are managed by a team leader. Communication between the leader and team members is vertical.

Because a centralized structure completes tasks faster, it is the most adaptable in handling simple problems. Decentralized teams generate more and better solutions than individuals. Therefore such teams have a greater probability of success when working on difficult problems. Since the CD team is centralized for problem solving, either a CD or CC team structure can be successfully applied to simple problems. A DD structure is best for difficult problems.

**Seven project factors that should be considered when planning the best team structure are:**

- ❑ The difficulty of the problem is to be solved.
- ❑ The size of the resultant program (s) in lines of code or function points.
- ❑ The time the team will stay together (team lifeline).
- ❑ The degree to which the problem can be modularized.
- ❑ The required quality and reliability of the system to be built.
- ❑ The rigidity of the delivery date.
- ❑ The degree of sociability (communication) required for the project.

The length of time the team will 'live together' affects team morale. It has been found that DD team structure result in high morel and job satisfaction and are therefore good for long lifeline teams.

The DD team structure is best applied to problems with relatively low modularity because of the higher volume of communication that is needed. When high modularity is possible (and people can do their own thing). The CC or CD structure will work well.

CC and CD teams have been found to produce fewer defects than DD teams, but these data have much to do with the specific quality assurance activities that are applied by the team. Decentralized teams generalized require more time to complete a project than a centralized structure and at the same time are best when high sociability is required.

**(b) What is a waterfall model? Explain, with an example why programs, which are developed using the waterfall model, are likely to be difficult to maintain.**

**Water Model:** The most familiar model is the waterfall model, which is given in figure. The model has five phases; Requirements analysis and specification, design, implementation and unit testing, integration & system testing, and operation & maintenance. The phases always occur in this order and do not overlap. The developer must complete each phase before the next phase begins. This model is named "Waterfall Model", because its diagrammatic representation resembles a cascade of waterfall.

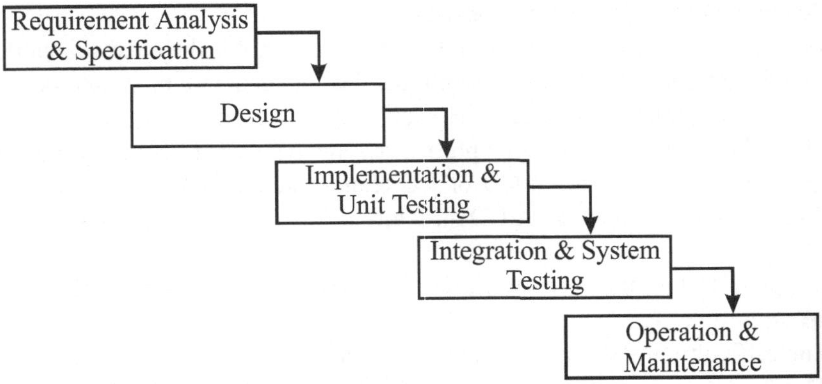


Problems that occur when waterfall is applied are:

**1.** Real projects rarely follow the sequential flow that the model proposes. Although the linear model can accommodate iteration, it does so indirectly. As a result, change can cause confusion as the project team proceeds.

**2.** It is often difficult for the customer to state all requirement explicitly. The linear sequential model requires this and has difficulty in accommodating the natural uncertainly that exists at the beginning of many projects.

**3.** The customer must have patience. A working version of the programs will not be available until the working program is reviewed, can be disastrous.

**Programs developed using waterfall model are difficult to maintain, is correct.** When a system is produced using the waterfall model, features tend to be added without regard to an overriding design. With each modification, the software becomes increasingly disorganized. System maintenance (fixing bugs; or adding new features after the system has been released) is hampered by these problems, as it is harder to identify the source of bugs in poorly designed systems. Poor documentation also makes maintenance more difficult.

**Q6(a). List five advantages of CASE tools.**

**Advantages of CASE Tools**

Current trends are showing a significant decrease in the cost of hardware with a corresponding increase in the cost of computer software. This reflects the labor intensive nature of the software. Developing effective software packages takes the work of many people and can take years to complete. Furthermore, small errors in the logic of the programs can have huge consequences for the user. CASE tools are an important part of resolving the problems of application development and maintenance. CASE tools significantly alter the time taken by each phase and the distribution of cost with in the software life cycle. Software engineers are now placing greater emphasis on analysis and design. Much of the code can now be generated automatically with the development of detailed specifications. Improvements in both these areas made possible through the use of CASE tools are showing dramatic reductions in maintenance costs. The power of CASE tools lies in their central repository which contains descriptions of all the central components of the system. These descriptions are used at all stages of the cycle; creation of input/output designs, automatic code generation, etc. Later tasks continue to add to and build upon this repository so that by the conclusion of the project it contains a complete description of the entire system. This is a powerful device which was not feasible before the introduction of CASE tools.

More specifically CASE tools:

- ensure consistency, completeness and conformance to standards
- encourage an interactive, workstation environment
- speeds up development process
- allows precision to be replicated
- reduces costs, especially in maintenance
- increases productivity
- makes structured techniques practical

**(b) What do you mean by Coupling and Cohesion? Explain why maximizing cohesion and minimising coupling lead to more maintainable systems.**

**Coupling is the measure of the degree of** interdependence between modules. Two modules with the high coupling are strongly interconnected and thus, dependent on each other. Two modules with low coupling are not dependent on one another. "Highly coupled" systems share a great deal of dependence between modules.

Cohesion is measure of the degree to which the elements of a module are functionally related. A strongly cohesive module implements functionality that is related to one feature of the solution and requires little interaction with other modules. Thus, we want to maximize the interaction with other modules. Hence an important design object is to maximize the module cohesion and minimize the module coupling.

Lower coupling is better. Low coupling tends to create more reusable methods. It is not possible to write completely decoupled methods, otherwise the program will not work. Low coupling leads to high reusability, and as the levels of reusability within my infrastructure are high it must demonstrate that my implementation is more than adequate. The degree of interaction within a module. Higher cohesion is better. A high cohesion method will be simpler to reuse, and to extend, so it will maximize reusability and extendability.

**(c) Explain atleast 3 attributes of design that might influence system maintainability.**

**The design process should not suffer from "tunnel vision":** A good designer should consider alternative approaches judging each based on the requirement of the problem the resources available to do the job.

**The design should be traceable to the analysis model:** Because a single element of the design model often traces to multiple requirement, it is necessary to have a means for tracking how requirements have been satisfied by the design model.

**The design should 'minimize the intellectual distance' between the software and the problem as it exists in the real world:** That is, the structure of the software design should (whenever possible) mimic the structure of the problem domain.

**The design should exhibit uniformity and integration:** A design is uniform if it appears that one person developed the entire thing. Rules of style and format should be defined for a design team before design work begins. A design is integrated if care is taken in defining interfaces between design components.

**The design should be structured to accommodate change:** The design concepts discussed in the next section enable a design to achieve this principle.

**The design should be reviewed to minimize conceptual errors:** There is sometimes a tendency to focus on smallest when the design is reviewed, missing the forest for the trees. A design team should ensure that major conceptual elements of the design have been addressed before worrying about the syntax of the design model.

# CS-70 : INTRODUCTION TO SOFTWARE ENGINEERING
## DEC - 2005

**Note:** *Questions no. 1 is* ***Compulsory****. Answer any* ***three*** *from the rest.*

**Q1(a). What is software maintenance? Describe briefly three types of maintenance. [8]**

**SOFTWARE MAINTENANCE**

Software maintenance is task that every development group has to face when the software is delivered to the customer's site, installed and is operational. Therefore, delivery or release of software inaugurates the maintenance phase of the life cycle. The time spent and effort required keeping software operational after release is every significant and consumes about 40-70% of the cost of the entire life cycle.

Software Maintenance is a very broad activity that includes error corrections, enhancements of capabilities, deletion of obsolete capabilities, and optimization. Because change is inevitable, mechanisms must be developed for evaluating, controlling and making modifications. So any work done to change the software after it is in operation is considered to be maintenance. The purpose is to preserve the value of software over time.

**1. Corrective Maintenance**

This refers to modifications initiated by defects in the software. A defect can result from design errors, logic errors and coding errors. Design errors occur when, changes made to the software are incorrect, incomplete, wrongly communicated or the change request is misunderstood. Logical errors result from invalid tests and conclusions, incorrect implementation of design specifications, faulty logic flow or incomplete test data. Coding errors are caused by incorrect implementation of detailed logic design and incorrect use of the source code logic. Defects are also caused by data processing errors and system performance errors.

**2. Adaptive Maintenance**

It includes modifying the software to match changes in the ever-changing environment. The term environment in this context refers to the totality of all conditions and influences which act from outside upon the software, for example, business rules, government policies, work patterns, software and hardware operating platforms. A change to the whole or part of this environment will require a corresponding modification of the software.

**3. Perfective Maintenance**

It means improving processing efficiency or performance, or restructuring the software to improve changeability. When the software becomes useful, the user tends to experiment with new cases beyond the scope for which it was initially developed. Expansion in requirements can take the form or enhancement of existing system functionally or improvement in computational efficiency; for example, providing a Management Information System with a data entry Module or a new message handling facility.

**(b) What is 4GL? Explain atleast three areas, which are impacted by the advent of 4GLs. [7]**

A fourth-generation programming language (abbreviated 4GL) is a programming language designed with a specific purpose in mind, such as the development of commercial business software. Such languages arose after the introduction of modern, block-structured third-generation programming language, which improved the process of software development.

All 4GLs are designed to reduce programming effort, the time it takes to develop software, and the cost of software development.

**Areas, which are impacted by the advent of 4GLs :**

**(i) Report Generation :** Report generators take a description of the data format and the report to generate and from that they either generate the required report directly or they generate a program to generate the report.

**(ii) Forms Generation :** Similarly, forms generates, manage online interactions with the applications system users or generate programs to do so.

**(iii) Interface Generation :** 4GLs gave a much impact on the GUI development. With advent of 4GLs it becomes easier to make better GUI which further enhances the look and feel of the software developed.

**(c) What is benchmark testing? Why is necessary? [7]**

The term "benchmark" was derived from the days when the machinist in factory would use measurement at each bench to determine if the parts he was machining were satisfactory in the computing field, to compare one system with another, you would run the set of "benchmark" programs, each system. A benchmark is a sample program specially designed to evaluate the performance of different computers and their software. This is necessary because computers will not generally use the same instruments, words of memory or machine cycle to solve particular problem. As regard, evaluation of software, benchmarking is mainly concerned with validation of vendor's claims in respect of following points:

- ❑ Minimum hardware configuration needed to operate a package.
- ❑ Time required execute a program in an ideal environment and how the

performance of own package and that of program under execution is affected, when running in a multi-programming mode.

The more elaborate the benchmarking, the more costly is the evaluation. The user's goals must be kept in mind. Time constraints also limit how through the testing process can be there must be compromise on how much to test while still ensuring that the software (or hardware) meets its functional criteria. Benchmarks can be in run almost all type of systems environment including batch and online jobs streams and with the users linked to the system directly or through telecommunications methods.

Common benchmarks test the speed of the central processor, with typical instructions executed in a set of program, as well as multiple sterns of jobs in a multiprogramming environment. The same benchmark run on several different computers will make apparent any speed and performance differences attributable to the central processor.

Benchmark can also be centered around an expected language mix for the program that will be run, a mix of different set of programs and applications having widely varying input and output volumes and requirements. The response time for sending and receiving data from terminals is an additional benchmark for the comparison of system.

**(d) Apply Waterfall model for development of a Telephone Directory Search system. Indicate in detail, each of the steps. [8]**

The models consists of six distinct stages, namely:

**1.** Requirements analysis phase

**a.**The problem is specified along with the desired service objectives (goals)

**b.** The constraints are identified

In Telephone Directory Search System, the main goal's is to search a number by its name, phone no, or form its address.

**2.** Specification phase the system specification is produced from the detailed definitions of (a) and (b) above. This document should clearly define the product function. In specification phase of TDSS, the goals are property defined & mentioned that waterfall model can be implemented efficiently to design and develop or well-defined system.

**3.** Software design phase, the system specifications are translated into a software representation. The software engineer at this stage is concerned with:

- ❑ Data structure
- ❑ Software architecture
- ❑ Algorithmic detail and
- ❑ Interface representations.

The hardware requirements are also determined at this stage along with a picture of the overall system architecture. By the end of this stage the software engineer should be able to identify the relationship between the hardware, software and the associated interfaces. Any faults in the specification should ideally not be passed 'down stream'.

In TDSS, the engineer has several questions that has to be resolved: what type of data structure to be used? What platform for the system, has to be used? How to create algorithms for the different process of the system? And what type of interface has to produced?

**4.** Implementation and testing phase stage the designs are translated into the software domain.

* Detailed documentation from the design phase can significantly reduce the coding effort. TDSS is made well documented, all the details are note down in the document file.

* TDSS is tested by inputting the dummy data and matching the output manually whether it is correct or incorrect.

**5.** Integration and system testing phase all the program units are integrated and used to ensure that the complete system meets the software requirements. After this stage the software is delivered to the customers in TDSS, the complete system is being tested, so as to make search fastest as possible by different fields of the software.

**6.** Maintenance phase the usually the longest stage of the software. In this phase the software in update to:

- ❑ Meet the changing customer needs
- ❑ Adapted to accommodate changes in the external environment
- ❑ Correct errors and oversights previously undetected in this testing phases.
- ❑ Enhancing the efficiency of the software.

**Q2(a). Consider the following team structure.**
**A senior programmer and some junior programmers form a team that is called a Chief Programmers team. Compare the communication paths in this structure with controlled decentralized structure. What are the advantage and disadvantage of this structure? Under what conditions will you suggest that this structure be used? [7]**

This structure is centralized controlled structure (CC)

**Controlled Decentralized (CD)** – This software engineering team has a defined leader who coordinates specific tasks and secondary leaders that have responsibility for subtasks. Problem solving remains a group activity, but implementation of solutions is partitioned among subgroups by the team leader. Communication among subgroups and individual is horizontal. Vertical communication along the control hierarchy also occurs.

**Controlled Centralized (CC)** – Top-level problem solving and internal team coordination are managed by a team leader. Communication between the leader and team members is vertical.

Because a centralized structure completes tasks faster, it is the most adaptable in handling simple problems. Decentralized teams generate more and better solutions than individuals. Therefore such teams have a greater probability of success when working on difficult problems. Since the CD team is centralized for problem solving, either a CD or CC team structure can be successfully applied to simple problems. A DD structure is best for difficult problems.

**Seven project factors that should be considered when planning the best team structure are:**

- The difficulty of the problem is to be solved.
- The size of the resultant program (s) in lines of code or function points.
- The time the team will stay together (team lifeline).
- The degree to which the problem can be modularized.
- The required quality and reliability of the system to be built.
- The rigidity of the delivery date.
- The degree of sociability (communication) required for the project.

The length of time the team will 'live together' affects team morale. It has been found that DD team structure result in high morel and job satisfaction and are therefore good for long lifeline teams.

The DD team structure is best applied to problems with relatively low modularity because of the higher volume of communication that is needed. When high modularity is possible (and people can do their own thing). The CC or CD structure will work well.

CC and CD teams have been found to produce fewer defects than DD teams, but these data have much to do with the specific quality assurance activities that are applied by the team. Decentralized teams generalized require more time to complete a project than a centralized structure and at the same time are best when high sociability is required.

Since the CD team is centralized for problem solving, either a CD or CC team structure can be successfully applied to simple problems. A DD structure is best for difficult problems.

A controlled centralized (CD) structure originally called the *chief programmer team*. The nucleus of the team was composed of a *senior engineer* (the chief programmer), who plans, coordinates and reviews all technical activities of the team; *technical staff* (normally two five people), who conduct analysis and development activities, and a *backup engineer* who supports the senior engineer in his or her activities an can replace senior engineer with minimum loss in project continuity.

The chief programmer may be served by on or more specialists (e.g., telecommunication expert, database designer), support staff e.g., technical writer, clerical personnel a *software librarian*. The librarian serves many teams and performs the following functions: maintains and controls all elements of the software configuration (i.e., documentation, source listings, data, storage media); helps collect and format software productivity data; catalogs and indexes reusable software components; and assists the teams in research, evaluation, and document preparation. The importance of a librarian cannot be overemphasized. The librarian acts as a controller coordinate and potentially, and potentially an evaluation of the software configuration.

A variation on the democratic decentralized team who advocates teams with creative independence whose approach to work might best be termed *innovative anarchy*. Although the free spirited approach software work has appeal, channeling creative energy into a high performance team must be a central goal of a software organization.

To achieve high performance team: high-performance

- ❑ Team members must have trust on one another.
- ❑ The distribution of skills must be appropriate to the problem.
- ❑ Mavericks may have to be excluded from the team, if team cohesiveness is to be maintained.

**Advantage and Disadvantages**

**1.** A frenzied work atmosphere in which team members waste energy and lose focus on the objectives of the work to be performed.

**2.** High frustration caused by personal, business, or technological factors that causes friction among team members.

**3.** "Fragmented or poorly coordinated procedures: or a poorly defined r improperly chosen process model that becomes a roadblock to accomplishment.

**4.** Unclear definition of roles resulting in a lack of accountability and resultant finger-pointing.

**5.** Continuous and repeated exposure to failure" that leads to a loss of confidence and a lowering of morale.

**(b) Who is a System Analyst/ Elaborate on the technical and interpersonal skills required of a Systems Analyst. What is one skill favoured over the other? Why? [8]**

A system analyst studies the problems and needs of an organization to determine how people, data, process communications, and information technology can best accomplish improvements for the business.

When information technology is used, the analyst is responsibility for the efficient capture of data from its business source, the flow of that data to the computer, the processing and storage of the data by the computer, and the flow of usual and timely information revolution. They were industrial engineers whose responsibilities centered on the design of efficient and effective manufacturing systems. Information system analysis involved from the need to improve the use of computer resources for the information processing needs of business applications.

The system analyst must possess various skills to effectively carry out the job. The skills (attributes) to be possessed by the system analysts are broadly divided in to following categories. These are

**1** Interpersonal Skills

**2** Technical skills

**The Interpersonal skills in context with the system are as follows:**

• **Communication :** The system analyst should have a very good communication skill. He is supposed to interact with the other person of the organisation. Communication means listening others, feeling what other says and coming to one another.

• **Understanding:** Identifying the problems and assessing their solutions with the consideration and constraints proposed by the organisation.

• **Teaching:** Educating the people to understand computer, its user how it works, what more and more can be obtained through the computer.

• **Selling:** Selling ideas and promoting innovations in problem solving using computers.

• **Creativity:** Helping users model ideas into concrete plans and developing candidate systems to match user requirements.

• **Project management:** Scheduling, performing well under time constraints, coordinating team efforts and managing costs and expenditure.

• **Dynamic interface:**

• Questioning attitude and inquiring mind.

• Knowledge of basic of the computer and business functions.

**Technical Skills:** In order to develop computer based information systems, systems analyst must understand information technologies, their potentials and their limitations. In general, a systems analyst should be familiar of technologies such as :

Microcomputers, workstations, minicomputers, and mainframe computers,

Programming languages,

Operating systems, both for PC's and networks.

Database and File management system,

Data communication standards and software for local and wide area networks,

System development tools and environments (such as forms & report generators and graphical user interface design tools), and

Decision support systems and data analysis tools.

**Situation where greater interpersonal skills are required than technical skills from a system analyst are following :**

• During analysis, there is greater need for interpersonal skills – working with the user to determine requirements and transact them into design criteria.

• During design, it requires highly technical procedures and methodologies.

• During implementation, analyst / user interface and user participation is more emphasized.

• During program construction, loading and testing are carried out with some user participation.

**Situation where greater technical skills are required than interpersonalskills from a system analyst are following :**

• During design, when input, output screen design, module design etc.

• During implementation, when system developed is implemented at the client site

• During system testing, where it is worked out that which hardware / supporting software configuration will be the best to run the proposed system

• During maintenance, also technical skills are needed to make the system error free or update according to the current changed requirements.

**Q3(a). State atleast five risks in Software Engineering. How will you manage them? [5]**

**Following are the five risks in Software Engineering :**

**(i)** Personnel Shortfalls

Staffing with top talent; job matching; team-building; morale-building; cross-training; pre-scheduling key people.

**(ii)** Unrealistic Schedules and Budgets

Detailed, multi-source cost & schedule estimation; design to cost; incremental development; software reuse; req. scrubbing.

**(iii)** Developing the wrong software functions

Organizational analysis; mission analysis; operational concept formulation; user surveys; prototyping; early users' manuals.

**(iv)** Developing the wrong user interface

Prototyping; scenarios; task analysis.

**(v)** Gold-plating

Requirements scrubbing; prototyping; cost-benefit analysis; design to cost

**General Managing Methods**

• Elimination: Risk exposure reduced to 0

• Retention: Risk kept, but perhaps made more tolerable

• Avoidance: Rearrange to remove risk

• Transfer: Pass risk to third party• Insurance• Contracts

**(b) What are the ten causes of failure of CASE in some projects? [10]**

Two following list has been inspired by actual mistakes encountered in real-word systems projects.

**1.** Don't use a specific methodology because coding is all that is really important.

**2.** Create the project plan by working backwards from a drop-dead system completion date.

**3.** Don't bother with a data model. Just build whatever tables you need.

**4.** Use a Technical Lead that has never built a similar system. Hiring such talent is too expensive.

**5.** Hire forty developers to make the coding go faster.

**6.** Build the system in Java, even though most of the development team still thinks that Java is coffee and you have no intention of ever deploying to the Web.

**7.** Three months before the system goes five, assign one junior developer to handle the data migration.

**8.** Skip the testing phase because the project is way behind schedule.

**9.** Change the system to support critical new requirements discovered during final development.

**10.** Busy a commercial, off-the-shelf package and customize it…a lot.

**Q4(a). How are MIS and DSS related. How do they differ from each other? [8]**

It is viewed that DSS is an extension of MIS or can be defined as a second generation of MIS =>MIS is generated when we add predefined managerial reports that are span out of transaction processing, report generation and online inquiry capabilities - all integrated with a given functional area such as production or personnel MIS => DSS results from adding external data sources, accounting and statistical modules and interactive query capabilities, the outcome is system designed to serve all levels or management.

**Management level** **Information level System support**

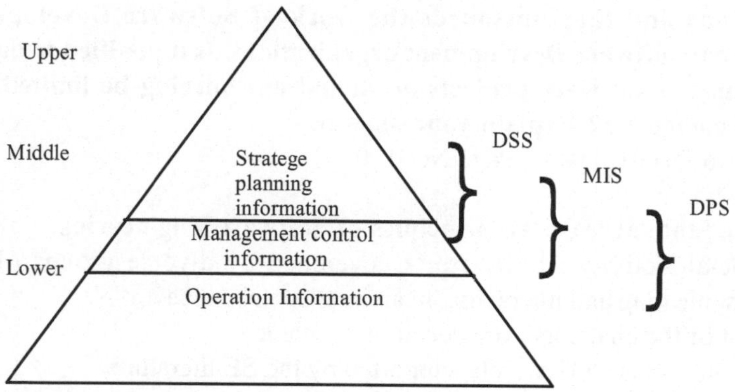


| | CATEGORY | CHARACTERISTICS |
|---|---|---|
| 1. | Management Information System | Provides input to be used in the managerial decision process. Deals with supporting well Structured decision situations. Typical Information requirements can be anticipated. |
| 2. | Decision Support System | Provides information to managers who must make judgements about particular situations. Support decision makers in situation that are not well-structured. |

**Difference between MIS and DSS :**

The MIS has the characteristics of a decision support system. The decision support system (DSS) concept is an evolution of the term MIS. However, the DSS focuses more on support leading to decisions.

The term DSS became popular in late 70's due to the wide and diverse computer applications. Operations carried out under DSS may range from retrieving information, analyzing and aggregating data, evaluating the consequences of decisions, and proposing decisions.

The distinction between MIS and DSS is basically a difference in focus. With the DSS the focus is on top decision makers to provide them with sound judgements and visions. On the other hand, MIS is focused on the flow of information, regardless of the user.

The DSS is a part of a larger concept where computer-based knowledge is used to make decisions. The computer operations and their linkages to data and decisions.

**(b) Several organizations don't have their own software development divisions and they outsource the work of Software Development to External Software Development organizations. Is it justified to outsource all types of software projects or should outsourcing be limited to only some categories? Explain your answer. [7]**

Refer to Dec01, Q4(a), Page No.-170

**Q5(a). State at least ten principles of Software Engineering. [10]**

**1.** Social Activity : Software is developed by diverse groups of people communicating and interacting in an intellectual endeavor.

· Most of the challenges are social, not technical

· This notion is NOT widely supported by the SE literature

**2.** Uncertainty Rules : If it were a sure thing, it's questionable whether it's worth doing. There is always uncertainty in worthwhile software endeavors

·Some people believe that software projects are more predictable than they are

· Plan to deal with uncertainty

**3.** Fail Early, Fail Cheaply: Software Engineering is inherently a risky business—count on some failure.

· Make canceling a project a success, not a failure

**4.** Software is Invisible : Software is one of the few media which cannot in and of itself be directly observed.

· "Strive to make invisible things visible"

· Not just code—requirements, designs, progress, responsibility

**5.** Invest Proportionally : Invest in organization and infrastructure proportionally to the potential value of the targeted system.

· Systems with greater value merit greater investment

**6.** Clean As You Go : The longer a problem lingers,the harder and more expensive it is to solve.

· Scrub bugs out as quickly as possible

**7.** Smart People # Smart Groups : Just because smart people gather together does not mean they will act smart as a group.

· Good teams are deliberately forged—they don't just happen.

**8.** Rumor Rules : Rumor naturally trumps knowledge. Assume that rumor is the rule, not the exception.

· People see what they want to see and hear what they want to hear

· Continually test what you believe

· Knowledge is a much stronger ally than rumor

**9.** Ambiguity Rules: Assume that every aspect of the endeavor is ambiguous to the stakeholders.

· People naturally have their own point of view

· Resolving ambiguity is a major source of conflict

**10.** Don't Reinvent : Build only what you must.

· Reuse or recycle everything you can

**(b) List at least five guidelines, which will help prevent problems during. Analysis and Design phases. [5]**

✓ **The design process should not suffer from "tunnel vision":** A good designer should consider alternative approaches judging each based on the requirement of the problem the resources available to do the job.

✓ **The design should be traceable to the analysis model:** Because a single element of the design model often traces to multiple requirement, it is necessary to have a means for tracking how requirements have been satisfied by the design model.

✓ **The design should "minimize the intellectual distance" between the software and the problem as it exists in the real world:** That is, the structure of the software design should **(whenever possible)** mimic the structure of the problem domain.

✓ **The design should exhibit uniformity and integration:** A design is uniform if it appears that one person developed the entire thing. Rules of style and format should be defined for a design team before designing work begins. Designs integrated if care is taken in defining interfaces between design components.

✓ **The design should be structured to accommodate change:** The design concepts discussed in the next section enable a design to achieve this principle.

✓ **The design should be reviewed to minimize conceptual errors:** There is sometimes a tendency to focus on minutiae when the design is reviewed, missing the forest for the trees. A design team should ensure that major conceptual elements of the design have been addressed before worrying about the syntax of the design model.

# CS-70 : INTRODUCTION TO SOFTWARE ENGINEERING
## JUNE - 2006

**Note:** *Questions no. 1 is* ***Compulsory.*** *Answer any* ***three*** *from the rest.*

**Q1(a). Explain the importance of problem identification in software development. Explain how a data flow diagram represents work flow in a typical Library Management System. [8]**

**Importance of Problem Identification:**

The quality of a software product is only as good as the process that creates it. Requirements engineering is one of the most crucial steps in this creation process. Without well-written requirements specifications, developers do not know what to build, customers do not know what to expect, and there is no way to validate that the built system satisfies the requirements.

· Identification and documentation of customer's and user's needs

· Creation of a document that describes the external behaviour and the associated constraints that will satisfy those needs

· Analysis and validation of the requirements document to ensure consistency, completeness, and feasibility

· Evolution of needs

**DFD (Library Management System) :**

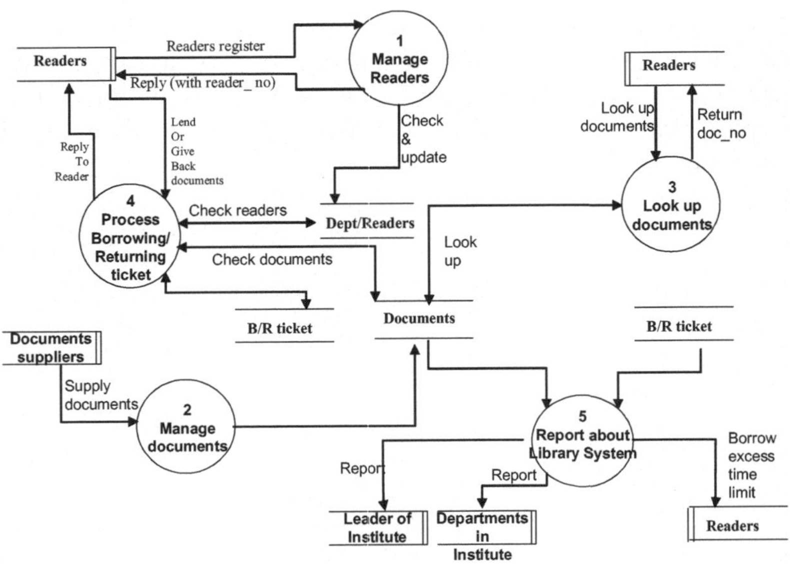


Data flow diagram high level

**(b) What is the concept of project outsourcing Give two examples each, with justification, of where outsourcing is recommended and where outsourcing is not recommended. [7]**

In concept, outsourcing is extremely simple. Software engineering activities are contracted to a third party who does the work at lower cost and, hopefully, higher quality. Software work conducted within a company is reduced to a contract management activity.

The decision to outsource can be either strategic or tactical. At the strategic level, business managers consider whether a significant portion of all Software work can be contracted to others. At the tactical level, a project manager determines whether part or all of a project can best accomplished by subcontracting the Software work.

Refer to Dec01, Q4(a), Page No.-170

**(c) Explain the term 'quality of software'. Consider any software for Desk Top Publishing. Give three factors which can affect the quality of this software. Justify your answer. [7]**

***Software quality*** is defined as:

Conformance to explicitly stated functional and performance requirements, explicitly documented development standards, and implicit characteristics that are expected of all professionally developed software.

**1.** Software requirements are the foundation from which quality is measured. Lack of conformance to requirements is lack of quality.

**2.** Specified standards define a set of development criteria that guide the manner in which software is engineered. If the criteria are not followed, lack of quality will almost surely result.

**3.** A set of implicit requirements often goes unmentioned (e.g., the desire for ease of use and good maintainability). If Software conforms to its explicit requirements but fails to meet implicit requirements, Software quality is suspect.

**Factors which can affect the quality of "DTP" Software :**

Program size, (empirically measured) programmer ability, and disciplined processes significantly affect software quality. Factors frequently used as surrogates for programmer ability, e.g., years of experience, and technology, e.g., programming language, do not significantly impact software quality, although they may affect other important software attributes such as productivity.

**(d) Explain the concept of object oriented programming. List four important features each of Oracle and Ingres. [8]**

The fundamental idea behind object-oriented languages is to combine both

data and the functions that operate on that data into a single unit called ***an object***. An object's functions, called member functions which typically provide the only way to access its data. If you want to read a data item in an object, you call only way to access its data. If you want to read a data item in an object, you call a member function in the object. It will read the item and return the value to you it can't access the data directly. The data is hidden, so it is safe to accidental alterations. Data and its functions are said to be encapsulated into a single entity, ***data encapsulation and data hiding*** are key terms in the description of object-oriented languages.
No other functions can access the data. This simplifies writing, debugging, and maintaining the program.
An Object oriented paradigm based program typically consist of a number of objects, which communicates with each other by calling one another's member functions.
Data items are referred to as ***instance variables***. Calling an object's member function is referred to as ***sending a message to the object***.

**Features of Oracle**

**(i)** Partitioning
Applies to tables and indexes. If a table or an index is partitioned, several pieces of the same object can be 'scattered' in separate segments and even on different tablespaces.
**(ii)** Objects
Refers to the ability to create user defined types.
**(iii)** Real Application Clusters (RAC)
Previously known as Parallel Server.
**(iv)** Advanced replication
This options is a requirement for updateable materialized views and writeable materialized views.
**(v)** Bit-mapped indexes
Bit-mapped indexes is one of the possible indexing methods.
**(vi)** Connection multiplexing

**Ingres Features** : is a Open source database solutions that provide enterprise-level functionality, services and support are revolutionizing today's marketplace.

**1.** The Fastest Query Optimization in Open Source
- Parallel Query Support allows complex queries to be executed in parallel

**2.** Most Secure Open Source Database
- C2 certified relational database management system (RDBMS)
- Ability to backup data online or offline and customize recovery process

· Built-in redundancy allows workload to be spread across multiple nodes in a cluster with automatic fail-over

**3.** Improved Performance and Scalability

· Key Range Table Partitioning enables parallel I/O operations across partitions

**4.** Better Web Integration

· Ingres 2006 provides support for all of the latest web application development technologies as well as supporting traditional standards based application development and deployment technologies

**5.** Easier implementation process

· Only one file to download

· Five-minute installation process

**Q2(a). What are the possible S/W team structures? In which of these is communication horizontal? Use examples of such teams to explain your answer. [6]**

Refer to Dec05, Q2(a), Page No.-219

In Democratic Decentralized (DD) structure communication is horizontal.

In case of managing the development of the next generation version of its widely used word processing software, we will use DD (horizontal communication) structure. Because competition is intense, light deadlines have been established and announced by the market. So following points advocate for the DD team structure if the professional involved with the project are from the organization itself.

**1.** Since project is large more number of personnel will participate.

**2.** Since project is complex it will require expert professional.

**3.** Expert professional need to have freedom to wash, they are first needed the deadlines to meet, should be having free hand to dead with, since they know this job and have maturity and experience so horizontal communication is appropriate structured.

**(b) What is software upgradation? What are the processes to be followed for upgradation? Explain four problems that could be encountered by not following the proper methodology for upgradation. [9]**

**Software Upgradation** is the analysis of existing Software system and modifying them to constitute a new form. The goal of upgradation is to understand the functionality and implementation of existing Software and re implement to improve System functionality, performance. System Replacement cost is expensive. Hence software upgradation is often a better choice. The four general software upgradation objectives:

· Improve maintainability

· Migration
· Improve reliability
· Functional enhancement

Although these principles focus on the rebuilding of a house, they apply equally well to the reengineering of computer-based systems and applications. Software reengineering, process model defines six activities.

**1. Inventory analysis.** Every software organization should have an inventory of all applications. The inventory can be nothing more than a spreadsheet model containing information that provides a detailed description (e.g., size, age, business criticality) of every active application. By sorting this information according to business criticality, longevity, current maintainability, and other locally important criteria, candidates for reengineering appear. Resources can then be allocated to candidate applications for reengineering work. It is important to note that the inventory should be revisited on a regular cycle.

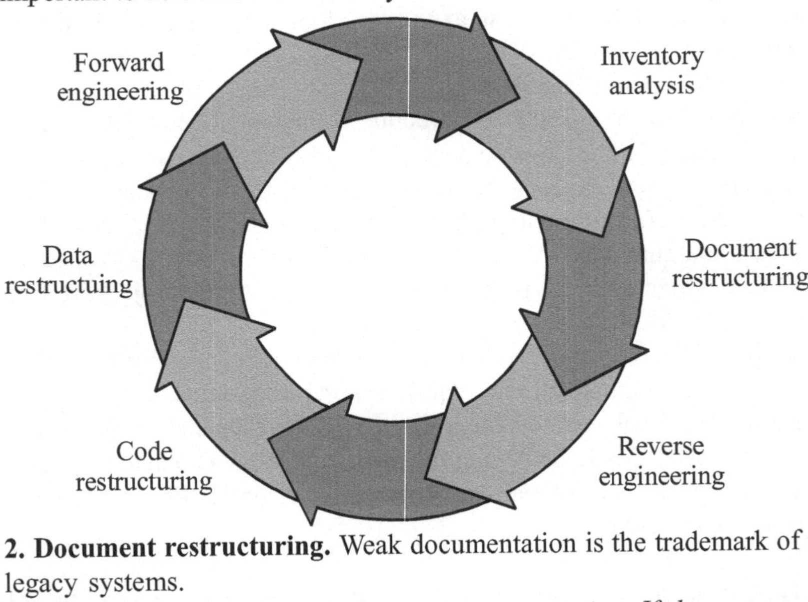


**2. Document restructuring.** Weak documentation is the trademark of many legacy systems.

**A.**.*Creating documentation is far too time consuming. If the system works, we'll live with what we have.*

**B.** *Documentation must be updated, but we have limited resources. We'll use a "document when touched" approach.*

**C.** *System is business critical and must be fully redocument.*

**3. Reverse engineering.** Reverse engineering is a process of design recovery. Reverse engineering tools extract data, architectural, and procedural design information from an existing program.

**4. Code restructuring.** Some legacy systems have a relatively solid program architecture, but individual modules were coded in a way that makes them difficult to understand, test, and maintain. In such cases, the code within the suspect modules can be restructured. To accomplish this activity, the source code is analyzed using a restructuring tool. Violations of structured programming constructs are note and code is then restructured (this can be done automatically). The resultant restructured code is reviewed and tested to ensure that no anomalies have been introduced. Internet code documentation is updated.

**5. Data restructuring.** A program with weak data architecture will be difficult to adapt and enhance. In fact, for many applications, data architecture has more to do with the long-term viability of a program that the source code itself.

**6. Forward engineering.** Forward engineering also called renovation or reclamation, not only recovers design information form existing software, but uses this information to alter or reconstitute the existing system in an effort to improve its overall quality. In most cases, reengineered software reimplements the function of the existing system and also add new functions and/or improves overall performance.

**Problems :**

1. system structure will not be understandable and maintainable
2. The understandability of data-driven programs may not be improved
3. Low acceptance in the organization
4. lack of commitment at organization level

No understanding of implications.

**Q3(a). Describe briefly four major functions of a Systems Analyst. Also describe four important attributes that a Systems Analyst must have.[8]**

Refer to June05, Q2(b), Page No.-207

**(b) Describe four problems encountered in applications development.[4]**

**I.** Gathering application requirements.

**II.** Application cost and time estimation of application.

**III.** Risk analysis property of different stages of software development.

**IV.** Software quality assurance

**(c) How does minimization of intellectual distance make software maintenance easy? Which design approach is developed using this concept.[3]**

The design should "minimize the intellectual distance" between the software and the problem as it exists in the real world. That is, the structure of the software design should (whenever possible) mimic the structure of the problem domain

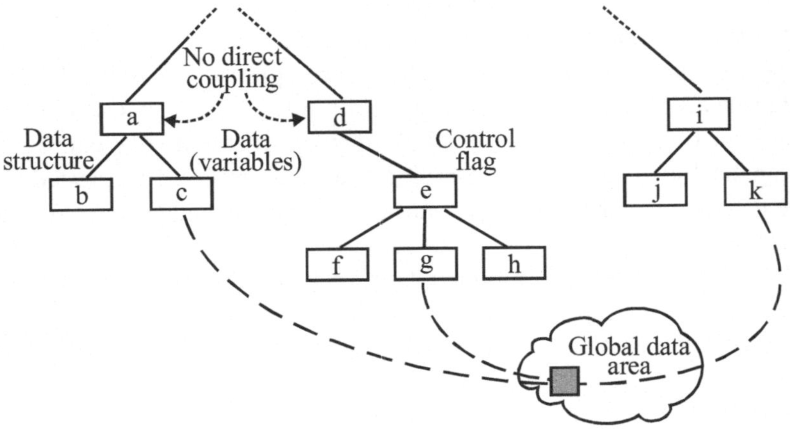


**(Coupling)**

Coupling is a measure of interconnection among modules in a software structure. Coupling depends on the interface complexity between modules, the point at which entry or reference is made to a module, and what data pass across the interface.

In software design, se strive for lowest possible coupling. Figure provides examples of different types of module coupling. Modules *a* and *d* are subordinate to different modules. Each is unrelated and therefore no direct coupling occurs. Module *c* is subordinate to module a and is accessed via a conventional argument list, through which data are passed.

As long as a simple argument list is present (i.e., simple data are passed; a one-to-one correspondence of items exists), low coupling (called data coupling) is exhibited in this portion of structure. A variation of data coupling, called stamp coupling, is found when a portion of data structure (rather then simple arguments) is passed via a module interface.

Control coupling is very common in most software designs where a "control flag" (a variable that controls decision in a subordinate or super ordinate module) is passed between module.

**Q4(a). What is project scheduling? Describe at least three functions associated with project scheduling. Explain four options available to a project manager when a project is behind schedule. [8]**

After selecting an appropriate process mode, identify the software engineering tasks that have to be performed estimate the amount of work and the number of people, know the deadline, even consider the risks. To create a network of software engineering tasks that will enable to get the job done on time. Once the network is created, assign responsibility for each task, make sure it gets done, and adapt the network as risks become reality. In a nutshell, that's software project scheduling.

**Function Options.**

**A.** Perform a detailed estimate using historical data from past projects. Determine the estimated effort and duration for the project.

**B.** Using an incremental process model, develop a software engineering strategy that will deliver critical functionality by the imposed dead-line but delay other functionality until later. Document the plan.

**C.** Meet with the customer and (using the detailed estimate), explain why the imposed deadline is unrealistic.

**Options.**

**I. Time allocation.** Each task to be scheduled must be allocated some number of work units (e.g., person-days of effort). In addition, each task be assigned a start date and a completion date that are a function of the interdependencies and whether work will be conducted of a full-time or part-time basis.

**II. Effort validation.** Every project has a defined number of staff members. As time allocation occurs, the project manager must ensure that no more than the allocated number of people have been scheduled at any given time.

**III. Defined responsibility.** Every task that is scheduled should be assigned to a specific team member.

**(b) Prepare an SRS document for an airline reservation system. Explain how design reviews can uncover deficiencies in this. [7]**

**1. System Objectives**

**1.1** The Airline Reservation System (ARS), which is a Large Scale Interactive Database, is a software application to handle all the requests coming from the customers (travelers) which are related to travelling by air.

**1.2** ARS should satisfy the following objectives:

**1.2.1** Reduce effort and frustration in interacting with ARS.

**1.2.2** Provide convenience to travelers.

**1.2.3** Preserved individuals' privacy concerning aspects of their traveling information that they don't want to be accessed by unauthorized persons.

**2 Functional Requirements**

**2.1** Checking flight information

**2.1.1** ARS shall present the person checking the flight information (henceforth called the Customer) with a selection of the following choices:

**2.1.2** ARS shall obtain the following flight information from the ARS' database:

**2.1.2.1** flight number **2.1.2.2** flight status

**2.1.2.3** gate/terminal **2.1.2.4** plane model

**2.2** Reservation

**2.2.1** ARS shall present the person making the flight reservation (henceforth called the Traveler) with a selection of the following choices:

**2.2.2** ARS shall display all the flight information for the flights with the lowest fare on the given dates.

**2.2.3** ARS shall use to obtain and display the flight information for the flights with the lowest currently available fare.

**2.3** Cancel a reservation **2.4** Change options **2.5** Customer Servicing

**Future Requirements**

• Provide more services to the Customer; for example give links for hotel reservation, car rental and other services.

• Support dynamic ticket pricing which will depend on various factors, such as service during peak flight season.

• Support not only the Customer, but also the airline, including such services as: Help airline maximize plane utilization

Design review can uncover deficiency to SRS because following points are clarified using proper design of the airlines reservation system.

1. Understanding of the project
2. Methodology and tools (if any) to be used for Software Design
3. Methodology and tools (if any) to be used for Software Development
4. Methodology and tools (if any) to be used for Software Testing
5. Detailed Project Plan including Gantt Charts and Resource Assignments
6. Details of assigned team members with their availability for the project
7. Detailed CV of each assigned project team member
8. On-site deployment plan
9. End User Service, support and training
10. Detailed Breakdown of price for project

☐ Resource Allocation ☐ Development Effort ☐ Quality Assurance

**Q5(a). How is 'risk management' performed in a software project ? List any six risks of a s/w project and the corresponding risk management techniques. [8]**

Refer Chapter-2, Q17 and Q18.

An effective strategy must consider three issues:

**1.** risk avoidance

**2.** risk monitoring

**3.** risk management and contingency planning

**1.** If a software team adopts a proactive approach to risk, avoidance is always the best strategy. This is achieved by developing a plan for *risk mitigation.* For example, assume that high staff turnover is noted as a project risk.

High turnover will have a critical impact on project cost and schedule.

To mitigate this risk, project management must develop a strategy for reducing turnover. Among the possible steps to be taken are.

Meat with current staff to determine causes for turnover.

**2.** As the project proceeds, risk monitoring activities commence. The project manager monitors factors that may provide an indication of whether the risk is becoming more or less likely. In the case of high staff turnover, the following factors can be monitored:

· General attitude of team members based on project pressures.

· The degree

· Interpersonal relationships among team members.

**3.** *Risk management and contingency planning* assumes that mitigation effort have failed and that the risk has become a reality. If the mitigation strategy has been followed, backup is available, information is documented, and knowledge has been dispersed across the team.

**(b) What are the considerations of evaluating a CASE tool ? Also list five benefits of using CASE tools. [7]**

This is the criteria list in making an early assessment of which tools will potentially fulfill the requirements identified and prioritized the criteria list to ensure that important objectives are satisfied by selecting the appropriate case tools. Non-prioritized or vague user requirements extend the search process resulting in a potential lose of time, money and training. This step will prevent the customer from evaluating CASE tools which will not meet user requirements.

Refer to June05, Q6(a), Page No.-213

| Characteristic | Must Have | Nice to Have |
|---|---|---|
| Supports Multiple Structured Methodologies | | * |
| Supports one well known structured methodology | * | |
| Supports Multiple Methodologies, Object Oriented and Structured | | * |
| Supports Objected Oriented Methodology | | * |
| Supported under multiple Operating Systems | | * |
| Supports DOS/Windows Environment | * | |
| Large installed product base | * | |
| Has active user group | * | |
| Provides Telephone Support | * | |
| Provides On Line Tutorial | * | |
| Intuitive Interface | * | |
| Supports both single user as well as work group in a network environment | * | |
| Provides Reverse Engineering Capability | | * |
| Provides Links to GUI tools and Code Generators | | * |

# CS-70 : INTRODUCTION TO SOFTWARE ENGINEERING
## December, 2006

**Note :** Question number 1 is **compulsory.** Answer any **three** questions from the rest.

**Q1(a). Explain the role of the software development team Normally, who is responsible to select and build the software team for a new project. Also mention the various options that are available in order to assign / allocate "x" people to work for "y" years on a newly arrived software project.** *10*

**Ans.** The software development team is responsible for development of a software process. There are several tasks that needs to be carried out for development of a software. There are several models for such process, each describing approaches to a variety of tasks or activities that take place during the process of software development.

**Process activities / steps are :**

**1) Software element analysis :** The most important tasks in creating a software product is extracting the requirements.

**2) Specification :** Specification is the task of precisely describing the software to be written, possibly in a rigorous way.

**3) Software Architecture :** The architecture of a software system refers to an abstract representation of that system. Architecture is concerned with making sure the software system will meet the requirements of the product, as well as ensuring that future requirements can be addressed. The architecture step also addresses interfaces between the software system and other software projects, as well as the underlying hardware or the best operating system.

**4) Implementation (or coding) :** Reducing a design to code may be the most obvious responsibility of the software development team, but it is not necessarily the largest portion.

**5) Testing :** Testing of parts of software, especially where code by two different engineers must work together, falls to the software team.

**6) Documentation :** An important task is documenting the internal design of software for the purpose of future maintenance and enhancement.

**7) Maintenance :** Maintaining and enhancing software to cope with newly discovered problems or new requirement is an important task of software development team, not only may it be necessary to add code that doesnot fit the original design but just determining how software works at some point after it is completed may require significant effort by a software engineer.

**Software manager** is responsible to select and build the software team for a new project. Software manager is project manager plans, monsters, and control the work of a team of software engineers senior managers coordinate the interface between the business and software professionals.

**The following options are available for applying human resources to a project that will require x people working for y years.**

**1)** x individuals are assigned to m different functional tasks; relatively little combined work occurs; coordination is the responsibility of a software manager who may have six other projects to be concerned with

**2)** x individuals are assigned to m different tasks so that informal "teams" are established; an ad hoc team leader may be appointed; coordination among team members is the responsibility of the projects manager.

**3)** x Individuals are organised into t terms; each team is assigned one or more functional task; each team has a specific structure that is defined for all teams working on the project; coordination is done by both the team and project manager.

**(b) Explain the significance of the project planning and control. Also describes the four major steps for the project planning.** *10*

**Ans.** Project planning is part of project management, which relates to the use of schedules such as Gantt charts to plan and subsequently report progress within the project environment.

Initially, the project scope is defined and the appropriate methods for completing the project are determined. Following this step, the durations for the various tasks necessary to complete the work are listed and grouped into a work breakdown structure. The logical dependencies between tasks are defined using an activity network diagram that enables identification of the critical path. Float or slack time in the schedule can be calculated using project management software. Then the necessary resources can be estimated and costs for each activity can be allocated to each resource, giving the total project cost. At this stage, the project plan may be optimized to achieve the appropriate balance between resource usage and project duration to comply with the project objectives. Once established and agreed, the plan becomes what is known as the baseline. Progress will be measured against the baseline throughout the life of the project. Analyzing progress compared to the baseline is known as earned value management.

**For four major steps for the project planning,**

**Now -** Refer to Jan-2001, Q.No-1(e), Page No.-191

**(c) With the help of a suitable example. Explain the concept of re-**

**application of the software modules.** **5**

**Ans. Reapplication of the software models :** A way to reduce the amount of code that must be written in any application is to identify tasks that must be done in several phases and write one low-level module to perform the common tasks. As a simple example, in designing a wagon, we might start from the general concept of "wagon". Once we decide that a wagon must be supported in four places, we will not try to invent the wheel four times. In the programming content, we might determine the details of a task just once, document pre-conditions and post-conditions for this task. Then, refer to that common task from several places.

For example, the some type of input or output may be needed in several places within a program, and we may write some procedures to perform standard input and output tasks.

In Pascal language, we regularly rely on the read and write procedures in virtually every program. A similar approach can be applied to many programs when we want to read data and place them in a standard form in a particular field of a data record on array. One data entry procedure can ensure that all terminal or file input will be handled in a consistent manner throughout the program.

**(d) What is the 4GL ? List and explain different advantages of the 4GL over the 3GL.** **5**

**Ans.** Fourth-generation language, also known as a 4GL, is a higher-level programming language that automates many of the basic functions that must be spelled out in conventional languages, and can obtain results with an order-of-magnitude less coding because of its richer content of commands. 4GLs are closer to human language than other high-level languages and are accessible to people without formal training as programmers. They allow multiple common operations to be performed with a single programmer-entered command. They are intended to be easier for users than machine languages (first-generation), assembly languages (second-generation), and older high-level languages (third-generation).

A fourth-generation programming language (abbreviated 4GL) is a descriptive term used for programming languages and environments designed with a specific purpose in mind, such as the development of commercial business software. In the evolution of computing, the 4GL followed the 3GL in an upward trend toward higher abstraction and statement power. The 4GL was followed by efforts to define and use a 5GL.

The natural-language, block-structured mode of the third-generation programming languages improved the process of software development.

However, 3GL development methods can be slow and error prone. It becomes clear that some applications could be developed more rapidly by adding a higher-level programming language and methodology which would generate the equivalent of very complicated 3GL instructions with fewer errors. In some senses, software engineering arose to handle 3GL development. 4GL and 5GL projects are more oriented toward problem solving and systems engineering.

All 4GLs are designed to reduce programming effort, the time it takes to develop software, and the cost of software development. They are not always successful in this task, sometimes resulting in inelegant and unmaintainable code. However, given the right problem, the use of an appropriate 4GL can be spectacularly successful. The usability improvements obtained by some 4GLs (and their environment) allowed better exploration for heuristic solutions than did the 3GL.

**Some successful fourth-generation languages**

**(1) Database query languages**

**(i)** FOCUS

**(ii)** NATURAL

**(iii)** Informix-4GL

**(2) Report generators**

**(i)** BuildProfessional

**(ii)** GEMBase

**(iii)** LINC

**Q2(a). List and explain the important qualities of the software product and the process.** ***10***

**Ans. The important quantities of the software product and Process are as follows :**

**(1) Correctness :** A program is functionally correct if it behaves according to the specification of the functions it should provide (called functions requirements specification). Correctness can be assessed through a variety of methods, some stressing an experimental approach (e.g. testing), others stressing an analytic approach (e.g., formal verification of correctness).

**(2) Reliability :** Software reliability may be defined as the ability of the system to perform its required functions under stated conditions for a specified period of time. Informally, software is reliable if the user can depend on it.

**(3) Robustness :** Software Robustness is the degree to which the software can function correctly in the presence of invalid input or stressful environmental conditions (e.g. when a program encounters incorrect input data or some hardware malfunction say, a disk crash). Informally, a program is robust if it behaves reasonably even in circumstances that were not anticipated in the requirements specification.

**(4) User friendliness, verifiability and maintainability :** A software is said to be user friendly if it was designed with that primary objective and the same was met. The process of evaluating software to determine whether the products of a given development phase satisfy the conditions imposed at the start of that phase is known as software verification and if it is possible to do the same, then we say that the software is verifiable.

The ease with which a software system can be modified to correct faults, improve performance or other attributes, or adopt to a changed environment, is known as software maintainability.

**(5) Reusability :** Reusability may be defined as the degree to which a software module can be used in more than one computer program or a software system. Reusability is aim to evolvability. In product evolution, we modify a product to build a new version reuse, we use it-perhaps with minor changes to build another product. A good example of a reusable product is the UNIX shell. Scientific libraries are best known reusable components. Reusability applies to the software process as well. Indeed, the various software methodologies can be viewed as attempts to reuse the same process for building different products. Example of reusability in a process is the replay approach to software maintenance. In this approach, the entire process is repeated when mailing a modification. That is, at first the requirements are modified, and then the subsequent steps are followed as in the initial product development.

**(6) Portability :** The ease with which a software can be transferred from one hardware or software environment to another is known as portability. Software is portable if it can run in different environments. The term environment can refer to a hardware platform or a software environment such as a particular operating system.

**(7) Data Abstraction :** Abstraction is a process whereby we identify the important aspects of a phenomenon and ignore its details. Thus, abstraction is a special case of separation of concerns wherein we separate the concern of the important aspects from the concern of the unimportant details. Data abstraction is a concept which encapsulates (collects) data structure and well defined procedure/ function in a single unit. This encapsulation forms a wall which is intended to shield –the data representation from computer used.

**(8) Modularity :** Modularity may be defined as the degree to which a computer program is composed of discrete components such that a change to one component has a minimal impact on other components. A complex system may be divided into similar pieces called modules. A system that is composed of modules is called modular. The main benefit of modularity is that it allows the principle of separation of concerns to be applied in two phases. When dealing with the details of each module in isolation (and ignoring details of other modules), and when dealing with the overall characteristics of all modules and their relationship in order to integrate them into a coherent system.

**(b) Describe the integrated structure methodologies briefly.** *5*

**Ans. Integrated structured methodologies specify :**

**(1)** A set of activities that are to be carried out in developing an information system.

**(2)** The sequence and the interrelationships of these activities.

**(3)** The tools and techniques that will be used for accomplishing these activities, and the way to record the results of these tasks.

Structured analysis considers new goals and structured tools for analysis. The goals of structured methodology of system analysis and design are as follows : -

**(i)** Graphics should be used wherever it is possible to well communicated with the uses and help the user also.

**(ii)** Differentiate between the logical and physical system.

**(iii)** A logical system model should be build to familiarize the uses with the system characteristics and inter-relationships before implementation.

A methodology integrates the activities of SDLC. The completion of the earlier phase is a pre-condition to the start of the later phases. Of course, some amount of controlled iteration is also allowed within or across phases in order to correct errors or to accommodate changes owing to better understanding of the system as the cycle proceeds.

Thus, structured methodologies go well beyond merely clubbing a set of tools. They have a well defined scope coverage, prescribing standards and connections and providing a reference framework applicable to all projects. They enforce simultaneous documentation and define the deliverables from the system clearly. Estimates can be made easily, and a clear work breakdown structure facilitates project management. Structured methodologies are thus beneficial to a whole host of constituents like the management, end-users, system management, analysts, programmers and quality assurance personnel.

**Q3(a). Consider to design a system for the inventory and billing operations of a "Retail Medical Outlet", draw the context level and first level data flow diagrams (DFDs) for the system and also prepare a SRS document.** *9*

**Ans.**

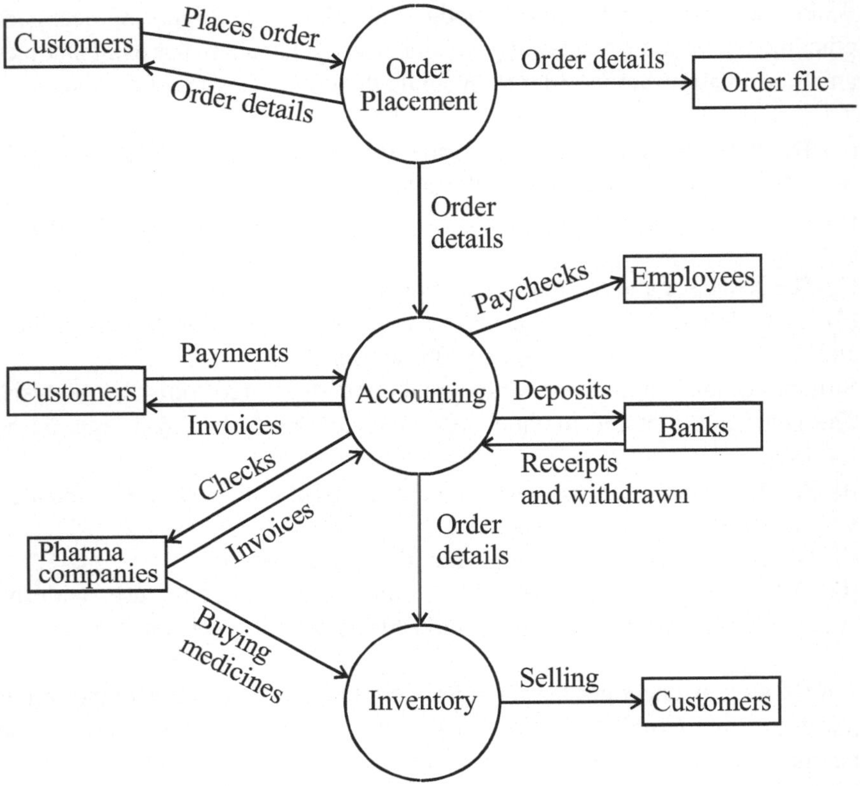


Context level Diagram
Retail Medical Outlet

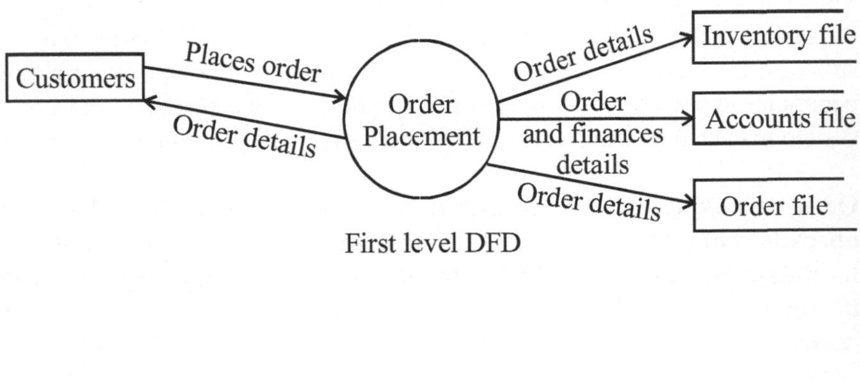


First level DFD

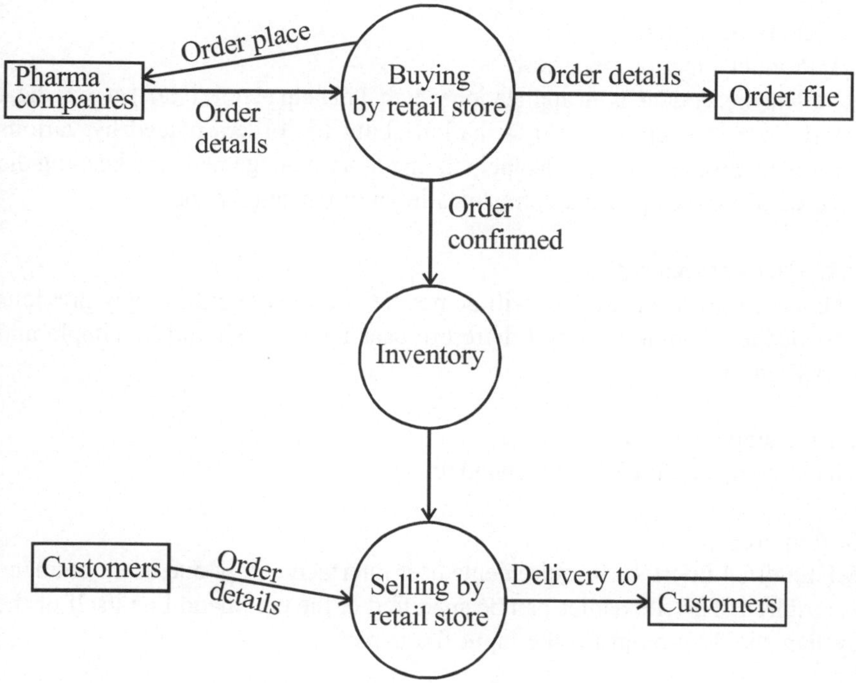


First level DFD

**SRS (Software Requirements Specification)**

**1.** Introduction

**1.1** Retails medial outlet, which is an interactive database, is a software application to handle all the requests coming from customers and seeing to various details related to different pharmaceutical companies.

**1.2** Scope : This document is the only one that describes the requirements of the system. It is meant for use by developers and will be the basis for validating the final delivered system. Any changes made to the requirements in the future will have to go through a formal change approval process. The developer is responsible for asking for clarification, where necessary and will not make any alternations without the permission of the client.

**1.3** References

Not applicable

**1.4** Developer's responsibilities

the developer is responsible for

**(a)** Developing the system

**(b)** Installing the software on the client's hardware.

**(c)** Conducting any user training that might be needed for using that system.

**(d)** Maintaining the system for a period of one year after installation.

**2.** General Description

**2.1** Product function overview.

Retail medical outlet, is an application which will help people (staff) at a medical retail store in keeping the information about the orders placed by various customers properly. It will also help in inventory management and keeping the records of various pharma companies in an organized manner.

**2.2.** User characteristics

The main uses of the system will be people, who may not have any previous knowledge of computers and therefore user interface should be simple and user friendly.

**2.3** General constraint

The system should be OS independent

**3.** Requirements.

**3.1** External Interface Requirements user interface : Only one user command is required. The file names can be specified in the command line itself or the system should prompt for the input file names.

**3.2** Performance Constraints

For input files containing 30 names, the reports should be printed in less than 1 minute.

**3.3** Design constraints.

Hardware constraints : The software will be run on a workstation with 256 MB RAM running OS (eg UNIX). It will be connected to an 8 page per minute printer.

**Security :** The file in which the information is contained must be secured against malicious deformation .

**Fault Tolerance :** Data should not be corrupted in case of system crash or power failure.

**4.** Future Extension

The possible future extension would be to make it multi user.

**5.** Acceptances Criteria

Before accepting the system, the developer must demonstrate that the system works on the data of the retail store. The developer will have to show last cases that all conditions are satisfied.

**(b) Explain the software crisis from the programmer's point of view.** *6*

**Ans.** The software crisis was a term used in the early days of software engineering, before it was a well-established subject. The term was used to describe the impact of rapid increases in computer power and the complexity of the problems which could be tackled. In essence, it refers to the difficulty of writing correct, understandable and verifiable computer programs. The roots of the software crisis are complexity, expectations, and change.

Conflicting requirements have always hindered the software development process. For example, while users demand a large number of features, customers generally want to minimize the amount they must pay for the software and the time required for its development.

The causes of the software crisis were linked to the overall complexity of the software process and the relative immaturity of software engineering as a profession. The crisis manifested itself in several ways from a programmer's point of view:

- Projects running over-budget.
- Projects running over-time.
- Software was of low quality.
- Software often did not meet requirements.
- Projects were unmanageable and code difficult to maintain
- Problem of compatibility.
- Problem in documentation.
- Problem in portability.
- Problem in coordination of work of different people when a team is trying to develop software.
- Problems that arise during actual run time in the organization. Sometimes the errors are not detected during sample run.
- Problem of piracy of software.
- Customers normally expand their specifications after program design and implementation has taken place.

**Q4(a). Describe the life cycle of a computer based system. Also explain the concept of waterfall model of software life cycle.** *7*

**Ans.** The waterfall model is a sequential software development model (a process for the creation of software) in which development is seen as flowing steadily downwards (like a waterfall) through the phases of requirements analysis, design, implementation, testing (validation), integration, and maintenance.

To follow the waterfall model, one proceeds from one phase to the next in a purely sequential manner. In the waterfall model one should move to a phase only when its preceding phase is completed and perfected. Phases of development in the waterfall model are thus discrete, and there is no jumping back and forth or overlap between them.

**Now :** Refer to Chapter-1, Q.No.-11&12, Page No.-9

**(b) List various management risks in the software engineering and the corresponding techniques to manage them.** *8*

**Ans.**

| Risk | Risk Management Techniques |
|---|---|
| a) Individual shortfalls | Staffing with top talent; job matching; teambuilding; key-personnel agreements; cross-training pre-scheduling key people. |
| b) Unrealistic schedules and budgets | Detailed cost & schedule estimation; cost of design, incremental development, software reuse, requirements scrubbing. |
| c) Developing the wrong software functions | Organisation analysis; mission analysis; concept formulation; user surveys; prototyping early user manuals. |
| d) Developing the wrong user interface | Prototyping; scenarios; tasks analysis; user characterization. |
| e) Continuing stream of change requests | High change threshold; information hiding; incremental development (defer change to later increments) |
| f) Shortfalls in externally furnished components | Benchmarking; inspections; reference checking; compatibility analysis. |
| g) Shortfalls in externally performed task | Reference checking; per-ward audits; award-fee contract; competitive design or prototyping; teambuilding. |
| h) Real-time performance shortfalls | Simulation; benchmarking modeling; tuning. |

**Q5(a). What are CASE tools ? Explain the two generations of the CASE tools. With the help of an example for each, explain the broad classification / categories of the CASE tools.** *10*

**Ans.** CASE (Computer Aided Software Engineering) tools are the programs that provide support in one or more stages of system development process. The objective of CASE tools is to help system analysts and designers in developing good quality systems within the specified time and budget constraints.

Case tools are available for most of the analysis and designing work and they allow the system analysis and designers to concentrate on the creative aspects of the design.

There are two generations of CASE tools: the first generation of CASE tools are broadly classified into three groups:

**(1)** Information generation or 4GL.

**(2)** Front-end design/analysis tools.

The variety of 4GL products include the following: report generators, query languages, DBMS frontends and modeling languages. Most suffer from shortcomings they are tied too closely to a proprietary database system thereby offering a very restricted solution; they are functionally too weak to be more than a building block in a large application solution or they are not easily integrated with existing production system and data.

Design tools (first generation of CASE tools) help a user to draw blueprints or design diagrams based on some predetermined methodology. Typically, high level design documentation is provided automatically. The flow in these tools is that are standalone and their results are not easily integrated into the subsequent phases of the life cycle.

A major shortcoming of the first generation CASE products is their inability to bridge the gap between design and application generation.

The second generation CASE tools evolved into two major categories: life cycle automation and solution software.

Life cycle automation tools is aimed at data processing profession to provide general solutions to their problems.

Solution software of tools is aimed at analyst or application specialist, in a restricted domain of application, to provide fast solution to the end user. Electronic spread sheets represent such tools in the very restricted domain of financial analysis.

**Categories of CASE Tools :**

CASE tools might be classified into four broad categories according to the CASE problems on which they focus.

**(1) Front-end CASE Tools, or Upper CASE Tools**

These deal with the high-level design, specification and analysis of software and requirements. These tools include computer-aided diagramming tools oriented towards a particular programming design methodology, more recently including object-oriented design.

**(2) Back-end CASE Tools, or Lower CASE Tools**

These deal with the detailed design, coding, assembly, and testing of software. These tools may help the programmer directly.

**(3) Maintenance Tools**

These deals with software after initial release. These tools may assist in tracking, fixed and enhancement requests, porting to new platforms or performing new releases.

**(4) Support Software and Frameworks**

These provide basic functionality required in tools of type 1,2 and 3. Support software includes basic operating-system functionality as well as higher-level support such as project management and scheduling software, and database support to track different versions of software releases. Various project have been directed towards standardizing framework to support and integrate CASE applications.

**(b) Describe the concept of software reliability, software reviews and software upgradation.** ***5***

**Ans. Software Reliability :**

**First :** Refer to Chapter-7, Q.No-5, Page.No-95

**Software Reviews :** Software reviews are a : "filter" for the software process that is, reviews are applied at various points during software engineering and serve to uncover errors and defects that can then be removed. Software reviews "purify" the software engineering activities namely analysis, design, and coding. Software reviews are needed because of following reasons :

**(1)** Technical work needs reviewing for the same reason that pencil need erasers. [To err is human]

**(2)** We need reviews because although people are good at catching some of their own errors, large classes of errors escape the originator more easily than they escape anyone else.

May different types of reviews can be conducted as part of software engineering. An informal meeting around the coffee machine is a form of review, if technical problems are discussed. A formal presentation of software design to an audience of customers, management, and technical staff is also a form of review. A formal technical review (FTR) is the most affective filter from a quality assurance standpoint.

**Software Upgradation :**

Like other engineering products, software products are modified over time to provide new functions or to change existing functions. Indeed, the fact that software, is so malleable makes modification extremely easy to apply to an implementation. There is, however, a major difference between software modification and modification of other engineering products. In the case of other engineering products, modification starts at the design level and then proceeds to the implementation of the product.

In the case of software, unfortunately, people seldom proceed in an organized fashion. Although the change might be a radical change in the application, too often the implementation is started without doing any feasibility study, let alone a change in the original design. Still worse, after the change is accomplished, the modification is not even documented as specifications are not updated to reflect the change. This makes future changes more and more difficult to apply.

Successful software products are long lined. If the software is designed with care, and if each modification is thought out carefully, then it can evolve gracefully.

# CS-70 : INTRODUCTION TO SOFTWARE ENGINEERING
## June, 2007

**Note :** Question no. 1 is **compulsory**. Answer any **three** questions from the rest.

**1. (a) List the merits and demerits of Waterfall model.** *5*

**Ans. Merits :**

**Enforced discipline through documents**

- no phase is complete until the docs are done & checked by SQA group - concrete evidence of progress
- makes which costly phase easier?

**Testing is inherent in every phase**

- continuously as well as at end of phases

**Demerits :**

**1)** It is often difficult for the customer to state all requirements explicitly. Thus natural uncertainty is not covered that exists at inception of projects.

**2)** Customer must have patience as working session of program is only available later in the project. That means if a major defect is detected after delivery, it becomes nearly impossible to correct.

**3)** Importantly, rear projects rarely follow the sequential flow that this model proposes. There is iteration, but it is indirect. Thus changes can cause confusion as project proceeds. A software development life cycle(SDLC) model that is better one and overcomes disadvantages mentioned above is incremental model.

*Project which requires to be build on prototype, where end user required the first working model to be out and be tested and feedback upon that working model will give input for the next prototype to be built. Under this circumstances also, the water fall model will fail to accommodate the requirement.

* For the project development firm where many teams and team members are working at a time on many projects. Water fall model causes the personnel to wait till their turn comes. For example for certain project the requirement gathering phase is ON, so the programmer for that project need to be accommodated with some other project OR rather all the programmer have to wait till their phase started. The development firm can not afford to allow this sort of personnel (manpower) wastage.

Since, each of the above stated problems are real, however, the Water fall model paradigm has a definite and important place in software engineering work. But well suited where the requirements are rigid and know before the development start. Waterfall model is well suited for in the development of embedded softwares, and Operating System etc.

**(b) Design a system for the Hospital Management. Draw the context level and joint level data flow diagrams (DFDs) for the system and also prepare a SRS document for the same. Describe the necessary assumptions.** ***8***

**Ans.**

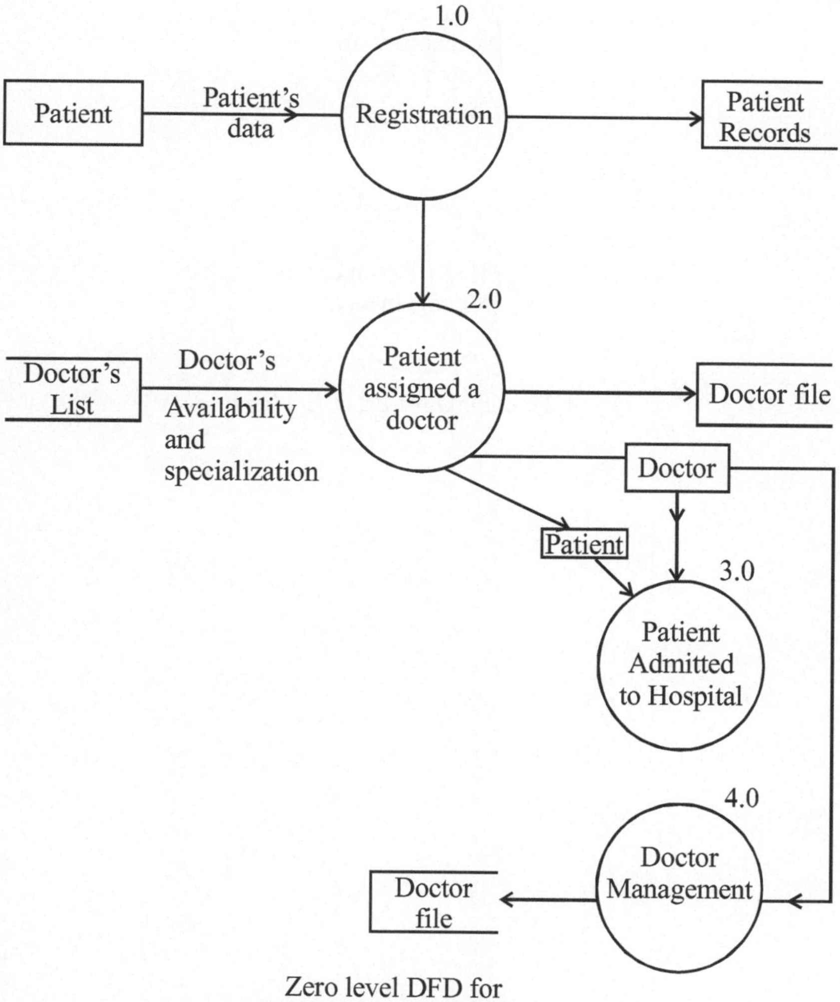


Zero level DFD for
Hospital Management System

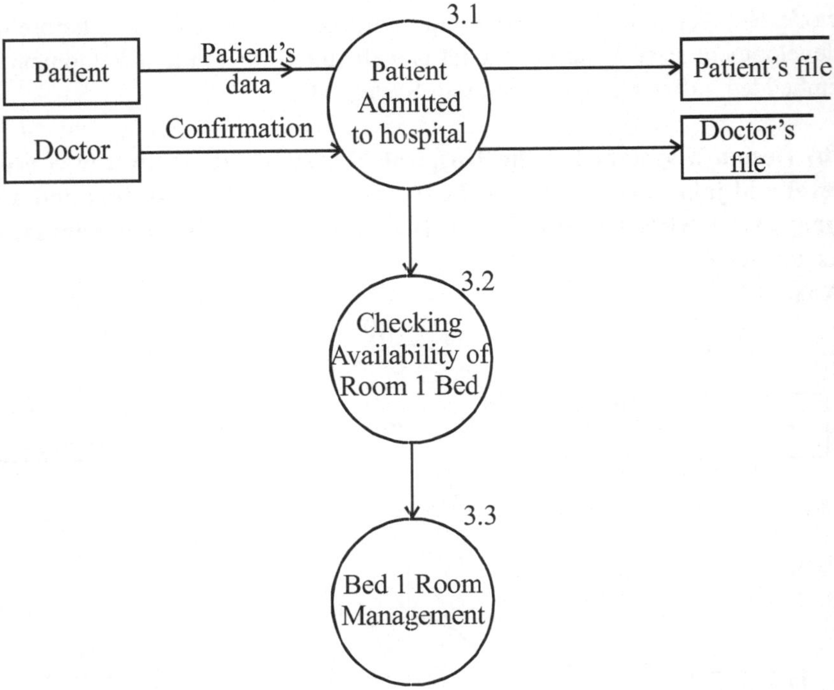


I" level DFD for Process 3.0

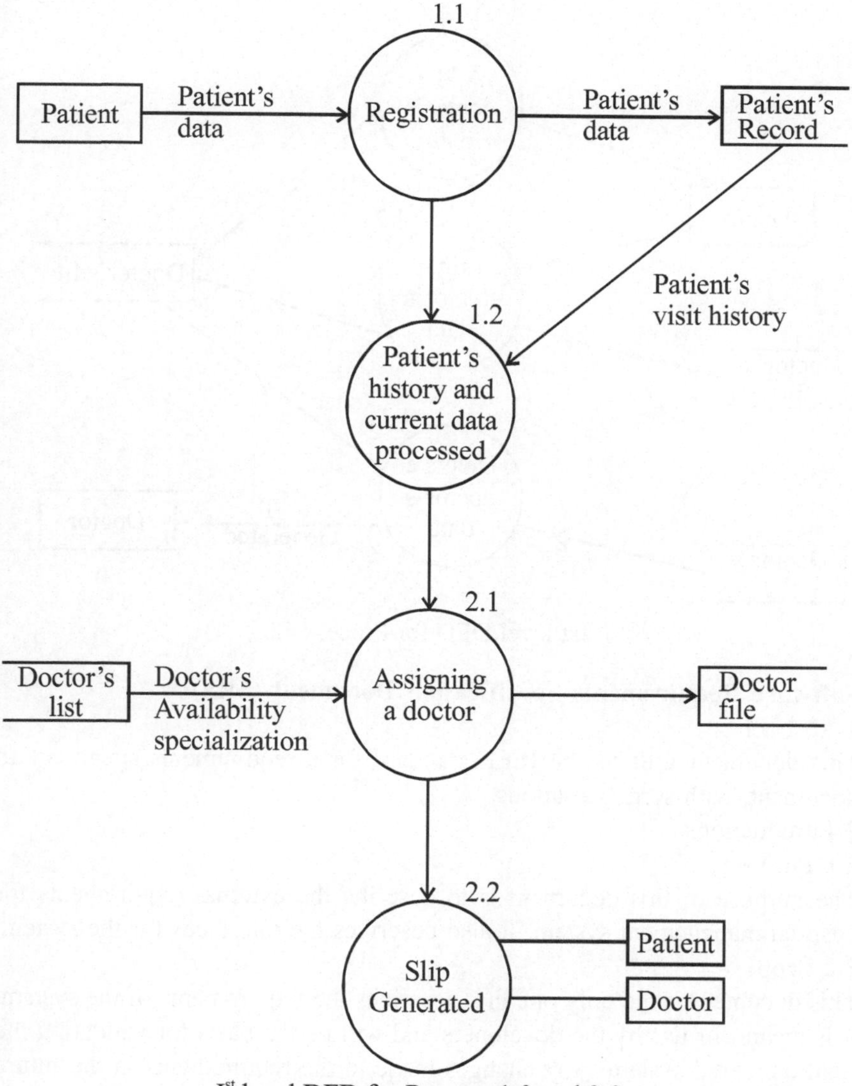


I[st] level DFD for Process 1.0 and 2.0

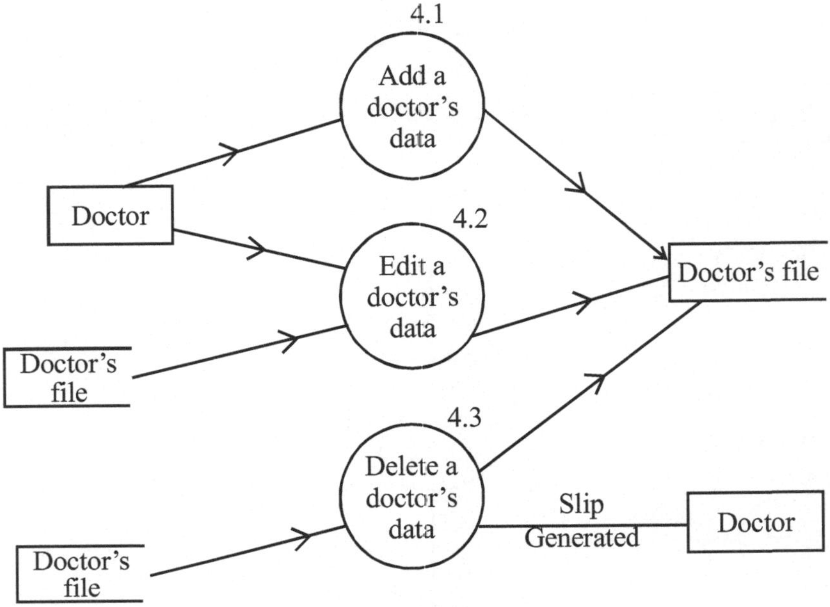


Ist level DFD for Process 4.0

**Software Requirements Specification Document (SRS)**

**1** Abstract

This document follows the IEEE standard for a requirements specification document, with some variations.

**2** Introductions

**2.1** Purpose

The purpose of this document is to describe the external requirements for hospital management system. It also describes the interfaces for the system.

**2.2** Scope

This document is the only one that describes the requirements of the system. It is meant for use by the developers and will be the basis for validating the final delivered system. Any changes made to the requirements in the future will have to go through a formal change approval process. The developer is responsible for asking for clarifications, where necessary, and will not make any alterations without the permission of the client.

**2.3** Definitions, Acronyms, Abbreviations

Not applicable.

**2.4** References

Not applicable.

**2.5** Developer's Responsibilities

The developer is responsible for (a) developing the system, (b) installing the software on the client's hardware, (c) conducting any user training that might be needed for using the system, and (d) maintaining the system for a period of one year after installation.

**3** General Descriptions

**3.1 PROBLEM STATEMENT**

Create a Management System for a hospital with the following features

- ***Registration*** - This feature allows to add/edit/delete patients in the system.
- ***Patient Management*** - Before we let a user to visit a doctor, we should classify whether he is an in-patient or an out-patient. Then basic symptoms should be captured and entered in the system. Existing patients can be searched by name, admission date, patient ID etc.
- ***Patient Visit History*** **-** Previous visit histories of the patient can be accessed
- ***Assign Doctor*** **-** Assign a patient to a doctor based on the basic information of the patient's problems. Based on the specialization and availability of the doctors, patients should be assigned.
- ***Doctor Management*** – Add/Edit/Delete the doctors working in the hospital.
- ***Bed/Room Management***– The beds or rooms in a hospital can be managed. Add/Edit/Update the rooms with details. Check availability and assign a room to in-patients
- Doctors can update the patient's record with their observations.

**3.2** User Characteristics

The main users of this system will be department secretaries, who are somewhat literate with computers and can use programs such as editors and text processors.

**3.3** General Constraints

The system should run on Sun 3/50 workstations running UNIX 4.2 BSD.(can vary)

**3.4** General Assumptions and Dependencies

Not applicable.

**4** Specific Requirements

**4.1** Inputs and Outputs

The system has inputs and produces outputs.

Input file 1: Contains the list of room numbers and their capacity; a list of all the patients in the patients file; and the list of various doctors. The format of the file is:

rooms
room1 : cap1
room2 : cap2

:

;

;

times

time1 , time2 , time3 ;

Input file 2: Contains information about the doctors visiting the hospital. For each doctor it specifies the code number, and various details.

**Reports:**

The following reports can be generated. You can implement more reports which you think can be useful.

- Utilization of doctors
- List of Patients diagnosed by a disease
- List of patients who visited during a given time period

**Output** : Error messages. At the minimum, the following error messages are to be given:

e1. Input file does not exist.

e2. Input-file-1 has error

e2.1. The code number has wrong format

e2.2. time has wrong format.

e2.3. room number has wrong format.

e2.4. capacity out of range.

e3. Input-file-2 has error

e3.1.code does not exist

..

.

**4.2** Functional Requirements

**4.3** External Interface Requirements

*The important roles associated with the system would be*

**Administrator** – Administrator will have complete control of the system. She/he can Add/Edit/Delete patients, Add/Edit/Delete Doctors, Add/Edit/Delete Beds, Search for patients, Assign patients to doctors.

**Doctor** – Doctor can access a patient's record and update his observations about the patient in that particular visit

**User Interface:** Only one user command is required. The file names can be specified in the command line itself or the system should prompt for the input file names.

**4.4** Performance Constraints

For input file 2 containing 10 patients details and their respective doctor's detail, the reports should be printed in less than 1 minute.

**4.5** Design Constraints

Software Constraints

The system is to run under the UNIX operating system.

Hardware Constraints

The system will run on a Sun workstation with 256 MB RAM, running UNIX. It will be connected to an 8-page-per-minute printer.

**5.** Acceptance Criteria

Before accepting the system, the developer must demonstrate to the user that the system works on the data for the last 4 years. The developer will have to show through test cases that all conditions are satisfied.

**(c) Define GUI and explain its various components. What types of errors do you anticipate while designing a user interface?** 7

**Ans.** Graphical user interfaces, also known as GUIs make it easier for people with little computer skills to work with and use computer software. It is a visual front to a piece of software. It links the user to the internal workings of a computer, or piece of software. Another common way of defining a GUI is by its visual elements. These visual elements simplify the job of the user.

**GUI, for example Microsoft Windows, has the following components :**

**(1)** Menus (pull down, pop up, etc)- A Menu displays a list of commands available within an application. Each menu item can be either a word or an icon representing a command or a function.

**(2)** Icons– Icons are used to provide a symbolic representation of any system/ user-defined object such or file, folder, address, book, applications and so on a specific type of icon represents different type of objects.

**(3)** Dialog Boxes – Are used to collect information from the user or to present information to the user. Dialog boxes for selecting files, options, and setting; when an option is selected, the one previously selected is turned off.

**(4)** Check lists form which the user can make multiple selections.

**(5)** Tiled windows (for views of multiple programs of data or for multiple views of single program of data block).

**(6)** Support for a pointing device, typically a mouse (especially to select and drag screen elements).

**(7)** Scroll Bars along the edges of windows to show the relative position of the content (such as end or beginning of the text) or to move to a different position (such as another part of worksheet).

**Types of errors you would anticipate while designing a user interface**

**(1)** Has each user interface been tailored to the intelligence, educational background and environmental pressures of the end user?

**(2)** Are the outputs of the program meaningful, non abusive, devoid of computer gibberish and so on?

**(3)** The input fields must have a validation check. In case the user, enters alphabets in a numeric field, an error message must be displayed.

These are fields that cannot be left blank by a user, appropriate messages must be generated if they are left blank.

**(d) Discuss the various steps to be followed for successful project implementation.** *10*

**Ans.** A crucial phase in the system left cycle is the successful implementation of the new system. The implementation includes all those activities that take place to convert from the old system to the new one the new system may be completely new or replacing an existing manual or automated system or it may be major modification to an existing system. In either case, proper implementation becomes necessary so that a reliable system based on the requirements of the organisation can be provided. Successful implementation may not guarantee improvement in the orgnaisation using the new system, but improper installation will prevent it. It has been observed that even the best system cannot show good result if the analysts managing the implementation do not attend to every important details. This is an area where the system analysts need to work with utmost care.

**Three aspects of implementation that should be considered are:**

- Training personnel
- Conversion procedures
- Post-implementation review

In each area, the particular elements of that aspect are discussed, along with the methods of handling each aspect efficiently and effectively.

**Training of personnel involved with system**

Even well designed system can succeed or fail because of the way they are operated and used. Therefore, the quality of training received by the personnel involved with the system in various capacities helps or hinders and may even prevent the successful implementation of management information system. Both systems operators and users need training.

**Systems Operators Training**

Running of the system successfully depend on the personnel working in the computer centre. They are responsible for providing the necessary support. Their training must ensure that they are able to handle all possible operations, both routine and extra-ordinary in nature.

**User Training**

Use may be trained on use of equipment, particularly in the case where, for example, a micro-computer is in use and the individual involved is both operator and user. In such cases, user must be given training on how to operate the system also. Questions that may be trivial to the analyst, such as how to turn on a terminal, how to insert a diskette into a micro-computer, or when it is safe to turn off equipment without danger of data loss, are significant problems to new users who are not familiar with computers.

**Training Methods :** Training of operators and users can be organised in several different ways. Most important are:
**(i)** Vendor and in-service training
**(ii)** In-house training

**Conversion Methods**

Conversion is the process of changing from the old system to the new one. It must be properly planned and executed. Four methods are common in use. They are: parallel systems, direct conversion, pilot system and systems phase-in. Each method should be considered in the light of the opportunities that it offers and problems that it may create. However, it may be possible that sometimes, we may be forced to apply one method over others, even though other methods may be more beneficial. In general, systems conversion should be accomplished in shortest possible time. Long conversion periods create problems for all persons involved including both analysts and users.

**Parallel Systems**

The most secure method of converting from an old to new system is to run both systems in parallel. Under this approach, users continue to operate the old system in the usual manner but they also start using the new system. This method is the safest one because it ensures that in case of any problems in using the new system, the organisation can still fall back to the old system without loss of time and money.

**Direct Conversion**

This method converts from the old to the new system abruptly, sometimes over a weekend or even overnight. The old system is used until a planned conversion day, when it is replaced by the new system. There are no parallel activities. The organisation relies full on the new system. The main disadvantages of this approach are: no other system to fall back on, if difficulties arise with new system. Secondly, wise and careful planning is required.

**Pilot System**

Pilot approach is often preferred in the case of the new system which involves new techniques or some drastic changes in organisation performance. In this method, a working version of the system is implemented in one part of the organisation, such as a single work area or department. The users in this area are aware that they are piloting a new system and that changes can be made to improve the system. Based on the feedback, changes are made and the system is installed in the remaining departments of the orgnaisation, either all at once (direct conversion method) or gradually (phase-in method). This approach provides experience and live test before implementation.

**Phase-in Method**

This method is used when it is not possible to install a new system throughout in organisation all at once. The conversion of files, training of personnel or arrival of equipment may force the staging of the implementation over a period of time, ranging from weeks to months. It allows some users to take advantage of the new system early. Also it allow training and installation without unnecessary use of resources.

**Conversion and Operation Plans**

After the system conversion is completed using any one of the methods mentioned above, the conversion plan starts. In the conversion plan, all the activities that must occur to implement the new system are properly defined and put it into operation. It identifies the persons responsible for each activity and includes a time schedule for each activity.

During the pre-implementation stages, when the conversion is being planned, analysts should prepare a list of all tasks, including the following:

- List all files of conversion
- Identify all data required to build new files during conversion
- List all new documents and procedures used during conversion
- Identify all controls to be made during conversion
- Assign responsibility for each task
- Verify conversion schedules

The conversion plan should anticipate possible problems and methods for controlling them. The missing documents, mixed data formats between current and new files, errors in data translation and situations that were overlooked during systems development are the common problems. The conversions manager must guard against the omission of steps in the conversion. This managers is also responsible for reviewing conversion plans, verifying the delivery of equipment, software and preparing the site.

**Site Preparation**

A major aspect of conversion is the preparation of the systems site. Preparation activities include electrical and air–conditioning preparation, site layout and installation of the equipment. It is the best to have the site preparation completed prior to the arrival of the equipment, since vendors are not in favour of delivering the system if the construction work is going on.

If the system is micro-computer, little sit preparation work is needed. However, the electric lines should be checked to ensure that they are free of static or power fluctuations. It is desirable to install a "clean" line that is not shared by any other equipment. Static electricity is very harmful for computers. Carpet should be avoided in the computer room. If carpet is necessary, it should be the anti-static type that will not allow static build-up.

The site layout should allow sufficient space for moving equipment in and setting it up for normal operation. Vendors will provide clearance requirements for performing service and maintenance and for air circulation. These requirements must be strictly adhered to or warranties can be voided and maintenance discontinued until specifications are met.

**File and Data Conversion**

Data and file preparation consumes a large proportion of conversion time. Not only must the data be converted to a format acceptable in the new system, but analysts must ensure that this is due without loss of detail or accuracy. By using record counts, financial controls and hash totals, analysts are able to detect correct problems quickly, before they get out of control, even if the conversion involves data transmission.

**Post Implementation Review**

After the system is implemented and conversions complete, a review should be conducted to determine whether the system is meeting expectations and where improvements are needed.

**2. (a) For the creation of a quality product, a quality process is necessary. Describe how CMM ensures the quality of software development process.** *6*

**Ans.** Refer to Chapter-1, Q.No.-9, Page No.-8

**(b) Differentiate between following:** *9*

**(i) Testing and Debugging**

**Ans. Testing – Debugging**

**(1)** Testing starts with the known conditions, users predefined procedures has predictable outcomes, only whether or not the program passes the test is unpredictable.

Debugging starts from unknown initial conditions and the end cannot be predicted except statistically.

**(2)** Testing can and should be planned, designed and scheduled. Procedures for debugging cannot be so constrained.

**(3)** Testing is a demonstration of errors whereas debugging is a deductive process it find out exact location of errors and remove it.

**(4)** Much of the test execution and design can be automated whereas automated debugging is still a dream.

**(5)** Testing can be done by an outsiders but debugging must be done by a person of the software company usually the programmers himself.

**(ii) Reverse Engineering and Re Engineering**

**Ans. Reverse engineering** (RE) is the process of discovering the technological principles of a device or object or system through an abductive analysis of its structure, function and operation. It often involves taking something (e.g. a mechanical device, an electronic component, a software program) apart and analyzing its workings in detail, usually to try to make a new device or program that does the same thing without copying anything from the original. Reverse engineering is the process of analyzing a subject system to create representations of the system at a higher level of abstraction.It can also be seen as "going backwards through the development cycle".In this model, the output of the implementation phase (in source code form) is reverse engineered back to the analysis phase, in an inversion of the traditional waterfall model.Reverse engineering is a process of examination only: the software system under consideration is not modified (which would make it reengineering).

Less formally, reengineering is the modification of a software system that takes place after it has been reverse engineered, generally to add new functionality, or to correct errors.

This entire process is often erroneously referred to as reverse engineering; however, it is more accurate to say that reverse engineering is the initial examination of the system, and reengineering is the subsequent modification.

**(iii) Compiler and Interpreter**

**Ans.**

| Compilers | Interpreter |
|---|---|
| 1) Scans the entire programs first and translates it into machine code.<br>2) Converts the entire program to machine code, when all the syntax errors are removed execution takes place.<br>3) Slow for debugging<br>4) Execution time is less | 1) Translates the programs line by line<br>2) Each time the program is executed, every line is checked for syntax error and then converted to equivalent machine code.<br>3) Good for fast debugging.<br>4) Execution time is more. |

**3. (a) Mention any five types of risks that a software development project faces and their management techniques.** *10*

**Ans.** Refer to Dec-2006, Q.No.-4(b), Page No.-248

**(b) Explain any five salient features of Object Oriented Programming with example.** *5*

**Ans. Object-oriented programming** (OOP) is a programming paradigm that uses "objects" to design applications and computer programs. It utilizes several techniques from previously established paradigms, including inheritance, modularity, polymorphism, and encapsulation. Object-oriented programming may be seen as a collection of cooperating *objects*, as opposed to a traditional view in which a program may be seen as a list of instructions to the computer. In OOP, each object is capable of receiving messages, processing data, and sending messages to other objects. Each object can be viewed as an independent little machine with a distinct role or responsibility.

**Fundamental concepts of Object Oriented Programming**

**1. Class :** A class defines the abstract characteristics of a thing (object), including the thing's characteristics (its attributes or properties) and the things it can do (its behaviors or methods or features). For example, the class Dog would consist of traits shared by all dogs, for example breed, fur color, and the ability to bark.

**2. Object :** A particular instance of a class. The class of Dog defines all possible dogs by listing the characteristics that they can have; the object Lassie is one particular dog, with particular versions of the characteristics. A Dog has fur; Lassie has brown-and-white fur. In programmer jargon, the object Lassie is an instance of the Dog class. The set of values of the attributes of a particular object is called its state.

**3. Inheritance :** In some cases, a class will have "subclasses," more specialized versions of a class. For example, the class Dog might have subclasses called Collie, Chihuahua, and Golden Retriever. In this case, Lassie would be an instance of the Collie subclass. Subclasses inherit attributes and behaviors from their parent classes, and can introduce their own. When an object or class inherits its traits from more than one ancestor class, and neither of these ancestors is an ancestor of the other, then it's called multiple inheritance. For example, independent classes could define Dogs and Cats, and a Chimera object could be created from these two which inherits all the (multiple) behaviour of cats and dogs.

**4. Encapsulation:** Conceals the exact details of how a particular class works from objects that use its code or send messages to it. So, for example, the Dog class has a bark() method. The code for the bark() method defines exactly how a bark happens (e.g., by inhale() and then exhale(), at a particular pitch and volume). Timmy, Lassie's friend, however, does not need to know exactly how she barks. Encapsulation is achieved by specifying which classes may use the members of an object. The result is that each object exposes to any class a certain interface — those members accessible to that class.

**5. Polymorphism:** Polymorphism is the ability of behavior to vary based on the conditions in which the behavior is invoked, that is, two or more methods, as well as operators (such as +, -, *, among others) can fit to many different conditions. For example, if a Dog is commanded to speak() this may elicit a Bark; if a Pig is commanded to speak() this may elicit an Oink. This is expected because Pig has a particular implementation inside speak() method. The same happens to class Dog. Considering both of them inherit speak() from Animal(), this is an example of Overriding Polymorphism.

**4. (a) What is 4GL? What are its limitations?** ***5***

**Ans.** Refer to June-2005, Q.No-3(b), Page No.-208

**(b) Explain any two project scheduling techniques with examples.** ***10***

**Ans. Project scheduling** is part of project management, which relates to the use of schedules such as Gantt charts and Pert chart to plan and subsequently report progress within the project environment

1.The **Program Evaluation and Review Technique** commonly abbreviated **PERT** is a model for project management. PERT is basically a method to analyze the tasks involved in completing a given project, especially the time needed to complete each task, and identifying the minimum time needed to complete the total project.

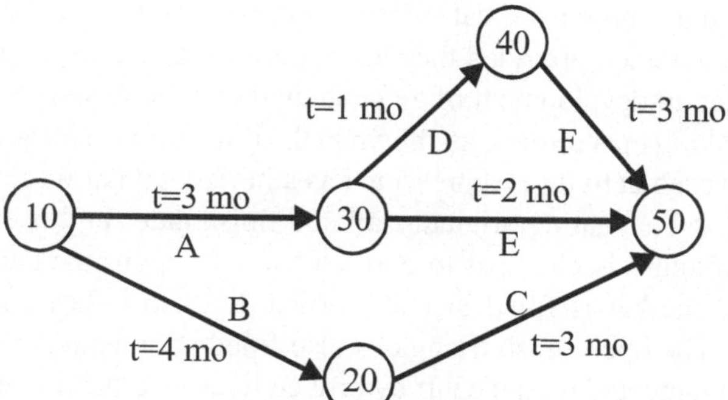


PERT network chart for a seven-month project with five milestones (10 through 50) and six activities (A through F).

The main feature of PERT analysis is a network diagram that provides a visual depiction of the major project activities and the sequence in which they should be completed. Activities are defined as distinct steps toward completion of the project that consume either time or resources. The network diagram consists of arrows and nodes and can be organized using one of two different conventions. The arrows represent activities in the activity-on-arrow convention, while the nodes represent activities in the activity-on-node convention. For each activity, managers provide an estimate of the time required to complete it.

The sequence of activities leading from the starting point of the diagram to the finishing point of the diagram is called a path. The amount of time required to complete the work involved in any path can be figured by adding up the estimated times of all activities along that path. The path with the longest total time is known as the critical path. The critical path is the most important part of the diagram for managers since it determines the completion date of the project. Delays in completing activities along the critical path will necessitate an extension of the final deadline for the project. If a manager hopes to shorten the time required to complete the project, he or she must focus on finding ways to reduce the time involved in activities along the critical path.

**2. Gantt chart:** A graphic device that depicts tasks, machines, personnel, or whatever resources are required to accomplish a job on a calendar-oriented grid. Charts may be provided for various managerial levels and responsibilities, but detailed planning occurs at the lowest organizational level. Performance may be monitored and controlled throughout the organization.

The Gantt chart is an effective tool for planning and scheduling operations involving a minimum of dependencies and interrelationships among the activities. The technique is best applied to activities for which time durations are not difficult to estimate, since there is no provision for treatment of uncertainty. On the other hand, the charts are easy to construct and understand, even though they may contain a great amount of information. In general, the charts are easily maintained provided the task requirements are somewhat static. An initial step in development of a Gantt chart may be to specify the tasks or activities making up a project, as shown in the illustration. The amount of time required for each activity is represented as a horizontal bar on the chart, with open triangles designating original start and finish dates in this example. The open start triangle is changed to a filled triangle upon inauguration of the activity, and the bar is filled in with vertical lines to indicate progress and completion. The open finish triangle is also filled upon completion. Slippage times are documented on the chart by broken lines, and the diamond symbols are employed to indicate rescheduled work. The vertical line on the chart is the current-date indicator and indicates present and future status of the project as of that date.

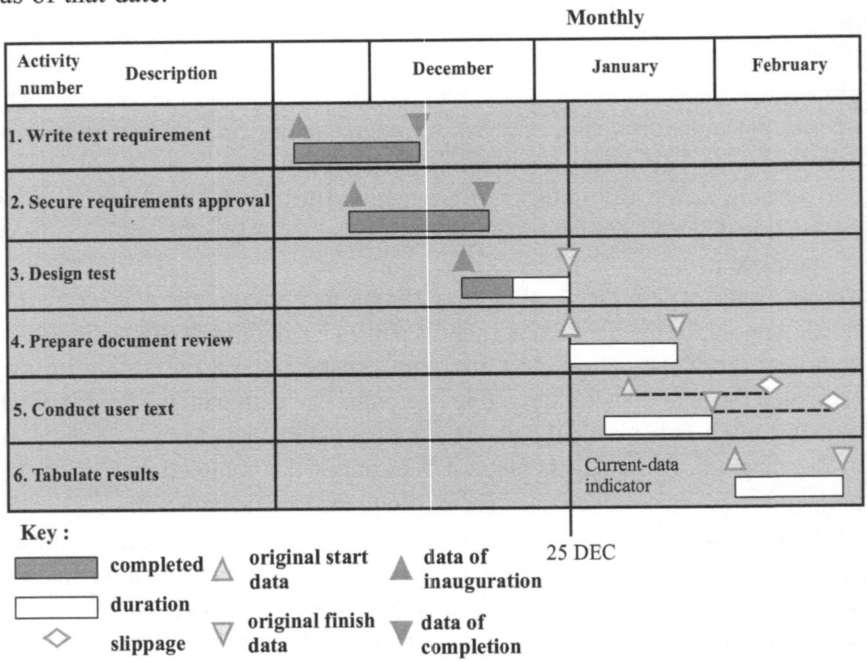


**Example of a Gantt bar Chart**

**5. Write short notes on the following with suitable example, if any:** *15*

**(a) Software Quality Assurance**

**Ans. Software Quality Assurance** (**SQA**) consists of the software engineering processes and methods used to ensure quality. SQA encompasses the entire software development process, which may include processes such as reviewing requirements documents, source code control, code reviews, change management, configuration management, release management and of course, software testing.

Software quality assurance is related to the practice of quality assurance in product manufacturing. There are, however, some notable differences between software and a manufactured product. These differences all stem from the fact that the manufactured product is physical and can be seen whereas the software product is not visible. Therefore its function, benefit and costs are not as easily measured.

**Now :** Refer to Chapter-3, Q.No.-5, Page No.-43

**(b) Software Crisis**

**Ans.** Refer to June-2005, Q.No.-1(c), Page No.-204

**(c) CASE Tools**

**Ans.** Refer to Chapter-8, Q.No.-1&2, Page No.-98

# CS – 70: INTRODUCTION TO SOFTWARE ENGINEERING
## December, 2007

*Note: Question number 1 is* ***compulsory****. Attempt any* ***three*** *questions from the rest.*

**Q1. (a) Design a system for the study center management for IGNOU. Draw the Data Flow Diagrams (DFDs) at least till level-2 and also prepare an SRS document for the same. If any assumptions are made, list them all.**

**Ans.** The software requirement specification is the produced at the culmination of the analysis task. The function and performance allocated to software as part of system engineering are refined by establishing a complete information description, a detailed functional description, a representation of system behavior, an indication of performance requirement and design constraint, appropriate validation criteria and other information pertinent to requirements. Software requirement specification (and/or prototype) is conducted by both the software developer and the customer. Because the specification forms the foundation of the development phase, extreme care should be taken in conducting the review.

The review is first conducted at a macroscopic level; that is reviewers attempt to ensure that the specification is complete, consistent and accurate when the overall information, function. And behavioral domains are considered.

Once the review is complete, the software requirement specification is "signed-off" by both the customer and the developer. The specification becomes a "contract" for software development. Request for changes in requirement after the specification is finalized will not be eliminated.

**1. Introduction of the software:** It specifies the goals and objectives of the software.

**2. Information description:** It provides the detailed description of the problem that the software must solve.

**3. Functional Description:** It deals with the each function design constraints are stated and justified performance and characteristics are stated one and more diagrams are included to graphically represent the overall structure of the software.

**4. Behavioral Description:** Behavioral description examines the operation of the software as a consequence of external events and internally generated control characteristics.

**5. Validation Criteria:** It is probably the most important and ironically the most often neglected section of software requirement specification validation criteria acts as an implicit review of all the requirements.

**6. Bibliography:** The bibliography contains references to all documents that relate the software. These include other software engineering documentation, technical references, vendor literature and standards.

**7. Appendix:** The appendix contains information that supplements the specifications. Tabular data, detailed description of the algorithms, charts, graphs and other material are presented as appendix.

**SRS of the IGNOU Study Centre Management:**

**Introduction:** Through this software I want to serve almost every information regarding Student Management System for IGNOU Study Centre to the general public as per their requirements.

**Information:** User can register as a vendor and customer. When user register as customer he will be given user id and password so that he can access in future to get information related about booking, enquiry and maintenance of all record of user as well as customer. When user registers as a vendor he/she will also be given a userid and password so that he can give the details related to the mobile.

**Function:** After the user gets registration he can access the facilities provided on this project. The entire user is search at a time in room as well as hotel facilities. User also can demand for another room to changing the types of current room.

**Behavior:** According to behavioral description this software will provide output in response of input, which is being provided by the user. Here output of the hotel description generated when the customer enroll the hotel.

**Validation criteria:** In this we describe the successful implementation, testing, functions, performance and constraints related to our software. The implementation will be done after completion of the entire software so that user can travel all around the website together the information contained in the site. The testing of the software will be done on various levels by providing the input constraints to check the validity of the required function. The overall performance of the software will be parameterized by above mentioned validation criteria.

**Appendix:** To specify the hotel description we have to use various types of tabular data, charts and other material during the course of software development. So that every user or vendor could know the real data references. These all will be included in report generation after the development of software. The proposed system contains the following main processes:

**PROJECT DESCRIPTION**

**PROJECT MODULES:** The proposed project will be mainly divided into partially dependent and partially independent modules as:

**1.** LOGIN SYSTEM

**2.** MRO DETAIL
**3.** COUNCELLOR DETAIL
**4.** PROGRAM DETAIL
**5.** STUDENT SCHEDULE
**6.** STUDENT ATTENDANCE
**7.** CHANGE PASSWORD
**8.** GENERATE BATCH & SERIAL NO.
**9.** COURSE DETAIL

**MODULES DESCRIPTION**

**1. LOGIN SYSTEM:**

· As the system is candidate dependent so proper username and password based candidate system is necessary to accomplish the fact. Whatever and however the system is to maintain the candidate status and specific user enabled services as well as to track the candidates surfing for security and privacy reason.

· Based on the login he is linked to the appropriate page.

· A login status and log is maintained to find who and from where login for which purpose and also to find the number of time a user logins.

**2. MRO DETAIL:**

· Mro means like a teacher Mrodetails, mroname, Mroid, Maddress, Mrostate.

· Different types of languages known by the teacher like .NET, JAVA2.0, C++ etc.

**3. COUNSELLOR DETAIL:** These modules define all the record of canceller like counselor unique id, counselor name counselor phone number, counselor address.

**4. PROGRAM DETAIL:** These modules define Program information. In this module academic can add new program record, update its existing record and deleted its Information. Program id, Program name, course code, theory class scheduling, practical class scheduling are the main attributes of the program modules.

**5. STUDENT SCHEDULE:** year, month, program, semester, coursecode, batch, time, days.

**6. STUDENT ATTENDANCE:** C_year, S_month, Program, CourseCode, batch.batchno, sdate, stime, sno.

**7. CHANGE PASSWORD:** This module provides forgotten password. If password is forgotten then we can change it.

**8. Batch Creating and Serial No.:** This module provides create a batch and serial number.

**9. COURSE DETAIL:** This module define course information. In this module academic can add new course record, update its existing record and deleted its Information. Course id, Course name, Course Code, Theory Class

Scheduling, Practical Class scheduling are the main attributes of the Course Modules.

**O LEVEL DFD:**

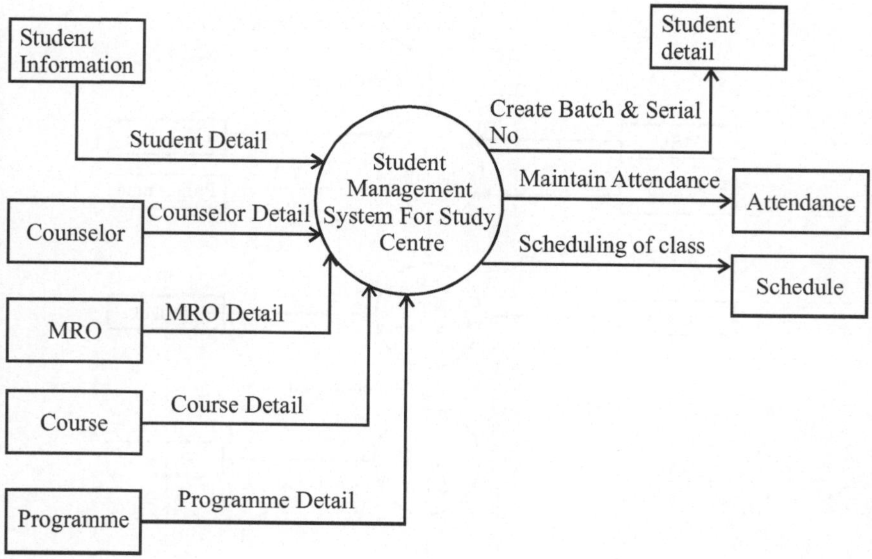


**1st LEVEL DFD:** This DFD shows all the processes together with all the data stores (tables). It shows the true data flow i.e. how data is actually flowing in the system. Data is coming from which table and going into which table is clearly shown by this DFD. This DFD is the main reference for the development of the system. After understanding the whole system, the application developer will fall back upon this DFD during the Development phase.

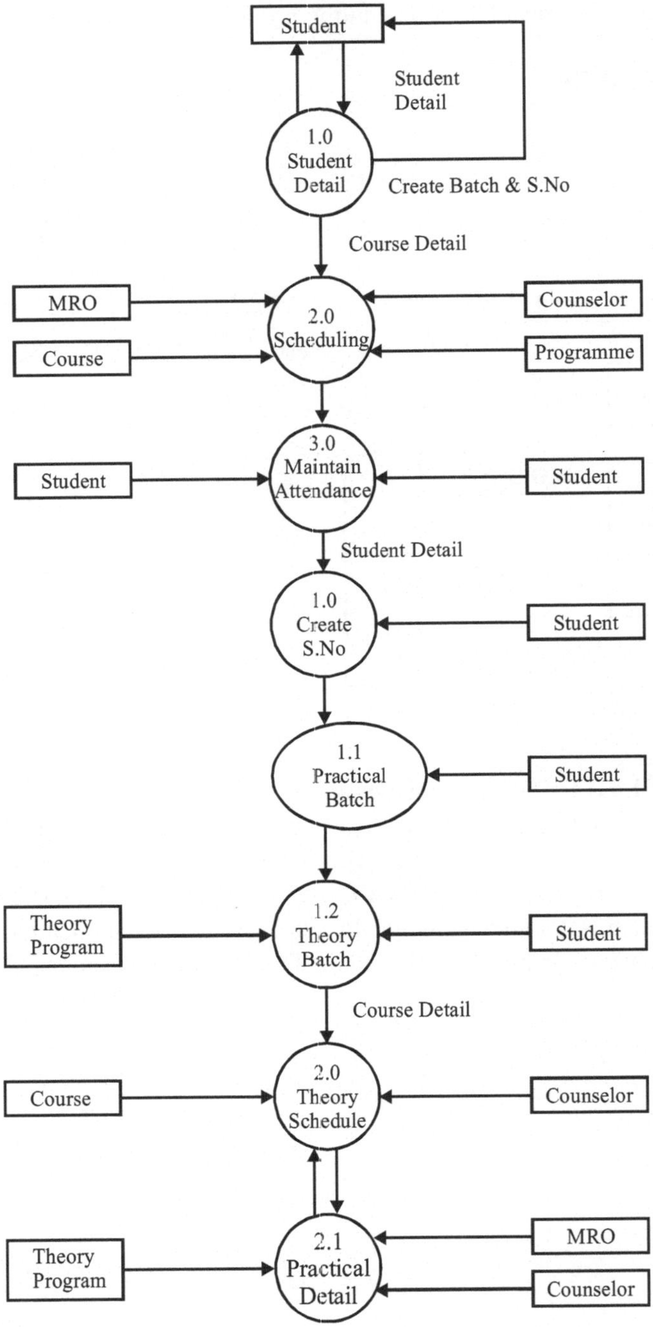


**(b) Design an ERD for the question 1(a). List the various entities and**

**the attributes used in it and describe how they are related. Also, show the cardinality on the ERD.**

**Ans. ENTITY RELATIONSHIP DIAGRAM:**

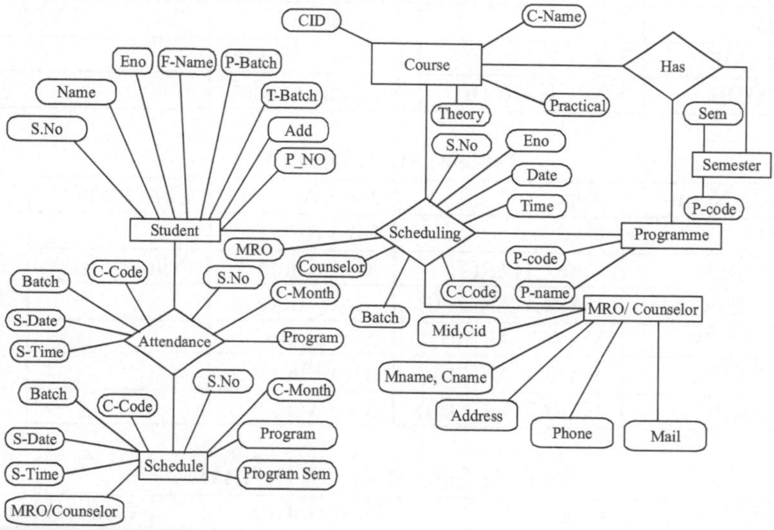


**DATABASE TABLE:**

**Table Structure:** There will be 9 tables in the STUDENT MANAGEMENT SYSTEM FOR IGNOU STUDY CENTRE the normalized form of the table with their structure is described as under:

**Table 1: User Login**

| Field Name | Type | Description | Constraint |
|---|---|---|---|
| USERNAME | VARCHAR(20) | User name | |
| PASSWORD | VARCHAR(20) | Password | |

**Table 2: Course Detail**

| Field Name | Type | Description | Constraint |
|---|---|---|---|
| PID | INT | Program ID | PRIMARY KEY |
| CNAME | VARCHAR(100) | Course name | |
| CCODE | VARCHAR(20) | Course Code | |
| TCLASS | NUMERIC(12) | Theory Class | |
| PCLASS | NUMERIC | Practical Class | |

**Table 3: Program Detail**

| Field Name | Type | Description | Constraint |
|---|---|---|---|
| PID | INT | Program Id | PRIMARY KEY |
| PNAME | VARCHAR(80) | Program Name | |
| PCODE | VARCHAR(10) | Program Code | |

**Table 4: MRO DETAIL**

| Field Name | Type | Description | Constraint |
|---|---|---|---|
| MID | INT | Mro Id | |
| MNAME | VARCHAR(50) | Mro Name | Primary Key |
| MADDRESS | VARCHAR(100) | Mro Address | |
| MSTATE | VARCHAR(50) | Mro State | |
| MPHONE | VARCHAR(50) | Mro Phone | |
| MMAIL | VARCHAR(100) | Mro Mail | |

**Table 5: COUNSELOR DETAIL**

| Field Name | Type | Description | Constraint |
|---|---|---|---|
| CID | INT | Counselor | |
| CNAME | VARCHAR(50) | Counselor Name | Primary key |
| CADDRESS | VARCHAR(100) | Counselor Address | |
| CPHONE | VARCHAR(21) | Counselor Phone | |
| CMAIL | VARCHAR(100) | Counselor Mail | |

**Type 6: PROGRAM DETAIL**

| Field Name | Type | Description | Constraint |
|---|---|---|---|
| PROGRAM | VARCHAR | Program | |
| BATCH | CHAR | Batch | |
| TIME | VARCHAR(50) | Time | |
| CON-CHARGE | INTEGER | ConCharge | |
| AMT-MRO | INTEGER | AmountMro | |
| AMT-CON | INTEGER | Amount Counselor | |

**Type 7: Study Center**

| Field Name | Type | Description | Constraint |
|---|---|---|---|
| NAME | VARCHAR(100) | Name | |
| CODE | VARCHAR(10) | Student Code | |
| ADDRESS | VARCHAR(100) | Student Address | |
| PHONE | VARCHAR(20) | Student Phone | |
| E_MAIL | VARCHAR(50) | Student mail | |
| SITE | VARCHAR(50) | Student Site | |

**Type 8: ATTENDANCE**

| Field Name | Type | Description | Constraint |
|---|---|---|---|
| C_YEAR | VARCHAR | Year | Primary key |
| S_MONTH | VARCHAR | Month | Primary key |
| PROGRAM | VARCHAR | Program | Primary key |
| BATCH | VARCHAR | Batch | Primary key |
| BATCH_NO. | INTEGER | Batch no. | Primary key |
| S_DATE | INTEGER | Date | Primary key |
| S_TIME | VARCHAR | Time | Primary key |
| SNO. | INTEGER | Sno. | Primary key |
| COURSE | VARCHAR | Course | Primary key |

**Type 9: DELETE STUDENT**

| Field Name | Type | Description | Constraint |
|---|---|---|---|
| SNO. | INTEGER | Serial No. | |
| YEAR | VARCHAR | Year | |
| ENMO | VARCHAR | Enrollment No. | |
| PROGRAM | VARCHAR | Program | |
| BATCH-P | VARCHAR | Batch Practical | |
| BATCH-T | VARCHAR | Batch Theory | |
| OLDPROGRAM | VARCHAR | Old Program | |
| MEDIUM | VARCHAR | Medium | |
| STUDY | VARCHAR | Study | |
| REG_CODE | VARCHAR | Region Code | |
| NAME | VARCHAR | Name | |
| FNAME | VARCHAR | Fname | |
| ADDRESS1 | VARCHAR | Address | |
| ADDRESS2 | VARCHAR | Address | |
| ADDRESS3 | VARCHAR | Address | |
| CITY | VARCHAR | City | |
| STATE | VARCHAR | State | |
| PIN | VARCHAR | Pin Code | |
| FAX | VARCHAR | Fax | |
| EMAIL | VARCHAR | Email | |

**(c) With the help of an example application, explain the prototyping model.**

Refer to Page-13, Q.No.-14

**Q2. (a) List the options that are available for applying human resources to a new software project that will require 'x' people working for 'y' years.**

Refer to Dec-2006, Q.No.-1(a)

**(b) "An application that is used by programmers qualifies as user friendly by virtue of different properties than an application that is used by expert programmers." In support of the above statement explain the features of the user-friendliness of any application.**

**Ans. User Friendliness of any Application:** If a program is not "User friendly", it is offer doomed to failure, even if the functions that it performs are valuable. Usability is an attempt to quantify "user friendliness" and can be measured in terms of following four characteristics:

**1.** The physical and intellectual skills required to learn the system.

**2.** The time required to become moderately efficient in the use of the system.

**3.** The net increase in productivity (over the approach that system replaces) measured when the system is used by someone who is moderately efficient.

**4.** A subjective assessment (sometimes obtained through a questionnaire) of users attitudes towards the system.

The programmer can depict better the various need for user friendliness for any software application as he has to design effective user interfaces accordingly in every process of development of software solution.

**Q3. (a) List and explain both the project scheduling tools (charting techniques). Also mention their pros and cons.**

Refer to June-2007, Q.No.-4(b)

**(b) Discuss the significance of the modularity with the help of an example application. In this context, also explain the "divide and conquer" technique.**

**Ans. Modularity:** Modularity is the single attribute of software that allows a program to be intellectually manageable.

Modularity is dividing software into separately named and addressable components, called modules that are integrated to satisfy problem requirements. The number of control paths, span of reference, number of variables and overall complexity would make understanding easy when we divide the software into small modules.

Let C(x) be a function that defines the perceived complexity of a problem x and E(x) be a function that defines the effort (in time) required to solve a problem x.

For two problems, p1 and p2, if

$C(p1) > C(p2)$

then it follows that

$E(p1) > E(p2)$

Now it will take more time to solve a difficult problem, i.e.

$C(p1 + p2) > C(p1) + C(p2)$

It implies that the perceived complexity of a problem that combines p1 and p2 is greater than the perceived complexity when each problem is considered separately.

Considering above problem, the new equation will be as follows:

$E(p1 + p2) > E(p1) + E(p2)$

This leads to a "divide and conquer" conclusion i.e., it is easier to solve a complex problem when you break it into manageable pieces.

The result expressed in inequality has important implications with regard to modularity and software.

Thus, if there is a number of M modules (divided) then that would result in minimum development cost (conquer) but we have to make necessary sophistications to predict M separate modules.

**Q4. (a) List and explain the four major tasks of the periodic review of a project under development.**

**Ans.** Refer Similar Question.

**(b) Define 4 GLs. Discuss how 4 GLs help to solve the complex problems. Also list the limitations.**

Refer to June-2005, Q.No.-3(b)

**Q5. (a) List the typical phases of the SDLC and their associated development tools.**

**Ans.**

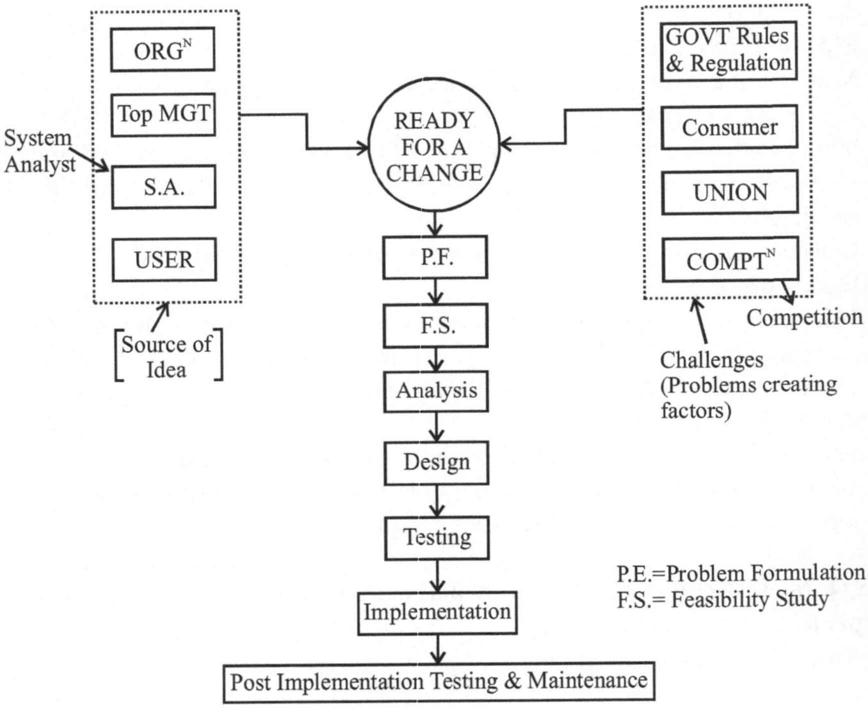


**System Development Life Cycle (SDLC):** It is the study of all phases of development from birth to death.

| Phase | Main Consideration/Key Question | Result/Output |
|---|---|---|
| **1. Problem Formulation/ Initial Study/ Preliminary Survey/ Recognition of Needs** | What problem is exactly? | Problem Specification Statement of scope and objectives |
| **2. Feasibility Study:** Evaluation of existing system and procedure, analysis of alternatives and cost estimation etc. | Whether the solution is possible? If not, then how can the problem be redefined. | **Approval of System:** Technical, behavioral, feasibility, economical feasibility. Final specification of the system on the basis of cost/benefit analysis and their performance. SRS is approved. |
| **3. Analysis:** Through the study of existing system and data collection and detailed evaluation. | What are the facts? In order to solve the problem what must be done? | **Logical model of the system:** Example: Data Dictionary, Data Flow-diagram, Decision tables etc. |
| **4. Design:** Do needful to design the system or to implement the logical model already developed in the previous phase. | How is it to be done? What is the system (processing flow)? | The physical system is ready as per the logical model for testing implementation specification. |
| **5. Testing:** Test whether the system is performing as per the expectations and needs or not? If not modify accordingly. | Whether the intended objective is fulfilled or not? How ready are programs for acceptance test? | System is ready for implementation security, quit and operating procedures formal system test. |
| **6. Implementation:** User training, file/system conversion | What is the actual operation? | User training, User manual and detailed documentation. |
| **7. Post Implementation and Maintenance:** Evaluation maintenance and up gradation | Is the system running properly? Is there any need of modification/up gradation? | End users are satisfied. User standards met. |

**(b) With the help of the ideal project progress and usual project progress charts explain the concept of project tracking.**

**Ans. Project Tracking:** The project schedule provides a road map for a s/w project manager. If it has been properly developed, the project schedule defines the tasks and milestones that must be tracked and controlled as the project proceeds. Tracking can be accomplished in a number of different ways:

**1.** Conduction periodic project status meeting in which each team member reports progress and problems.

**2.** Evaluating the results of all reviews conducted throughout the s/w engineering process.

**3.** Comparing actual start date to planned start date for each project task listed in the project table.

**4.** Meeting informally with practitioners to obtain their subjective assessment of progress to date and problems on the horizon.

| **Work Task** | **Planned Date** | **Actual Date** |
|---|---|---|
| **1.** Identify needs and benefits of customers and s/w product | Wk1, d1 | Wk1, d1 |
| **2.** Define desired output/control and inputs | Wk1, d4 | Wk2, d1 |
| **3.** Define the functionality and behavior of s/w project etc. | Wk2, d5 | Wk2, d6 |

# CS – 70: INTRODUCTION TO SOFTWARE ENGINEERING
## June, 2008

*Note: **Question number 1 is compulsory.** Attempt any **three** questions from the rest.*

**Q1. (a) A news magazine is published monthly and is sent by post to its subscribers. Two months before the expiry of subscription, a reminder is sent to the subscribers. If subscription is not received within a month, another reminder is sent. If renewal subscription is not received upto two weeks before the expiry of the subscription, the subscriber's name is removed from the mailing list and the subscriber is accordingly informed.**

**Design the DFDs (till level 2) and also prepare the SRS document for the same. List all assumptions, if any.**

**Ans.**

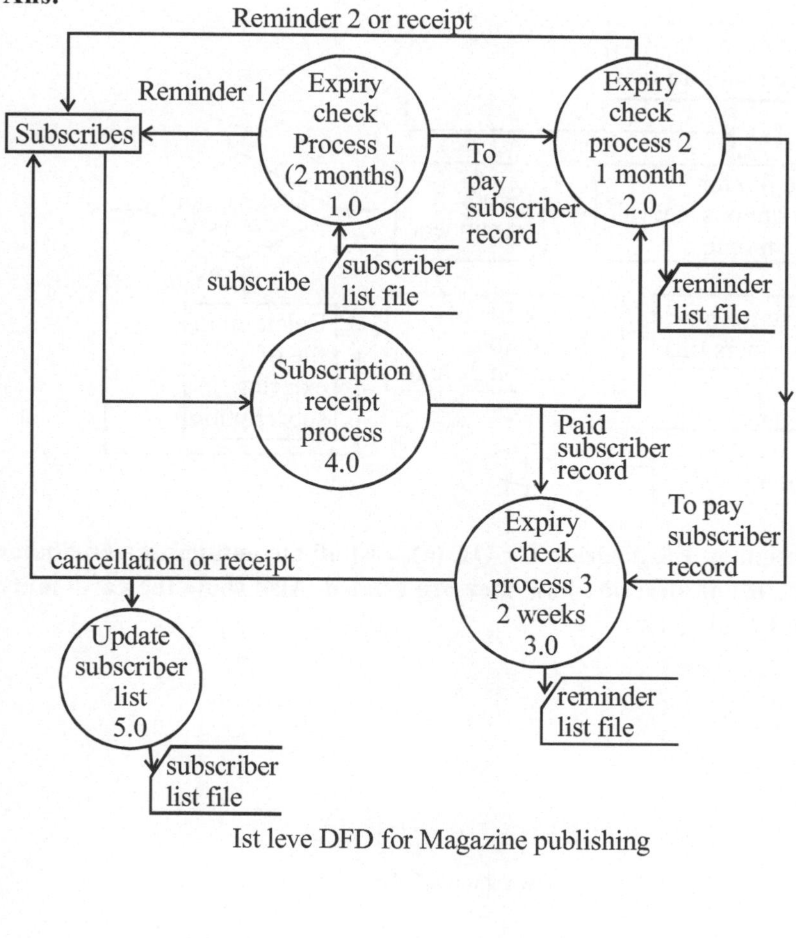


Ist leve DFD for Magazine publishing

**The SRS of Magazine Publishing house is based on the following functional activities** ***<u>Now Refer block 1 Cs-70 page No-13 Chapter-1</u>***

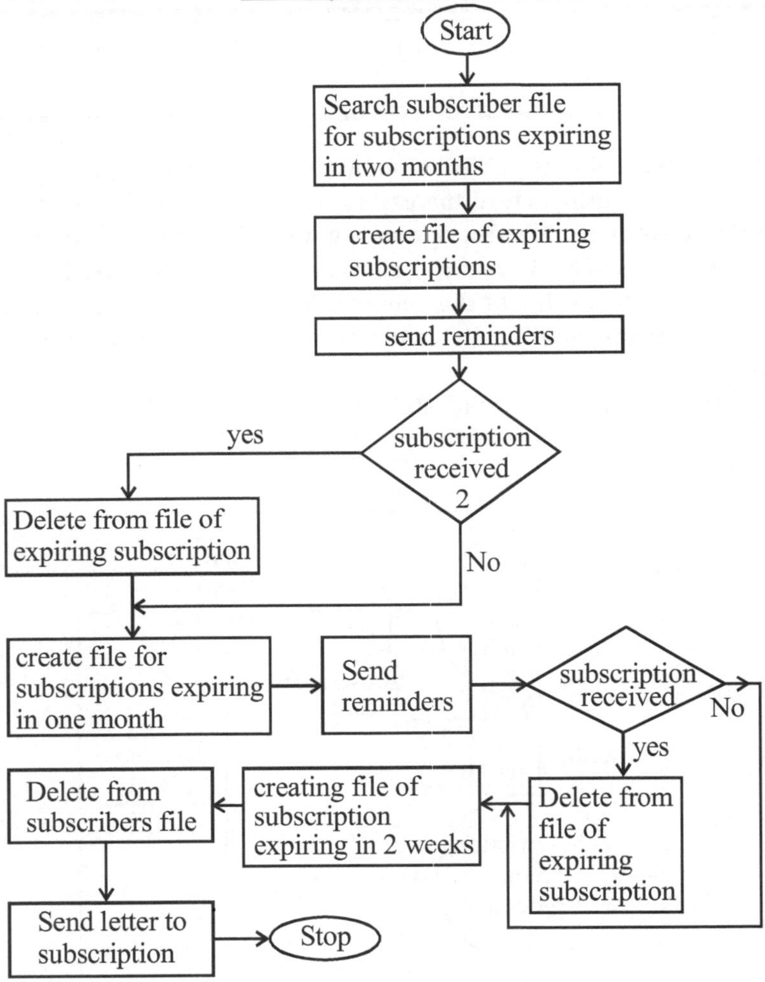


**(b) Design an ER diagram for Q1. (a). List all the entities, the attributes used in it and describe how they are related. Also show the cardinality on the ER diagram.**

**Ans.**

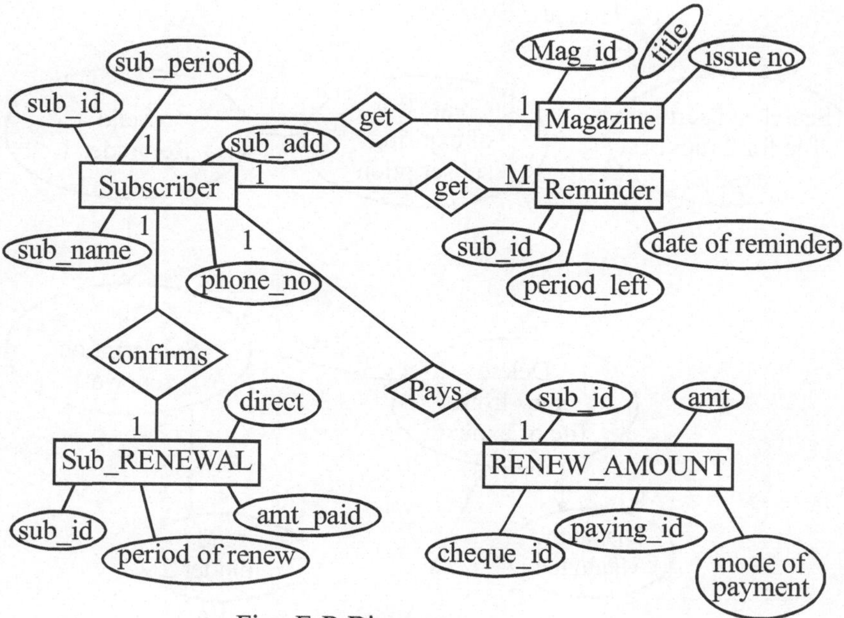


Fig : E-R Diagram

**The cardinality on ER Diagram is as follows**

**1)** Subscriber to Reminder is 1 : Many

**2)** Subscriber to sub_renewal is 1:1

**3)** Subscriber to magazine is 1:1

**4)** Subscriber to renew_amount is 1:1

**(c) Draw the PERT chart for the problem outlined in Q1. (a). Also, show the critical path.**

PERT chart

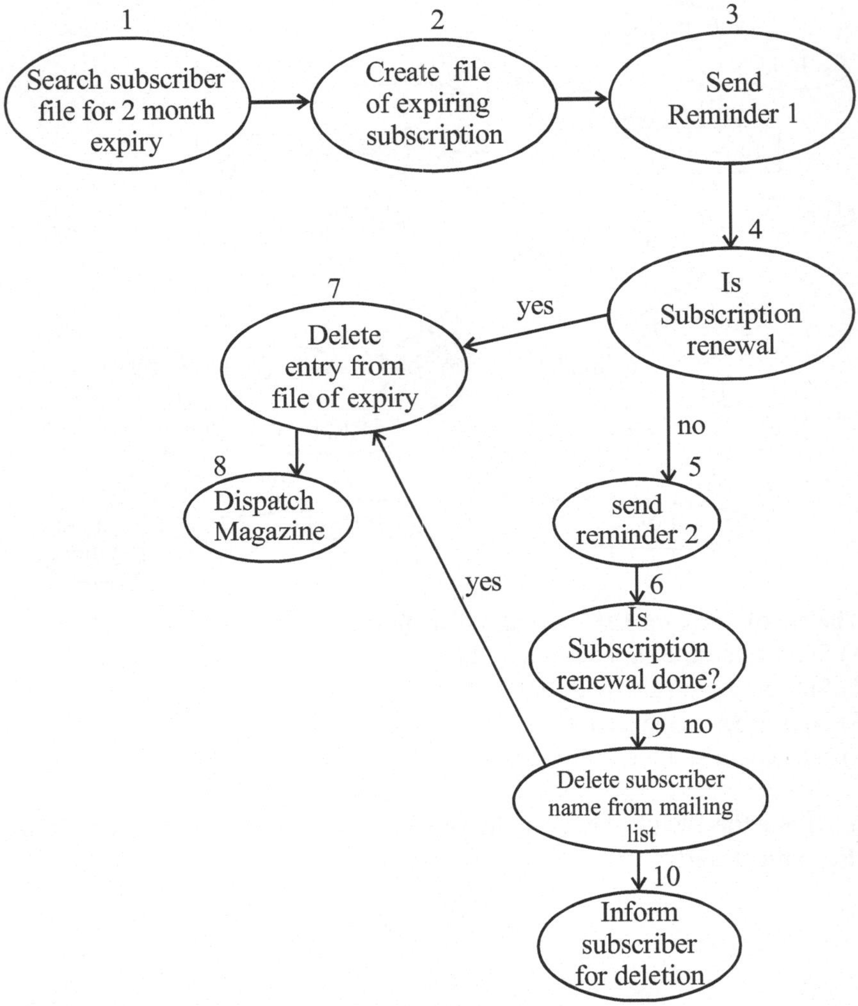


**The Critical Path**

| Process 1→2→3→4→7→8 |
|---|

i.e the shortest path for renewal of magazine subscription

**Q2. Explain the following terms, with appropriate examples:**

**(a) Data Abstraction**

**Ans.** It refers to the ability to define abstract data types or ADTs that encapsulates some data together with a set of well defined operations. Such user defined data types can represent objects in software.

In software engineering, data abstraction is the process of defining a data type together with the principle of data hiding. Data hiding ensures that the internal structure of the ADT can be altered without any fear of breaking the programs that call the functions provided for operations on that ADT.

**(b) Cohesion and Coupling**

Refer to Page-72, CS-70

**(c) Test Case**

**Ans.** A test case is one test that has a high probability of finding an as-yet undiscovered error. The essence of software testing is to determine a set of test cases for the item being tested. A test case has an identity and it is associated with program behaviour. A good test case is one that has a high probability of finding an as yet undiscovered error. Two different categories of test case design are:

**1.** White Box Testing

**2.** Black Box Testing

**(d) Class-diagram**

**Ans.** A class is an object oriented concept that encapsulates the data and procedural abstractions that are required to describe the context and behaviour of some real world entity.

The class diagram for defining attribute and operations in software engineering approach is as follows:

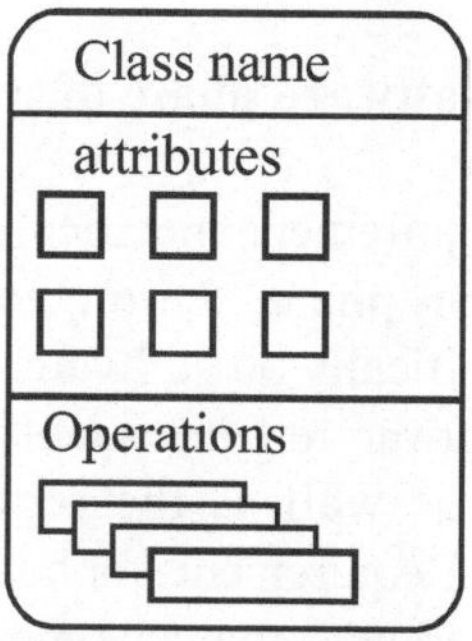


Fig : Class Diagram

Practically the class diagram in software development is implemented like this as shown in figure below:

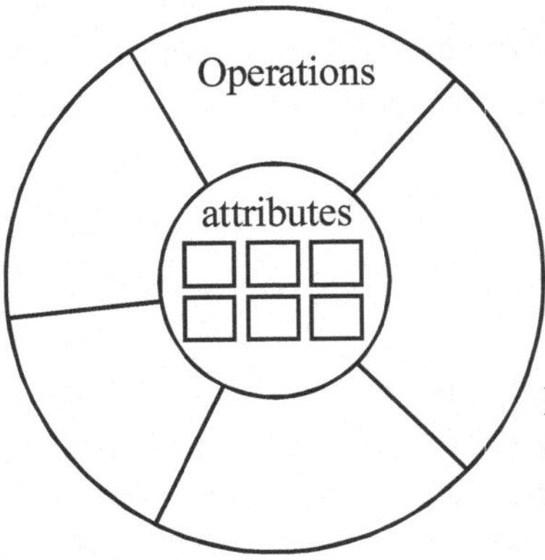


Fig : Class Diagram
(as Practically implemented in s/w engineering)

**(e) Project Scheduling**
Refer to Page-266

**Q3. Identify and elaborate all the risk factors in software project. Also, explain the techniques that can be used to manage them.**
**Ans. Risk Factors:** Refer to Page-33
**Techniques to Manage Risks:** Refer to Page-35

**Q4. (a) What are the different categories of CASE tools? What are its benefits? Also, write the limitations of CASE tools.**
**Ans. CASE Tools:** Refer to Page-99

**(b) Explain the following software phase of waterfall model:**
**(i) Design and specification**
**Ans.** This phase includes requirement specification phase and design phase. In **requirement specification phase,** the requirements gathering process is intensified and focused specifically on software. To understand the nature of programs to be built, the software engineer must understand the information domain for the software, as well as the required function, behaviour, performance and interfacing. Requirements for both the system and the software are documented and reviewed with the customer.
**Design Phase:** Software design is actually a multi step process that focuses on four distinct attributes of a program: data structure, software architecture, interface representations and procedural detail. The design process translates requirements into a representation of the software that can be accessed for quality before code generation begins. Design is documented and becomes a part of the software configuration.

**(ii) Delivery and maintenance**

**Ans.** Software will undergo change after it is delivered to the customer. Change will occur because errors have been encountered, because the software must be adapted to accommodate changes in its external environment (example: a change required because of a new operating system or peripheral device) or because the customer requires functional or performance enhancements.

Software maintenance is a task that every development group has to face, when the software is delivered to the customer's site, installed and it is operational.

The release of software inaugurates the operation and maintenance phase of the life cycle. Software maintenance includes error correction enhancement of capabilities, deletion of obsolete capabilities and optimization.

**Q5. (a) Discuss the concept of modularity with appropriate examples.**

**Ans. Modularity:** Refer to Page-71

**(b) Elaborate on the various steps required for successful project implementation.**

**Ans. Project Implementation Steps:** Refer to Page-260

## CS – 70: INTRODUCTION TO SOFTWARE ENGINEERING
**December, 2008**

*Note: **Question number 1 is compulsory.** Attempt any **three** questions from the rest.*

**Q1. A library (Audio & Video) has branches in different cities of India. Each branch has the popular/current sets of audio & video CDs, DVDs, cassettes etc. All branches have access to the database of all stock items available in the branch libraries. Each branch maintains the database of their customers which is updated weekly to the centralized database. Each branch can normally give items on rent as well as sell the items. Every branch can borrow the items from nearby branch, by taking permission from Head Office at Delhi.**

**Answer the following based upon the above given specifications:**

**(a) Design the DFDs upto two levels.**

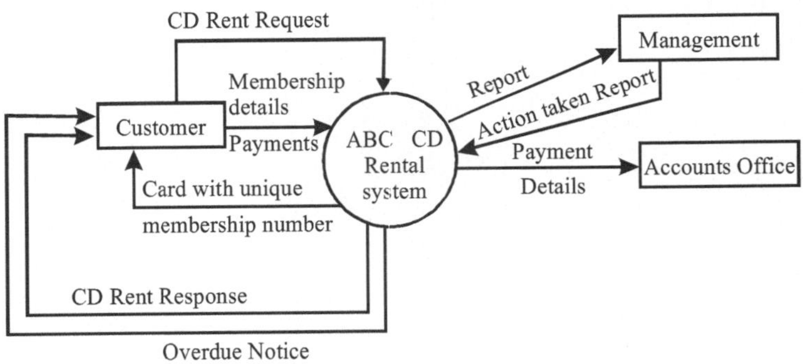


Context Level DFD

Level 1 DFD

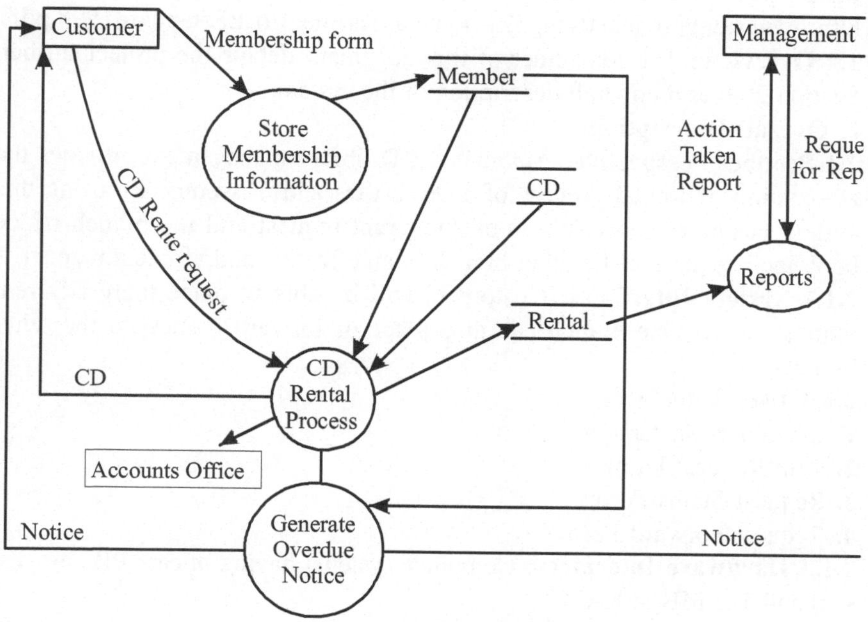


Level 2 DFD for CD Rental process

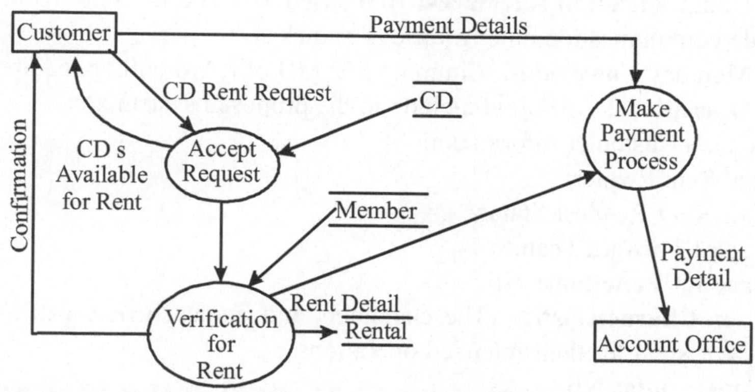


**(b) Prepare SRS document. List assumptions, if any.**

**Ans. SRS Document for CD Library:**

**1. Introduction:**

**1.1 Purpose:** The proposed system is used to develop automated library management of CDs. The intended audience fro this document is the developers who will be working on the project.

**1.2 Definitions, Acronyms and Abbreviations:**

CD – Compact Disc

DVD – Digital Versatile Disc

**1.3 References:**

IEEE Recommended Practice for SRS 30 May 07

http://www.engr.uvic.ca/seng321/home/assessment/IEEEstandard1998.pdf

**1.4 Overview:** The remainder of this document details the project further. Section 2 gives an overall description of the system.

**2. Overall Description:**

**2.1 Product Perspective:** Automated CD library management provides the automation of Rental process of CDs, DVDs and Cassettes. By using this system customer can easily book their rent request and the branch office book their request to the other branch in an effective and efficient manner.

**2.1.1 System Interfaces:** Customers will be able to place there CD rent request easily. One branch can also place or forward request to the other branch.

**2.1.2 User Interfaces:**

1. Customer Master Info
2. Rent Request Form
3. Request Status Form
4. Request Forward Form

**2.1.3 Hardware Interfaces:** Computer systems having atleast PIV processors and 512 MB of RAM.

**2.1.4 Software Interfaces:** NIL

**2.1.5 Communication Interfaces:** Web based user interfaces are required to provide communication among various branches.

**2.1.6 Memory Constraint:** Minimum 512 MB of RAM will be required.

**2.1.7 Operations:** Operation include in the proposed system are:

1. Maintain Customer Information
2. Place Rent Request
3. Show Rent Request Status
4. Request Forward Feature

**2.2 Product Functions:** NIL

**2.3 User Characteristics:** The customers and branch officer can interact with the system for their intended operations.

**2.4 Constraints:** NIL

**2.5 Assumption and Dependencies:** NIL

**2.6 Apportioning of Requirements:** NIL

**(c) Design an ER diagram. List all, the entities, attributes, cardinality keys, strong and weak entities etc.**

**Ans.**

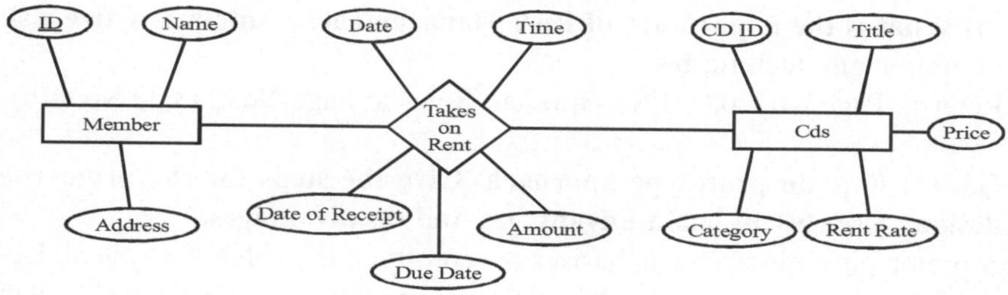


**(d) Draw PERT chart for the problem and show the critical path.**
**Ans.**

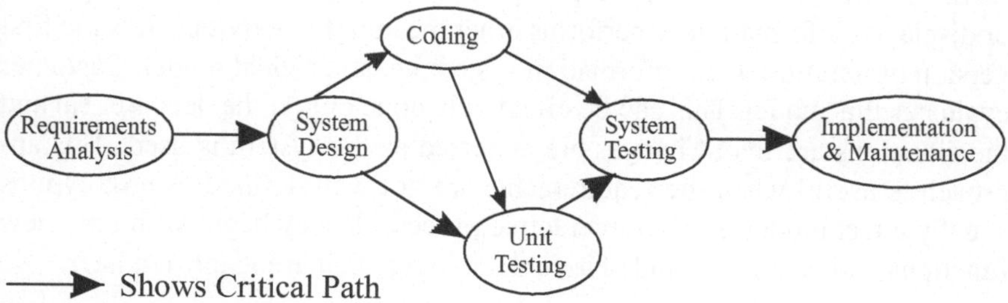


**(e) Specify the software life cycle model suitable for the specification. Also, explain briefly about the phases of this model.**

Refer to Page No.-190, Q.No.-1(b)

**Q2. (a) What is feasibility study? Why is it important for system design? How does cost benefit analysis contribute to it?**

It is an investigation to determine whether a proposed project, system, etc. would be desirable, cost effective, etc. to develop or put into operation or the analysis of a problem to determine if it can be solved effectively. The operation, economical and technical aspects are part of the study.

It is important for system design because the Results of the study determine whether the solution should be implemented. If not, then no need for system design.

Since cost plays quite an important role in deciding the new system, it must be identified and estimated properly. Costs vary by type and consist of various distinct elements. Benefits are also of different type and can be grouped on the basis of advantages they provide to the management. So, cost benefit analysis is done during economical feasibility study.

**(b) What is the importance of Risk Management? Explain any five risk management techniques.**

Refer to Page No.-208, Q.No.-3(a) and Refer to Page No.-248, Q.No.-4(b)

**Q3. (a) Explain prototype approach. Give the steps for the prototype design. Also, list its main advantages and disadvantages.**

A prototyping approach emphasizes the construction model of a system. Designing and building a scaled-down but functional version of a desired system is the process known as Prototyping. A prototype is a working system that is developed to test ideas and assumptions about the new system. It consists of working software that accepts input, performs calculations, produces printed or displayed information or performs other meaningful activities. It is the first version or iteration of an information system i.e. an original model. Customer evaluates this model. This can be effectively done only if the data are real and the situations are live. Changes are expected as the system is used. This approach is useful when the requirements are not well defined. A prototype is usually a test model. It is an interactive process. It may begin with only new functions and can be expanded to include others that are identified later.

**Typically, these are the steps in the prototype design:**

· Identify the user's known information requirements and features needed in the system.

· Develop a working prototype.

· Use the prototype, noting needed enhancements and changes. These expand the list of known system requirements.

· Revise the prototype based on information gained through user experience.

· Repeat these steps as needed to achieve a satisfactory system.

As these steps suggest, prototyping is not a trial-and-error development process. Before staring the system design work, user and system analyst sit together and discuss to identify the requirements. These discussions form the basis for the construction of the prototype. System analyst is fully responsible for the development of the working prototype.

**(b) Define software crisis and explain six cases which contribute to a software crisis.**

Refer to Page No.-197, Q.No.-4(b)

**Q4. (a) How is coupling and cohesion related? Explain each with an example.**

Refer to Page No.-73, Q.No.-4

**(b) Explain the cyclomatic complexity with a suitable example.**

Refer to Page No.-82, Q.No.-6

**(c) How are CASE tools useful for project management? List their disadvantages.**

Refer to Page No.-213, Q.No.-6(a)

**Disadvantages of CASE Tools:** The following are some of the disadvantages of CASE tools:

**1.** Complex functionality of an organization.

**2.** Many project management problems are not amenable to automation. Hence, CASE tools can't be used in such cases.

**3.** CASE tools cannot automatically provide a functional, relevant system.

**4.** They cannot easily interface with database and 4GL.

**5.** They cannot radically transform the systems analysis and design process.

**6.** They cannot automatically force analysts to use a prescribed methodology when one does not exist.

**7.** There can be many project problems which are not amenable to automation. Thus CASE tool implementation fails.

**Q5. Explain the following with an example:**

**(a) Bottom-up Design approach**

**Ans.** Refer to Page No.-85, Q.No.-9

**(b) LOC based estimation**

**Ans.** LOC based estimation is typically related with effort. It is easy to determine, automate and enforce. The LOC is counted excluding the comments and code created by application generators. Simple to measure estimation method and is more familiar and understandable

but is less accurate than FP. Stating the size of an application in LOC would not be a good measure for understanding any system. The basic assumption is that all lines would be of the same complexity. It is language dependent and may not be easily understood, as there is no way to express the difference between complexity and functionality! Especially for projects where a piece of application is getting modified, it is easier to measure the size of project using impacted lines of code rather than FP.

**(c) Project Scheduling**

Refer to Page No.-266, Q.No.-4(b)

**(d) Data Dictionary**

In database management systems, a file that defines the basic organization of a database. A data dictionary contains a list of all files in the database, the number of records in each file, and the names and types of each field. Most database management systems keep the data dictionary hidden from users to prevent them from accidentally destroying its contents.

Data dictionaries do not contain any actual data from the database, only bookkeeping information for managing it. Without a data dictionary, however, a database management system cannot access data from the database.

**(e) Test Cases**

Refer to Page No.-287, Q.No.-2(c)

# CS – 70: INTRODUCTION TO SOFTWARE ENGINEERING
## June, 2009

***Note: Question number 1 is compulsory.*** *Attempt any* ***three*** *questions from the rest.*

**Q1. (a) Discuss the types of problems which may contribute in maximum cases to a software crisis from the following points of view:**
**(i) Programmer (ii) User**
Refer to Page No.-204, June-2005, Q.No.-1(c)

**(b) Design a system for a courier company. Draw DFD's for the system till level 2 and also prepare the SRS document for the same. Describe the assumptions made if any.**
**Ans.**

Level O DFD

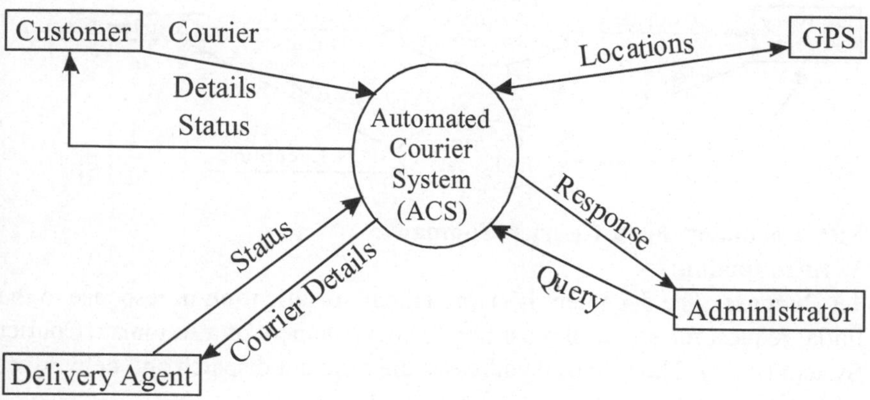

Level I DFD

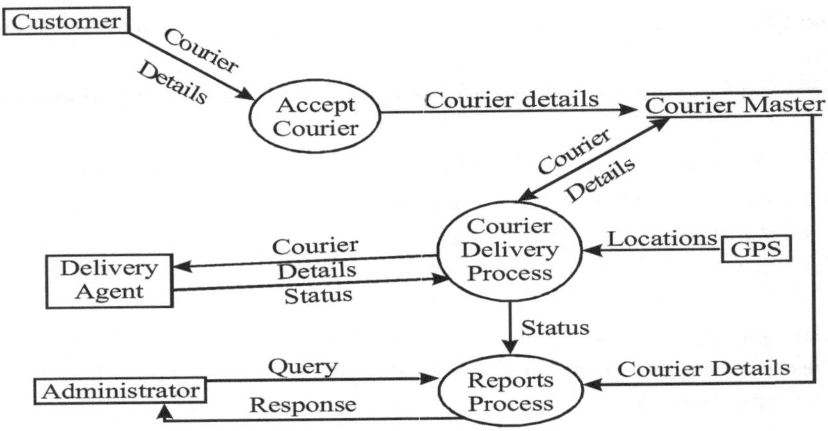


Level 2 DFD For Courier Delivery Process

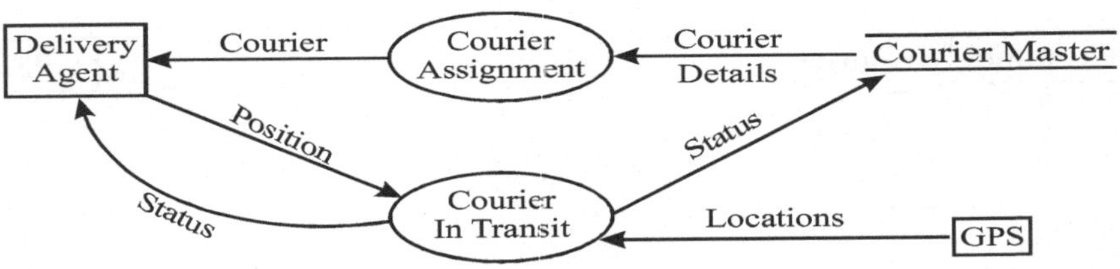


## SRS Document for a Courier Company:

### 1. Introduction:

**1.1 Purpose:** The document is **requirement specification** in response to the initial request for proposal regarding the development of a Automate Courier System (ACS). The proposal addresses the efficient dispatch and delivery of couriers.

The intended audience for this document is the developers who will be working on the project. The system will dispatch the couriers in an efficient manner to ensure the **courier** closest to the pickup location is dispatched.

The couriers carry a hard held device that is connected wirelessly to the ACS. The ACS monitors the location of the couriers.

**1.2 Definitions, Acronyms and Abbreviations:** Handheld – Device similar to a PDA that is used buy the bicycle couriers to receive pickup requests. ACS – Automated Courier System. The **software** system used to manage the delivery requests.

GPS – Global positioning system. Used to determine an exact location.
GUI – Graphical user interface.

**1.3 References:** IEEE Recommended Practice for **Software** Requirements Specifications. 30 May 2007 http://www.engr.uvic.ca/seng321/home/assessment/IEEE Standard 1998.pdf.
http://www.csc.uvic.ca/jtaekema/seng321/doc/cli/RFP.pdf.

**1.4 Overview:** The remainder of this document details the project further. Section 2 gives an overall description of the system.

**2. Overall Description:**

**2.1 Product Perspective:** Automated Courier System (ACS) provides an automated same day delivery service to the Recipients. Some components of the system allow users to place orders via web interface and track the location of their parcels; others instruct couriers on pick-up and drop-off locations as well as the most efficient route to take.

**2.1 System Interfaces:** On the client side of the ACS users will be able to place orders through the web interface. Their orders will be sent directly for processing and storage. Once processed, the order information will be passed to the ACS, which will use GPS data from handheld devices carried by couriers to determine where the order should be sent.

**2.1.2 User Interfaces:** Four classifications of user will have access to the ACS. The client will have access to the web interface allowing him or her to place orders and track their progress in real-time. The client will have password protected access to the status of their order and will be responsible for granting the recipients access to that information. Delivery agents will access the ACS through their handled devices, which they will use to manage all aspects of delivery.

**2.1.3 Hardware Interfaces:** The handheld device carried by the delivery agent will have an on board GPS system as well as a wireless transceiver. The GPS system will update the handheld devices current position each time it gets a new order from the ACS or sends an order status update to the server. It will also update its GPS coordinates once every 15 minutes to insure constant communication of the location of the **courier**. Upon completion of an order the recipients signature will be recorded using the touch screen on the handheld device. The recipients signature as well as a comment by the **courier** will be sent via cell phone transceiver to the ACS.

**2.1.4 Software Interfaces:** A Graphic User Interface (GUI) will allow customer representatives direct access to the ACS. Any order status changes through this GUI will be updated immediately in the ACS. The handheld device will automatically prioritize the curriers orders to simplify his or her interaction with the device. The current task will be displayed as being at the top of a list of all the orders for that currier. Priority of deliveries will be determined by the route calculator. Once the order has been placed they will be given an order number and password to be allowed access to the status and location of their assigned **courier** as well as their order status.

**2.1.5 Communications Interfaces:** The information will be used to update the web interface with the latest information on the status of the clients order.

**2.1.6 Memory Constraints:** The handheld devices will require enough memory to store the necessary map information as well as the order information. The only other memory requirements for the handheld devices will be for the storage of their operating system. The server will require enough memory to store all current orders as well as backups. An external memory device could be used to keep a history of all completed orders.

**2.1.7 Operations:** Operations performed within the ACS include:

· **Courier** status updates using their hand held devices.

· User order placement through the web interface.

· Tracking of placed orders through the web interface.

· Automatic route calculation and order prioritization by hand held devices.

**2.2 Product Functions:** The Hand-Held device will function as follows:

· Will interact with the existing system to assign the new order to the closest or the most available agent.

· Will notify the agent if there is a change in the order such as cancellation or change of address.

· Will have and input device or enter notes or special comment by the agent and also customer's signature upon a successful delivery.

· Will have a GPS navigation system that is constantly updated, with functionality of informing the agent with the shortest path to the destination.

**2.3 User Characteristics:** The intended users are the couriers who interact with the device to update the delivery status and use the GPS function to find the shortest path.

The device will uses a wireless connection to the main server and GPS satellites, so it will be beneficial for the user to have a previous experience with wireless devices such as cell phones.

**2.4 Constraints:** The following constraints are outlined in the RFP:

· The handheld device must be no bigger than 20cm by 15cm by 5cm and weigh no more than 3kg.

· The battery life of the handheld device must be at least 10 hours under the usage expected and must be fully rechargeable in 10 hours.

· The per-unit cost of the hand-held device must be below $500.

· Throughout the coverage area, the handheld must be able to reliably communicate with the server.

**2.5 Assumptions and Dependencies:** NIL

**2.6 Apportioning of Requirements:** NIL

**(c) Design an ER diagram for the Retail store. Make assumptions, if any. List all the entries (corresponding attributes), their relationships and also mention their cardinality.**

**Ans.**

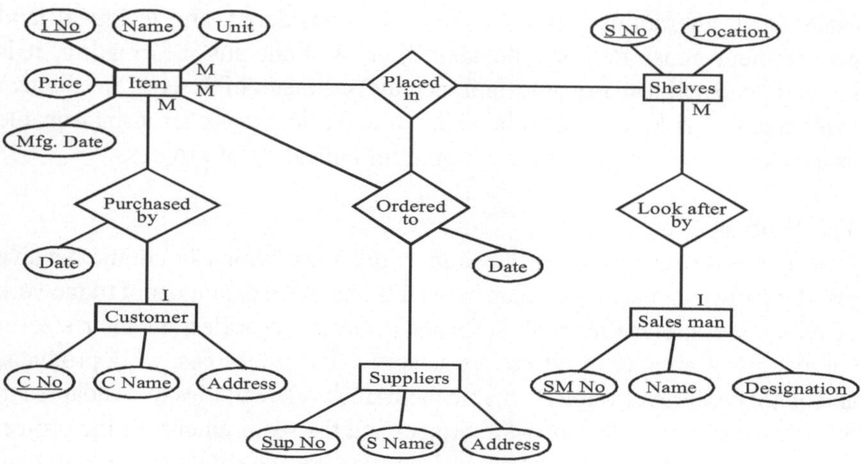


**Q2. (a) Explain the role and functions of a Systems Analyst in the overall project development.**

Refer to Page No.-122, Q.No.-4(a) and Refer to Page No.-150, Q.No.-3(a)

**(b) With the help of an illustration, explain the following scheduling techniques:**

**(i) Work breakdown structure**

**(ii) Flow Graph**

A work breakdown structure (WBS) is a chart in which the critical work elements, called tasks, of a project are illustrated to portray their relationships to each other and to the project as a whole. The graphical nature of the WBS can help a project manager predict outcomes based on various scenarios, which can ensure that optimum decisions are made about whether or not to adopt suggested procedures or changes.

When completed, a well-structured WBS resembles a flowchart in which all elements are logically connected, redundancy is avoided and no critical elements are left out.

Refer to Page No.-51, Q.No.-6

**Q3. (a) Define Benchmark testing. Explain its role in evaluating the performance of different computers and their software.**

**Ans.** Refer to Page No.-86, Q.No.-10

**(b) How product differs from Process? Discuss their qualities.**

**The Product**

Before a project can be planned, product objectives and scope should be established, alternative solutions should be considered, and technical land management constraints should identified. Without this information, it is impossible to define reasonable (and accurate) estimates of the cost, an effective assessment of risk, a realistic breakdown of project tasks, or a manageable project schedule that provides a meaningful indication of progress.

**The Process**

A software process provides the framework from which la comprehensive plan for software development can be established. A small number of framework activities are applicable to all software projects, regardless of their size or complexity. A number of different task sets-tasks, milestones, work products, and quality assurance points – enable the framework activities to be adapted to the characteristics of the software project and the requirements of the project team. Finally, umbrella activities – such as software quality assurance, software configuration management –overlay the process model. Umbrella activities are independent of any one framework activity and occur throughout the process.

Refer to Page No.-241, Q.No.-2(a)

**Q4. (a) Define the following terms with respect to Software Reviews:**

**(i) Software Verification**

Refer to Page No.-201, Q.No.-6(b)

**(ii) Software Evaluation**

**Ans. Software evaluation is the process of assessing the software.** Here, the software is assessed for the intended use (purpose, context, users) are well defined. One must become familiar with the software documentation as well as the software itself in order to make a fair and complete evaluation.

**(iii) Repairability**

**Ans.** Ability of a damaged or failed system to be restored to acceptable operating condition within a specified period (repair time).

**(iv) Adaptive Maintenance**

Refer to Page No.-216, Q.No.-1(a) 2nd Point

**(b) List all the questions which may be asked about each software development methodology before deciding on adopting it as a standard by any organization?**

**Ans. 1.** Is software already running?

**2.** Is software will be totally developed as new software or to upgrade existing software?

**3.** Whether the final outcome required after each step or at the end?

**4.** Whether all requirements are clearly specified?

**5.** Is risk factor involved?

**Q5. Explain the following with an example:**

**(a) Debuggers**

**Ans.** A **debugger** is a computer program that is used to test and debug other programs. The code to be examined might alternatively be running on an *instruction set simulator* (ISS), a technique that allows great power in its ability to halt when specific conditions are encountered but which will typically be much slower than executing the code directly on the appropriate processor.

When the program crashes, the debugger shows the position in the original code if it is a **source-level debugger** or **symbolic debugger**, commonly seen in integrated development environments. If it is a **low-level debugger** or a **machine-language debugger** it shows the line in the disassembly.

The importance of a good debugger cannot be overstated. Indeed, the existence and quality of such a tool for a given language and platform can often be the deciding factor in its use, even if another language/platform is better-suited to the task.

**(b) Software Robustness**

Refer to Page No.-241, Q.No.-2(a) 3rd Part

**(c) Fourth Generation Languages (4GL's)**

Refer to Page No.-16, Q.No.-18

**(d) Project Outsourcing**

Refer to June-2006, Q.No.-1(b)

**(e) Cohesion**

Refer to Page No.-72, 2nd Para

*Sweetness is a virtue that searches with patience for the good in every person and situation*

**Brahma Kumaris**

*People will naturally start trusting me when they see my reliability and consistency*

**Brahma Kumaris**

*When I notice a weakness in another, let me also aim to recognize their strengths*

**Brahma Kumaris**

## CS-70 : INTRODUCTION TO SOFTWARE ENGINEERING
## December, 2009

***Note : Question number 1 is compulsory.*** *Answer any* ***three*** *questions from the rest.*

**Q1. (a) Design a system for a University Information System. Draw DFD's for the system till level-2 and also prepare the SRS document for the same. Describe assumption made, if any.**

**Ans. DFD of University Information System**

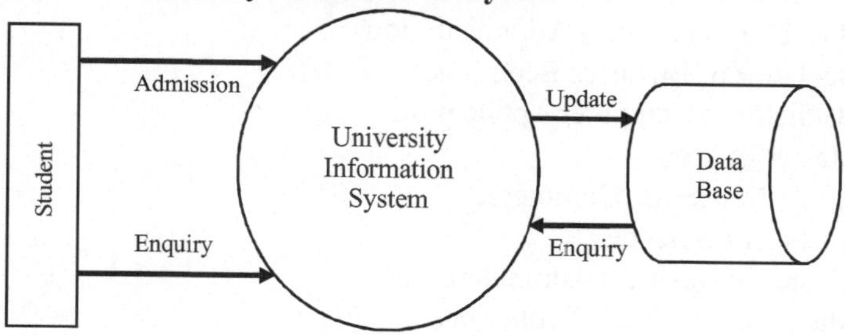


0 Level DFD

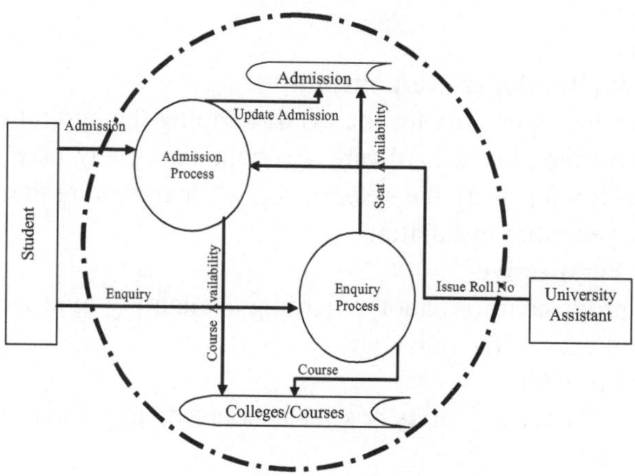


1 Level DFD

### SRS of University Information System

### 1 Introduction

The University Provides Admission to different courses in different colleges

### 1.1 Purpose

Facilitate Admission to different courses in different colleges

**1.2 Scope**

This document is the only one that describes the requirements of the system. This is meant for use by the developers and will be the basis for validating the final developed system. All future requirements will have to go through the formal change approval. The developer is responsible for asking clarifications, where necessary, and will not make any alterations without the permission of the client.

**1.3 Definition**

B.A. Bachelor of Arts
B.Com. Bachelor of Commerce
B.Sc. Bachelor of Science
BBA Bachelor of Business Administration
BBE Bachelor of Business Economics
BCA Bachelor of Computer Application
M.A. Master of Arts
M.Com. Master of Commerce
M.Sc. Master of Science
MBA Master of Business Administration
MBE Master of Business Economics
MCA Master of Computer Application

**1.4 References**

Not Applicable

**1.5 Overview (Developer Responsibility)**

The developer is responsible for the (a) developing the system (b) installing the software on the clients hardware, (c) conducting any user training that might be required for using the system, and (d) maintaining the system for a period of one year after installation.

**2.1 Product Perspective**

The product provides information regarding availability of seats and courses in different colleges of the university.

**2.2 Product Functions**

**(i)** Information about availability of seats in courses, **(ii)** Admission to courses, **(iii)** Cancellation of Admission,

**2.3 User characteristics**

User will be eligible students for different course, who are expected to be computer literate and highly qualified.

**3.1 External Interfaces**

The system should be OS independent and will be Web (Internet) based.

**3.2 Functional Requirements**

The system should be able to query the database of the colleges as well as the University.

**3.3 Performance Requirements (Performance Constraints)**

The query should be processed in less than 30 seconds when the internet connection running properly.

**3.4 Logical Requirements (Design Constraints)**

Hardware constraint: the software will be run on a workstation with 512 MB RAM and running OS (Unix or windows). It will be connected to the Internet with a high speed Internet Router.

Security: The database should be secured against unauthorized access and malicious deformation.

Fault tolerance: Data should not be corrupted in case of system crash or power failure.

**3.5 Acceptance Criteria**

Before acceptance the developer must demonstrate that the system works on the data of the University. The developer will have to show through test cases that all conditions are satisfied.

**(b) Design ER Diagram for the Library Management System. List all the entities, corresponding attributes, relationship. Also, mention cardinality.**

**Ans.** Entity Relationship Diagram for the Library Management System

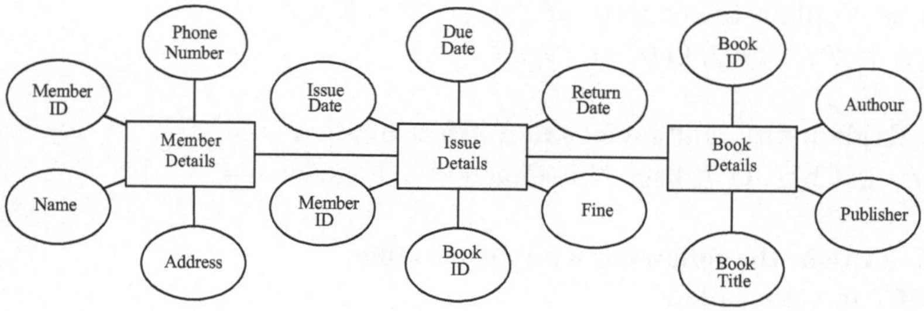


**(c) Define GUI and explain its components. Also, describe its significance in overall project design.**

Refer to June–2007, Q 1(c), Page No.-259

**Q2.(a) Explain the role of the Project Leader in Project Planning and control.**

**Ans. Role of the Project Leader**

**Plan:** Diagnose the technical and organizational Issues that are relevant and systematically structure a solution.

**Motivation:** The ability to encourage technical people to produce to their best of ability

**Organise:** Apply problem solving management style. Should concentrate on understanding the problem to be solved and manage flow of ideas.
**Control:** Letting everyone in the team know that quality counts and that it should not be comprised and motivate other professionals to develop a solution.

**(b) Explain "Iterative Enhancement Model". Also, suggest which kind of projects can be considered for development using this paradigm.**
**Ans.** Refer to Ch–1, Q 20, Page No.-17
**Suitable Projects**
Projects where less manpower is available and the release deadlines are tight. In-house Product development, where it is ensured that the user has something to start with.

**Q3. (a) Explain the principles of Coupling and Cohesion.**
Refer to Ch–5, Q 2, Page No.-72

**(b) How 4 GL's enable Online Application Development?**
Refer to Dec–2005, Q 1(b), Page No.-217 and;
Refer to June–2005, Q 3(b), Page No.-209

**Q4.(a) Explain the concept of Project Tracking.**
Refer to Dec–2002, Q 6(iii), Page No.-156

**(b) Explain any four factors that affect quality.**
Refer to Ch–3, Q 7, Page No.-45 and Q 6, Page No.-44

**Q5. Explain the following with an example:**
**(a) Code Generations**
**Ans.** The software development is a sequence of steps that transform a given problem description called a specification into another description called an implementation. In general, the later description is more formal, more detailed and of lower level than the formal. It is also more efficient. The transformation process eventually ends in machine executable code. Immediate steps may also be executable.
Derivation steps may require creativity and may be supported by tools to varying degree. A simple and fully automatic step is the transformation of specifications into an essentially a translator supporting the stepwise transformation of specifications into an implementation. The optimizer is also only partially automated. The clerical job of recording the transformation steps is automated in order to support later modifications. We also envision the case

where the optimizer plays the role of an intelligent assistant. The difficult and critical steps, however, cannot be automated; thus, even is this case, most of the creative tasks are the software engineer's responsibility.

Moving from the formal specification of a module to an implementation may also be viewed as a transformation that involves creative activities such as designing data structure of algorithms. Again, clerical parts of such transformation can be supported by automatic tools. Examples of generalized code generators are provided by several so-called fourth-generation tools, which automatically generate code for higher level language. Also, reports may be automatically generated from database definitions. In this case, the user can choose among several options to define the report formats.

**(b) Black Box Testing**

Refer to Ch–6, Q 4, Page No.-81

**(c) Software Development team structures**

Refer to Ch–2, Q 5, Page No.-20

**(d) Project Scheduling**

Refer to Dec–2004, Q 6(i), Page No.-144

**(e) LOC based estimation**

Refer to Dec–2008, Q 5(b), Page No.-295

# CS-70 : INTRODUCTION TO SOFTWARE ENGINEERING
## June, 2010

***Note : Question number 1 is compulsory**. Answer any **three** questions from the rest.*

**Q1. (a) Explain all the phases of SDLC. Does the role of System Analyst is confined to Analysis Phase? Comment.**

Refer to June–2005, Q 1(a), Page No.-202

Role of System Analyst differs from organization to organization. The role of the System Analyst is not confined to Analysis phase.

**(b) Design a system for an Insurance Company. Draw DFD's for the system till level-2 and also prepare the SRS document for the same. Clearly mention the assumption made, if any.**

**Ans.** **DFD of Insurance Company**

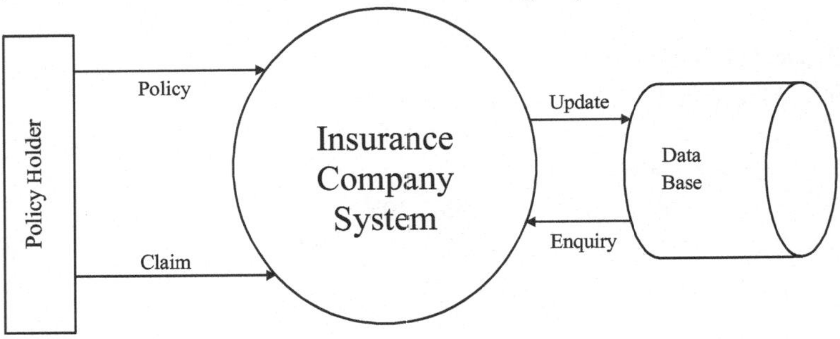


0 Level DFD

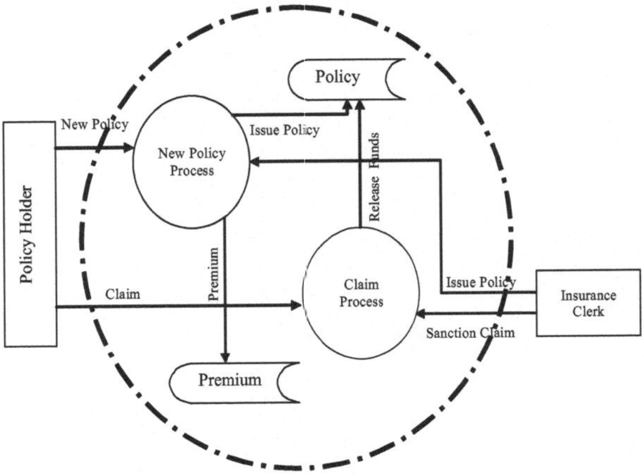


1 Level DFD

**SRS of Insurance Company**

**1 Introduction**

The Insurance company Provides Insurance cover for a variety of Insurance needs to Its Policy holders.

**1.1 Purpose**

Facilitate Insurance Cover to policy Holders for a variety of Insurance Needs.

**1.2 Scope**

This document is the only one that describes the requirements of the system. This is meant for use by the developers and will be the basis for validating the final developed system. All future requirements will have to go through the formal change approval. The developer is responsible for asking clarifications, where necessary, and will not make any alterations without the permission of the client.

**1.3 Definition**

**Client Policy Holder**

Policy Holder a person who has taken a Insurance Policy and has paid premium upto current month.

**1.4 References**

Not Applicable

**1.5 Overview (Developer Responsibility)**

The developer is responsible for the (a) developing the system (b) installing the software on the clients hardware, (c) conducting any user training that might be required for using the system, and (d) maintaining the system for a period of one year after installation.

**2.1 Product Perspective**

The product provides information regarding availability of different Insurance Policy and premium payable.

**2.2 Product Functions**

**(i)** Information about availability of different Policies for different Insurance requirements, **(ii)** Premium payable for different Insurance policies, **(iii)** Information regarding Insurance claims,

**2.3 User characteristics**

User will be prospective clients and may not be computer literate and of varying age groups. Hence information will have to be provided in easy to understand language with examples for simple understanding.

**3.1 External Interfaces**

The system should be OS independent and will be Web (Internet) based.

**3.2 Functional Requirements**

The system should be able to query the database of the Insurance Company.

**3.3 Performance Requirements (Performance Constraints)**

The query should be processed in less than 30 seconds when the internet connection running properly.

### 3.4 Logical Requirements (Design Constraints)

Hardware constraint: the software will be run on a workstation with 512 MB RAM and running OS (Unix or windows). It will be connected to the Internet with a high speed Internet Router.

Security: The database should be secures against unauthorized access and malicious deformation.

Fault tolerance: Data should not be corrupted in case of system crash or power failure.

### 3.5 Acceptance Criteria

Before acceptance the developer must demonstrate that the system works on the data of the Insurance company. The developer will have to show through test cases that all conditions are satisfied.

**(c) Design ER Diagram for the above system. Make assumptions, if any. List all entities along with their attributes and relationship.**

**Ans. Entity relationship Diagram of Insurance Company**

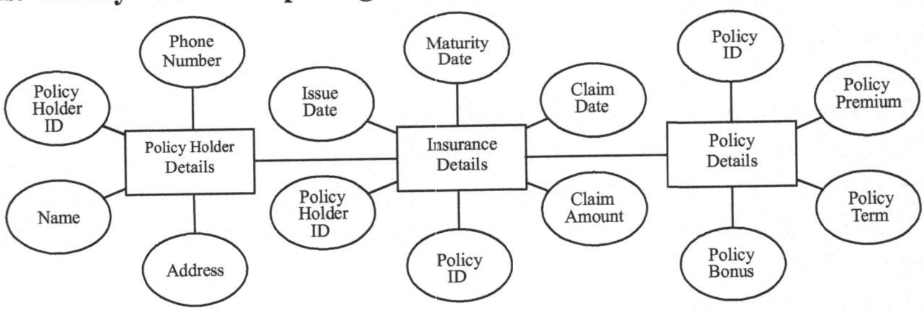


**Q2. (a) What is Integration Testing? What is its role and how it is performed?**

Refer to Ch–6, Q 9, Page No.-85

**(b) What is Risk Management? Further, discuss the areas of Risk that a software project manager must address.**

Refer to Dec–2004, Q 3(a), Page No.-105

**Q3. (a) List and explain Fault Finding Techniques.**

**Ans,** Following are the FFT :

1. Test the system, i.e. make measurements or collect other evidence
2. Analyse the readings
3. Locate fault based on analysis (step 2)
4. Determine the original cause of the fault. (i.e. find a method to prevent recurrence)
5. Repair the fault (bearing in mind step 4)
6. Retest the system

**(b) What is an Object Oriented Design? Discuss its advantages in developing a software system.**

**Ans.** Object-oriented design is a design strategy where system designers think in terms of 'things' instead of operations or functions. The executing system is made up of interacting objects that maintain their own local state and provide operations on that state information. They hide information about the representation of the state and hence limit access to it. An object-oriented design process involves designing the object classes and the relationships between these classes. When the design is realised as an executing program, the required objects are created dynamically using the class definitions. Object-oriented design is part of object-oriented development where an object-oriented strategy is used throughout the development process.

Advantages in developing a software system :

(i) Easier maintenance. Objects may be understood as stand-alone entities.

(ii) Objects are potentially reusable components.

(iii) For some systems, there may be an obvious mapping from real world entities to system objects

**Q4. (a) Differentiate between Coupling and Cohesion. What are the various types of Coupling?**

Refer to Ch–5, Q 2, Page No.-72 and Q 4, Page No.-73

**(b) What are CASE Tools? What are various types of CASE Tools ? Discuss its benefits?**

Refer to Ch–8, Q 1, Page No.-98 and Q 2, Page No.-99

**Q5. Explain the following with an example (any three)**

**(a) Validation and Verification**

Refer to Jan–2001, Q 6(b), Page No.-200

**(b) Principles of Software Engineering**

Refer to Dec–2005, Q 5(a), Page No.-226

**(c) Function Point Analysis**

Refer to Ch–2, Q 12, Page No.-27

**(d) Software Maintenance**

Refer to Dec–2005, Q 1(a), Page No.-216

**(e) White-Box Testing**

Refer to Ch–6, Q 5, Page No.-81

# CS-70 : INTRODUCTION TO SOFTWARE ENGINEERING
## December, 2010

*Note: Question number 1 is compulsory. Attempt any three from the rest.*

**Q1. (a) Differentiate between a spiral model and a waterfall model. Further discuss the exclusive significance of a spiral model.**

**Ans.**

| Spiral Modal | Waterfall model |
|---|---|
| (i) Evolutionary software process model. | Linear Sequential software process model |
| (ii) Controlled and iterative approach. | Controlled and systematic approach |
| (iii) Good for even large systems. | Good for small systems. |
| (iv) Preferred by Developers. | Preferred by customers. |
| (v) Incremental changes hence no confusion. | Changes can cause confusion. |
| (vi) No delay on account of evolutionary nature | Unnecessary delay for developers may occur due to sequential nature. |
| (vii) Requires considerable expertise in risk | A major blunder discovered early may cause much problem. |
| (viii) Customers changes can be accommodated easily in final stages | Changes are not possible in final stages |

**Significance of spiral model:**

**(i)** It is suitable for large systems.

**(ii)** Requires considerable expertise in risk control for some reason.

**(iii)** As the system is large it is highly likely that changes may be there in final stage or middle of the development so, this will not delay on account of evolutionary nature.

**(b) Design a system for University library. Draw DFD's for the system till level-2 and also prepare the SRS document for the same. Mention the assumption made if any.**

Visit us at www.Gullybaba.com\bca\CS-70

**(c) Design an ER diagram for above system. Make assumptions if any. List all the entities along with their attributes and relationship.**

Refer to Dec–2009, Q 1(b), Page No.- 307

**Q2. (a) Who is a system Analyst? Discuss the various skills required to be a system Analyst.**

Refer to Dec–2005, Q.2(b), Page No.- 221

**(b) Why Software Safety and hazard analysis is a major concern? Describe along with four Software Application Areas.**

Refer to June–2003, Q 5(b), Page No.- 143

**Q3. (a) Describe COCOMO model. Also explain its importance.**
Refer to Ch–2, Q 14, Page No.- 29
**(b)What do you mean by project outsourcing? Explain with any two applications of its implementation.**
Refer to June–2006, Q 1(b), Page No.- 229

**Q4. (a) Mention any five principles of S.E.**
Refer to Dec–2005, Q 5(a), Page No.- 226
**(b) Explain software crisis from programmer's and user's point of view.**
Refer to Page No.-204, Point (c)

**Q5. Explain the following terms: (any three)**
**(a) Benchmark Testing**
Refer to Ch–6, Q 10, Page No.- 86
**(b) Top down and Bottom up design**
**Ans.** Top down – integration produced down the invocation hierarchy, adding one module at a time until an entire tree level is integrated; and thus it eliminates the need for drivers. The bottom up strategy works similarly from the bottom and has no need of stubs. A sandwich strategy runs from top and bottom concurrently, meeting somewhere in the middle.
Integration should follow the lines of first putting together those subsystem that are of great concern. This prioritization might dictate top-down integration if control and the user interface were the most worrisome or complex part of software. This can occur, for instance, if the customer is anxious to see a running program early in the testing phase. In another situation, the machine interface and performance might be of special interest, and then bottom-up integration would be dictated. With bottom-up integration we stand better chance of experiencing a high degree of concurrency during our integration. It has also been said that top-down integration is an exercise in faith that everything will work out well, whereas bottom-up integration shows that things really do work.
**(c) 4GL**
Refer to Q 3(b), Page No.-208
**(d) Reverse engineering.**
Refer to Ch–8, Page No.- 96 [Reverse Engineering]

# CS-70 : INTRODUCTION TO SOFTWARE ENGINEERING
## June, 2011

*Note: Question number 1 is compulsory. Attempt any* ***three*** *from the rest.*

**Q1. (a) Design the following for a simple "Project Proposals Management System". The project proposals of BCA/MCA programmes are received at Regional centres, situated all over India. The final year students of BCA/MCA submit their project proposals to the respective regional centres in either of the 2 slots per year, i.e. (i) Apr. – June and (ii) Oct – Dec. The submitted synopsis details are entered and a PP NO. will be issued to each of the synopsis. Further, they are funded into lots of 50 proposals and are sent for evaluation by the approved project proposal evaluators. After receiving from them, the status and other remarks are noted and are sent back to the students.**

**(i) Design the DFDs upto second level.**

**(ii) Prepare SRS document. List assumptions, if any.**

**(iii) Design an ER diagram. List all the entities, their attributes, cardinality, key constraints etc.**

**(iv) Draw PERT chart for the problem and show the critical path.**

**(v) Specify the s/w development life cycle model for the given specifications. Also explain briefly about the phases of the model.**

Visit us at www.Gullybaba.com\bca\CS-70

**Q2. (a) Discuss all the key process areas (KPA) associated with the five levels of Capability Maturity Model (CMM)**

**Ans.** The Software Engineering Institute (SEI) has developed a comprehensive model predicated on a set of software engineering capabilities that should be present as organizations reach different levels of process maturity. To determine an on organization's current state of process maturity, the SEI uses an assessment that results in a five point grading scheme. The grading scheme determines compliance with a *capability maturity model* that defines key activities required at different levels of process maturity. The SEI approach provides a measure of the global effectiveness of a company's software engineering practices and establishes five process maturity levels that are defined in the following manner:

**Level 1: Initial.** The software process is characterized as ad hoc and occasionally even chaotic. Few processes are defined, and success depends on individual effort.

**Level 2: Repeatable.** Basic project management processes are established to track cost, schedule, and functionality. The necessary process discipline is in place to repeat earlier successes on projects with similar applications.

**Level 3: Defined.** The software process for both management and engineering activities is documented, standardized, and integrated into an organization wide software process. All projects use a documented and approved version of the organization's process for developing and supporting software. This level includes all characteristics defined for level 2.

**Level 4. Managed.** Detailed measures of the software process and product quality are collected. Both the software process and products are quantitatively understood and controlled using detailed measures. This level includes all characteristics defined for level 3.

**Level 5: Optimizing.** Continuous process improvement is enabled by quantitative feedback from the process and from testing innovative ideas and technologies. This level includes all characteristics defined for level 4.

**(b) Explain the concept of project tracking with the help of the following charts:**

**(i) Ideal Project progress chart**

**(ii) Usual Project progress chart.**

Refer to Dec–2007, Q 5(b), Page No.- 281

**Q3. (a) Discuss the role of a systems Analyst. What are the various attributes required to become an effective Systems Analyst?**

Refer to Ch–4, Q 4, Page No.- 49 & June–2002, Q 6(ii), Page No.-166

**(b) Define 4GL. Discuss how 4GLs help to solve the complex problems. Also, mention their limitations**

Refer to Dec–2007, Q 4(b), Page No.- 279

**Q4. (a) Discuss the concept of modularity with appropriate illustration. Also explain its significance.**

Refer to Ch–5, Q 1, Page No.- 71 & Page No.-242 [Modularity]

**(b) What are the various categories of CASE tools? What are their benefits? Also, mention their limitations.**

Refer to June–2008, Q 4(a), Page No.- 288

**Q5. Write short notes on the following :**

**(a) Software Reviews**

**(b) Software upgradation**

Refer to Dec–2006, Q.No.-5(b), Page No.- 250

**(c) Software Crisis.**

Refer to June–2005, Q.No.-1(c), Page No.- 204

●●●

## CS-70 : INTRODUCTION TO SOFTWARE ENGINEERING
**December, 2011**

*Note: **Question no. 1 is compulsory.** Answer any **three** questions from the rest.*

**Q1. A General Hospital consists of a number of specialized wards (Such as Maternity, Paediatry, Oncology etc). Each ward hosts a number of patients, who were admitted on the recommendation by their own specialist doctor and confirmed by a Sr. Consultant employed by the Hospital. On admission, the personal details of every patient are recorded. A seperate register is to be held to store information of the tests undertaken and the results of a prescribed treatment. A number of tests may be conducted for each patient. Each patient is assigned to one leading consultant but may be examined by another doctor, if required. Doctors are specialists in some branch of medicine and may be leading consultants for a number of patients, not necessarily from the same ward.**

**(a) Design the DFD's upto second level.**

**Ans.** **0th Level CFD (Context Free Diagram)**

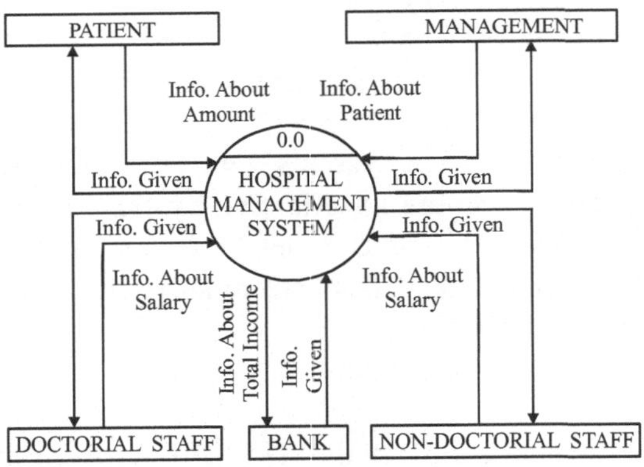


**1st Level**

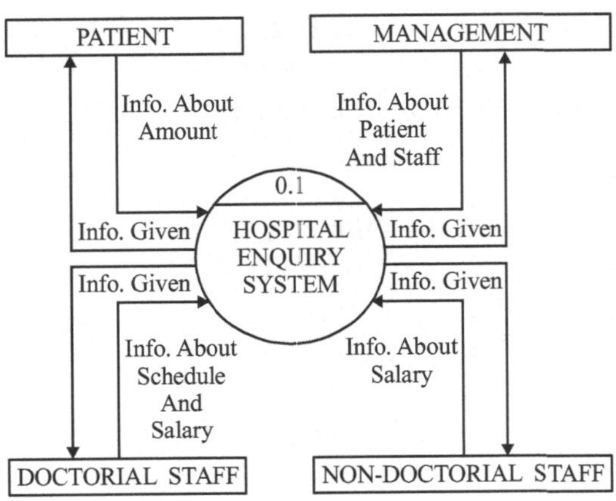

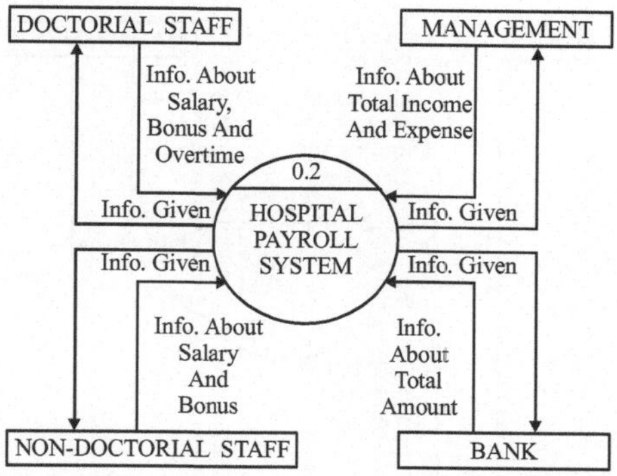
DOCTORIAL STAFF
MANAGEMENT
Info. About Salary, Bonus And Overtime
Info. About Total Income And Expense
0.2
HOSPITAL PAYROLL SYSTEM
Info. Given
Info. Given
Info. Given
Info. Given
Info. About Salary And Bonus
Info. About Total Amount
NON-DOCTORIAL STAFF
BANK

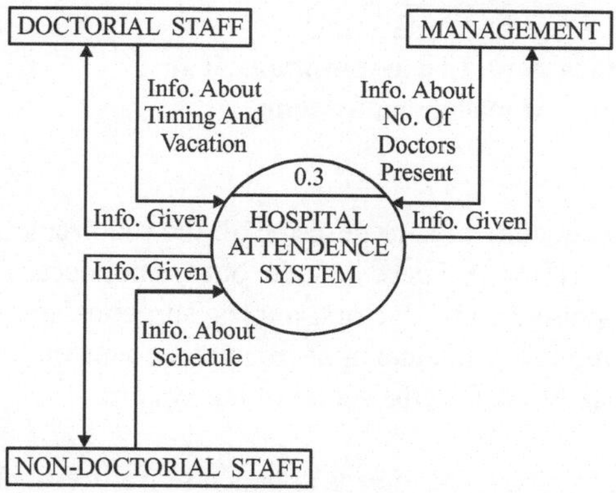
DOCTORIAL STAFF
MANAGEMENT
Info. About Timing And Vacation
Info. About No. Of Doctors Present
0.3
HOSPITAL ATTENDENCE SYSTEM
Info. Given
Info. Given
Info. Given
Info. About Schedule
NON-DOCTORIAL STAFF

**2nd Level**

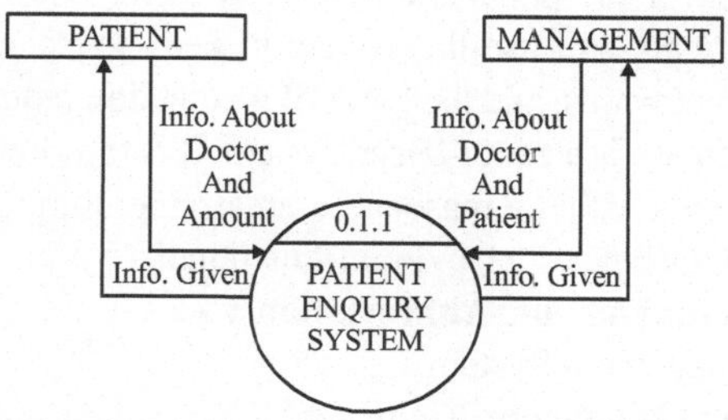
PATIENT
MANAGEMENT
Info. About Doctor And Amount
Info. About Doctor And Patient
0.1.1
PATIENT ENQUIRY SYSTEM
Info. Given
Info. Given

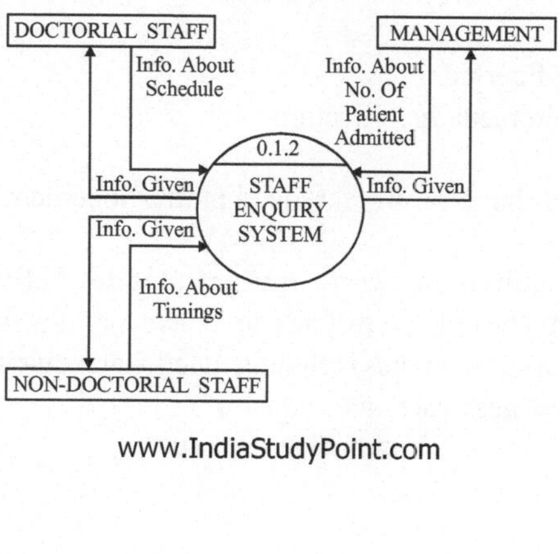
DOCTORIAL STAFF
MANAGEMENT
Info. About Schedule
Info. About No. Of Patient Admitted
0.1.2
STAFF ENQUIRY SYSTEM
Info. Given
Info. Given
Info. Given
Info. About Timings
NON-DOCTORIAL STAFF

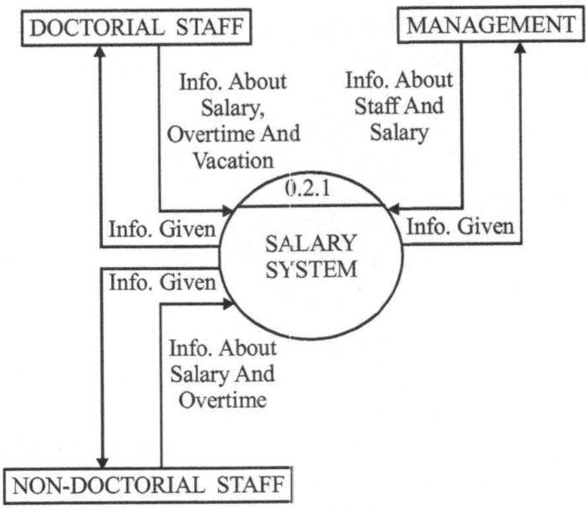


**(b) Prepare SRS document. List assumptions, if any.**

**Ans.** SRS for Hospital Management System:

**(1) Introduction**

**(1.1) Purpose**

The purpose of this document is to describe all the requirements for the Hospital Management System (HMS). These include, but are not necessarily limited to, the following: administrative staff, doctors, nurses, surgeons and developers. Please note that only the requirements that appears in this document or a future revision, however, will be used to define the scope of the system.

**(1.2) Scope**

The system will be used to allocate beds to patients on a priority basis, and to assign doctors to patients in designated wards as need arises. Doctors will also use the system to keep track of the patients assigned to them. Nurses who are in direct contact with the patients will use the system to keep track of available beds, the patients in the different wards, and the types of medication required for each patient. The current system in use is a paper-based system. It is too slow and cannot provide updated lists of patients within a reasonable timeframe. Requirement statements in this document are both functional and non-functional.

**(1.3) Definitions, Acronyms, and Abbreviations:**

HMS: Hospital Management System

PHN: Personal Health Number on health card

ID: Identification

GUI: Graphical User Interface

SRS: Software Requirement Specification

**(1.4) References**

No formal documents have been referenced in this document.

**(1.5) Overview**

This SRS is the requirement work product that formally specifies Hospital Management System. The objective of this document therefore is to formally describe the system's high level requirements including functional requirements, non-functional requirements and business rules and constraints.

**(2) General Description**

**(2.1) Product Perspective**

This Hospital Management System is a self-contained system that manages activities of the hospital as bed assignment, operations scheduling personnel management and administrative issues.

**(2.2) Product Functions**

(2.2.1) Registration
(2.2.2) Consultation
(2.2.3) Patient Checkout
(2.2.4) Report Generation

**(2.3) User Characteristics**

(2.3.1) Front desk staff
(2.3.2) Administrators
(2.3.3) Nurses
(2.3.4) Doctors

**(3) Specific Requirements**

**(3.1) Functional Requirements**

(3.1.1) Registration
(3.1.1.1) Add patients
(3.1.1.2) Assign ID
(3.1.2) Consultation
(3.1.2.1) Add ward
(3.1.2.2) Assign to waiting list
(3.1.3) Medical matter management
(3.1.3.1) Assign Doctor
(3.1.3.2) Assign Nurse
(3.1.3.3) Emergency case
(3.1.3.4) Surgery case

**(3.2) Design Constraints**

(3.2.1) Database
(3.2.2) Operating System
(3.2.3) Web-based

**(3.3) Non-functional Requirements**

(3.3.1) Security
(3.3.1.1) Patient Identification
(3.3.1.2) Logon Id
(3.3.1.3) Administrator's rights
(3.3.1.4) Doctor's rights
(3.3.1.5) Nurse's rights
(3.3.2) Performance Requirements
(3.3.2.1) Response time
(3.3.2.2) Capacity
(3.3.2.3) User interface
(3.3.3) Maintainability

(3.3.3.1) Back up
(3.3.3.2) Errors
(3.3.4) Reliability
(3.3.4.1) Availability

**(c) Design an ER diagram. List all the entities, their attributes, cardinality, key constraints etc.**

**Ans.**

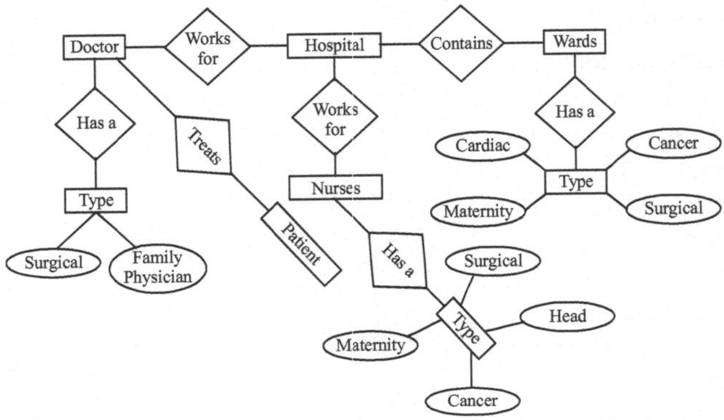


**(d) Draw PERT chart for the problem and show the critical path.**

**Ans.**

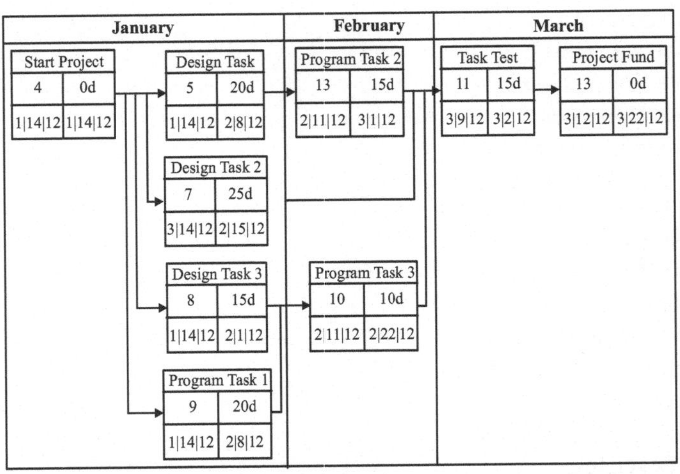


**(e) Specify the s/w development life cycle model for the given specifications. Also, explain briefly about the phases of the model.**

**Ans.** Software development life cycle model for the given specification is prototyping model.Phases of the model are:

**(1) Build and fix model:** It is simple two phase model. In one phase, code is developed and in another, code is fixed.

**(2) Waterfall model:** The waterfall approach, the whole process of software development is divided into separate process phases. The phases in waterfall model are:

• Requirement Specifications phase
• Software design
• Implementation and testing & maintenance

**(3) Iterative enhancement model:** An iterative enhancement model does not attempt to start with a full specification of requirements. Instead, development begins by specifying and implementing just part of the software, which can be than reviewed in order to identify further requirements.

**(4) Spiral model:** The spiral model, also known as spiral life cycle model, is a system development method used in information technology. This model of development combines the features of the prototyping model and waterfall model. The spiral model is intended for large, expensive and complicated projects.

**(5) RAD (Rapid Application Development):** It is a concept that products can be developed faster and of higher quality through:
• Gathering requirements using workshops
• Prototyping and early, reiterative user testing of designs
• Reuse of software components

**(6) Prototyping Model:** A prototype is a working model that is functionally equivalent to a component of the product. In many instances the client only has a general view of what is expected from the software product. In such a scenario where there is an absence of detailed information regarding the input to the system, the processing needs and the output requirements, the prototyping model may be employed.

**Q2. (a) What do you mean by Function Point Analysis? Mention its features.**

**Ans.** Simply stated function points are a standard unit of measure that represents the functional size of a software application. In the same way as a house is measured by the square feet its provides, the size of an application can be measured by the number of function points it delivers to the users of the application.

Features of function point analysis:
• The ability to accurately estimate:
  o project cost
  o project duration
  o project staffing size
• An understanding of other important metrics, such as:
  o Project defect rate
  o Cost per FP
  o FP's per hour
  o The productivity benefits of using new or different tools.

**(b) Describe cocomo model briefly.**

Refer to Ch–2, Q 14, Page No.-29

**Q3. (a) Explain s/w crisis from programmer's point of view.**

Refer to June–2005, Q 1(c), Page No.-204

**(b) With the help of an example application, explain the prototyping model.**

Refer to Ch–1, Q 14, Page No.-13

**Q4. (a) Identify and elaborate all the risk factors in a s/w project.**

Refer to Ch–2, Q 18, Page No.-33

**(b) What are the 3P's of S/W project management? Explain the factors that should be considered when planning the structure of a team.**

**Ans.** The 3P's of s/w project management are:

**P1:** If I had to pick one thing out that is most important in our organization, I'd say it's not the tools that we use. It's the people.

**P2:** The most important ingredient that was successful on this project was having smart people. The most important thing you do for a project is selecting the staff. The success of the software development organization is very much associated with the ability to recruit good people.

**P3:** The role I have in management is to ensure that I have good people and that I provide an environment in which they can be productive.

Factors are:

- The difficulty of the problem to be solved.
- The size of the resultant program in lines of code or function points.
- The time the team will stay together.
- The degree to which the problem can be modularized.
- The required quality and reliability of the system to be built.
- The rigidity of the delivery date.
- The degree of sociability required for the project.

**Q5. Write short notes on:**

**(a) Software Reliability**

Refer to Ch–7, Q 5, Page No.-95

**(b) Regression testing**

Refer to Ch–6, Q 13(a), Page No.-89

**(c) DEFT case tools**

**Ans.** DEFT Case Tools: DEFT supplies Computer Aided System Engineering products to engineers who works with RDBMS. RDBMS engineers use the DEFT case system to:

- assist them in gathering the initial requirements from end-user.
- analyze these requirements and determine their feasibility.
- designs the systems general algorithms.
- design an actual detailed implementation in terms of the target environment.
- automatically generates the RDBMS from the design.
- control their development efforts through the medium of our configuration management tools.

●●●

> When you build a house, every brick counts. When you build a character, every thought counts.

## CS-70 : INTRODUCTION TO SOFTWARE ENGINEERING
### June, 2012

*Note: Question number one is compulsory. Answer any **three** from the rest.*

**Q1. (a) What is need of different phases in SDLC? Explain in which phase of SDLC System Analysts are involved? List the responsibilities of a System Analyst.**

**Ans.** SDLC (Software Development Life Cycle) covers many activities across well defined phases. These include questioning why the information system needs to be built, to charting feasibility factors, analyzing issues that are expected to crop up, zeroing in on a certain design and architecture for the system, developing the system, implementing and testing it, and delivering it to the target customer. Each of these activities is carried out in an orderly manner in a set of well defined development phases. That is why SDLC is referred to as a process of gradual refinement. That is, each phase takes over where the previous phase left off, and refines what was done before.

In all phases of SDLC, System Analysts are involved.

The analyst understands the nature of the information and the functions of the software, which is required for the system. The analyst makes a brief survey of the requirements and tries to analyze the performance of the system, which is to be developed. He also makes sure that he gets enough information and resources for building the appropriate system.

**(b) Design a System for Student's Record Management by an Engineering College. Draw DFDs of system upto 2nd level. Also, briefly describe the processes of the system. Clearly mention the assumptions made if any.**

**Ans.** **0th Level (CFD)**

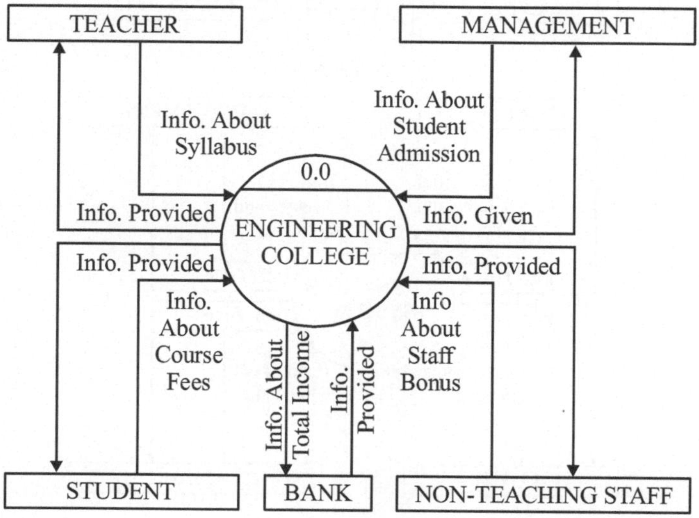

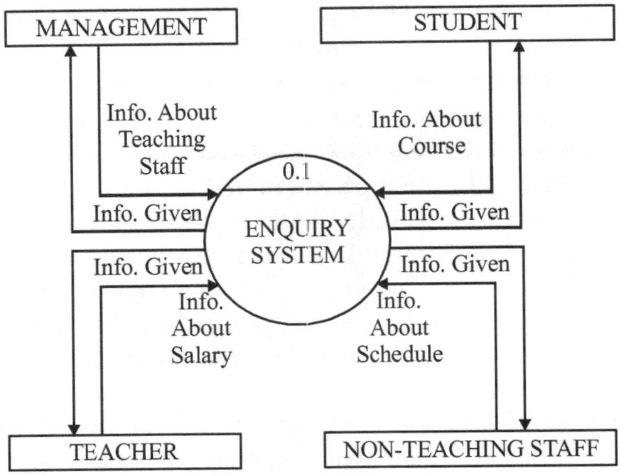
MANAGEMENT
STUDENT
Info. About Teaching Staff
Info. About Course
0.1
Info. Given
Info. Given
ENQUIRY SYSTEM
Info. Given
Info. Given
Info. About Salary
Info. About Schedule
TEACHER
NON-TEACHING STAFF

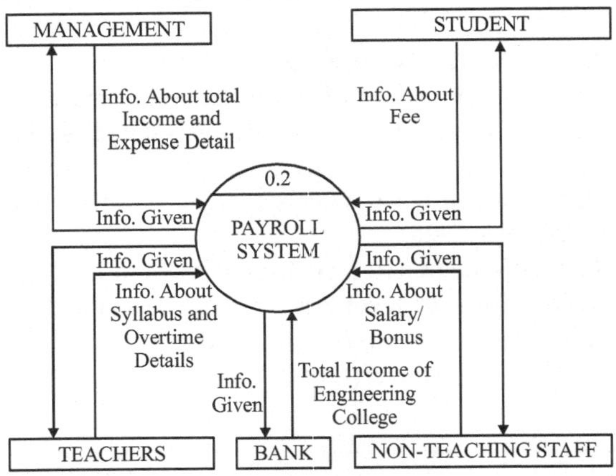
MANAGEMENT
STUDENT
Info. About total Income and Expense Detail
Info. About Fee
0.2
Info. Given
Info. Given
PAYROLL SYSTEM
Info. Given
Info. Given
Info. About Syllabus and Overtime Details
Info. About Salary/ Bonus
Info. Given
Total Income of Engineering College
TEACHERS
BANK
NON-TEACHING STAFF

**I - Level**

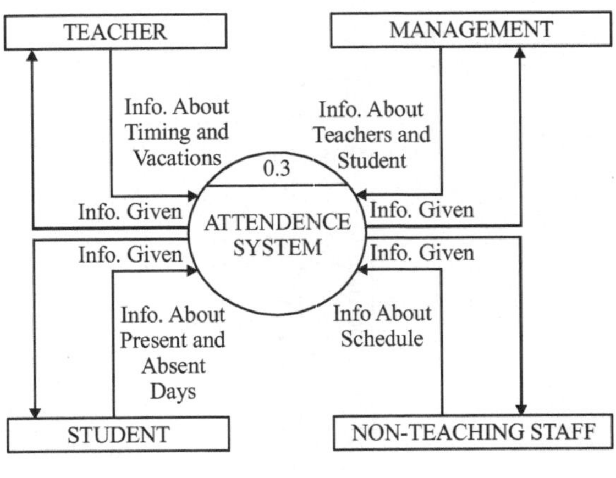
TEACHER
MANAGEMENT
Info. About Timing and Vacations
Info. About Teachers and Student
0.3
Info. Given
Info. Given
ATTENDENCE SYSTEM
Info. Given
Info. Given
Info. About Present and Absent Days
Info About Schedule
STUDENT
NON-TEACHING STAFF

## II- Level

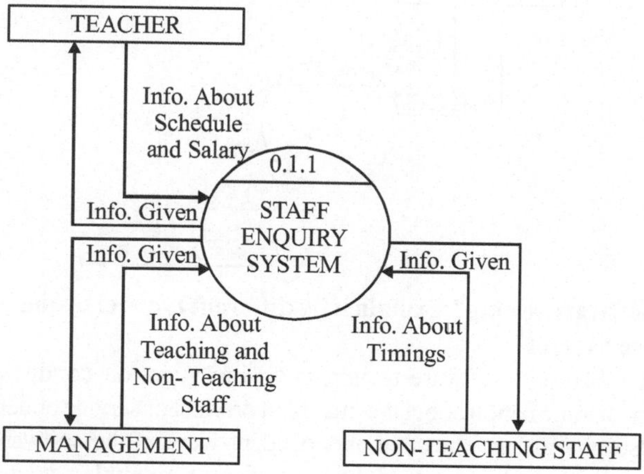
TEACHER
Info. About Schedule and Salary
0.1.1
STAFF ENQUIRY SYSTEM
Info. Given
Info. Given
Info. Given
Info. About Teaching and Non- Teaching Staff
Info. About Timings
MANAGEMENT
NON-TEACHING STAFF

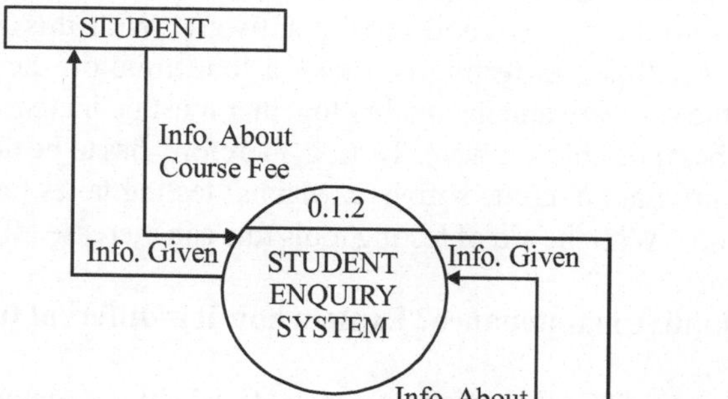
STUDENT
Info. About Course Fee
0.1.2
STUDENT ENQUIRY SYSTEM
Info. Given
Info. Given
Info. About Total No. of Students
MANAGEMENT

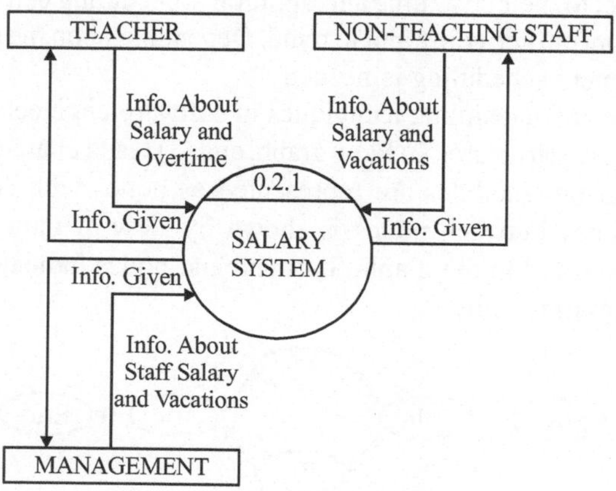
TEACHER
NON-TEACHING STAFF
Info. About Salary and Overtime
Info. About Salary and Vacations
0.2.1
SALARY SYSTEM
Info. Given
Info. Given
Info. Given
Info. About Staff Salary and Vacations
MANAGEMENT

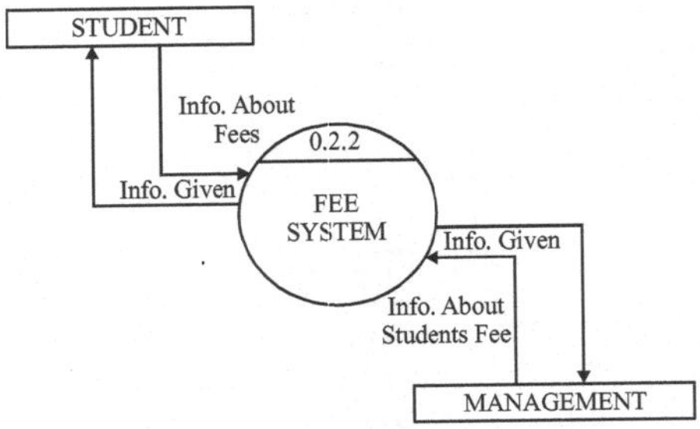


**(c) What is Software testing? Explain why different types of testings are required for a Software System?**

**Ans.** Software Testing: Software testing is an investigation conducted to provide stakeholders with information about the quality of product or service under test. Software testing can also provide an objective, independent view of the software to allow the business to appreciate and understand the risks of software implementation.

As the software industry grows, it becomes more and more competitive and advanced for business to produce such good quality software. With this also comes the reliability and deadlines as testing can take a long time on the software. The production of the software and the quality together must be increased for business to produce the best possible software. Testing, therefore, has to be done throughout the process of programming the software. Manual testing takes too long and can waste a lot of time. With the aid of testing tools this can increase efficiency and get the deadlines met.

**(d) What is adaptive maintenance? Explain how it is different from corrective maintenance?**

Refer to Page No.-216 [Corrective maintenance & Adaptive maintenance]

**Q2. (a) What is need of Software System Development Scheduling? Explain how scheduling is done in Flow Graph technique, with an example?**

**Ans.** Scheduling of a software project can be correlated to prioritising various tasks with respect to their cost, time and duration. Scheduling can be done with the resource constraint or time constraint in mind. Depending upon the project, software system development scheduling is needed.

The various types of scheduling techniques in software engineering are:

(1) Work breakdown structure, (2) Flow graph, and (3) Gantt chart or time line charts

Flow Graph: Various modules are represented as nodes with edges connecting nodes. Dependency between nodes is shown by flow of data between nodes. Cycles are not allowed in the graph. Start and end nodes indicate the source and terminating nodes of the flow.

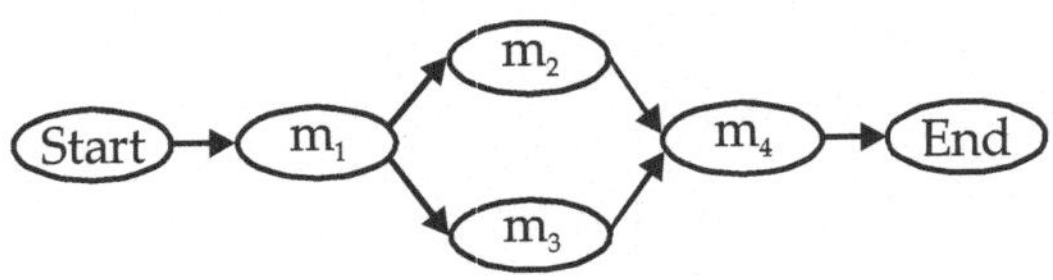

$M_1$ is the starting module and the data flows to $m_2$ and $m_3$. The combined data from $m_2$ and $m_3$ flow to $m_4$ and finally the project terminates. In certain projects, time schedule is also associated with each module. The arrows indicate the flow of information between modules.

**(b) Define 4GLs. Explain advantages of 4GLs over 3GLs.**

Refer to Dec–2006, Q 1(d), Page No.-240

**Q3. (a) What is Software fault? Explain how faults are detected found/in a Software System?**

**Ans.** Software fault is a possibly recoverable error that occurred because of a programming error. Such faults are usually detected by hardware, and are sent to the appropriate software handler for processing. For example, a division by zero error will generate a Divide By Zero fault, which will be sent to the software's try-catch block, or will eventually filter up to the operating system, at which point the program will cease execution. The detection process is modeled by constant probabilities, which are functions of the current level and the fault introduction. The probabilities are, of course, assigned values according to the effort that is put into fault detection mechanism on each level. This gives us the chance to study the impact of different parameters on the spreading and detection process.

Now Refer to June–2010, Q 3(a), Page No.-312

**(b) What is Software reliability? Explain the process of software review. Also explain how software review helps in finding software reliability**

Refer to Dec–2006, Q 5(b), Page No.-250

**Q4. (a) Mention any five principles of Software Engineering.**

Refer to Dec–2005, Q 5(a), Page No.-226

**(b) Explain the following terms in the context of Software Engineering.**

**(i) Debuger:** Refer to June–2009, Q 5(a), Page No.-303

**(ii) Repairability:** Refer to Page No.-303 [Repairability]

**(iii) Verification:** Refer to Page No.-201 [Verification]

**(iv) User Interface**

**Ans.** The user interface, in the industrial design field of human–machine interaction, is the space where interaction between humans and machines occurs. The goal of interaction between a human and a machine at the user interface is effective operation and control of the machine, and feedback from the machine which aids the operator in making operational decisions. Examples of this broad concept of user interfaces include the interactive aspects of computer operating systems, hand tools, heavy machinery operator controls, and process controls.

**Q5. (a) What is cohesion? Is a more cohesive system considered good (Yes/No) Justify your answer.**

**Ans.** Refer to Page No.-72 [Cohesion]

Yes, because cohesion is the functional strength of a module. Increasing dependencies on implementation details of other components isn't a good thing.

**(b) What are CASE tools? List various CASE tools in use. Explain briefly the advantages of using CASE tools.**

Refer to Ch–8, Q 1, Page No.-98 & Q 2, Page No-99

●●●